7.95x

D1403436

WITHDRAWN

RIVER OF GOLD

RIVER OF GOLD

The Story of the Palmer River Gold Rush

HECTOR HOLTHOUSE

ANGUS AND ROBERTSON

First published in 1967 by

ANGUS & ROBERTSON LTD

89 Castlereagh Street, Sydney
54 Bartholomew Close, London
107 Elizabeth Street, Melbourne

Copyright 1967 Hector Holthouse

Registered in Australia
for transmission by post as a book
PRINTED IN AUSTRALIA BY
HALSTEAD PRESS, SYDNEY

ACKNOWLEDGMENTS

The author wishes to thank the staff of the Oxley Memorial Library, Brisbane, and friends who helped him obtain material used in this book.

AUTHOR'S NOTE

In the course of writing this book I examined many conflicting contemporary reports in an endeavour to discover what really happened in those lively days of the Palmer River gold rush. If some details of this story vary from generally accepted views, it is because that is the way the men on the spot saw them at the time. Quotations from the letters, reports, and reminiscences of miners, carriers, Government officials, and others have in some instances been edited slightly to remove redundant material and make reading easier, and in places dialogue, based on the descriptive material, has been added, but in no instance has the original meaning been changed.

H.H.

CONTENTS

1 · CANNIBAL COUNTRY   1

2 · THE RUSH   14

3 · BATTLE CAMP   29

4 · SHORT RATIONS   40

5 · DEATH IN THE MUD   51

6 · HELL'S GATE   59

7 · GOLD FOR ALL   73

8 · THE ASIATIC INVASION   86

9 · ROBBERS AND KILLERS   98

10 · ROLLICKING REEFERS   111

11 · HANG MULLIGAN!   124

12 · ROARING DAYS   138

13 · MURDER ON THE REEFS   153

14 · THE CHINESE PANIC   170

15 · GOLDEN HORSESHOES   182

16 · THE BATTLE OF LUKINVILLE   194

17 · THE PALMER SLEEPS   205

INDEX   213

The photographs of Cooktown and the Palmer River today were taken by the author. The illustrations of the period have been reproduced from contemporary issues of the *Australasian Sketcher* and the *Queenslander*, except for the portrait of Mulligan, which is from a portrait in the possession of the Oxley Memorial Library, Brisbane; cradling for gold, from the *Picturesque Atlas of Australasia*; and Cooktown in 1874 and the approach to Hell's Gate, which are from the *Illustrated Sydney News*.

ILLUSTRATIONS

James Venture Mulligan   18

Mulligan and his mates prospecting on the Palmer   19

Sluicing for gold on the Palmer   19

Cradling for gold   34

Crowded quarters on a ship bound for Cooktown   34

Cooktown at the time of the Wet in February 1874   35

All kinds and all races took the track   35

Camped in the bush   66

The approach to Hell's Gate   66

Diggers fight for their lives on the track to the goldfields   67

A shower of spears comes flying from the trees   67

Mulligan and his party fight off a determined attack   82

The cannibals of the Palmer preferred Chinese food   82

Chinese were carried off bodily for the roasting fires   83

The first burial on the Hodgkinson   83

A punitive party sneaks up on a blacks' camp   114

A sampling of Cooktown's Chinese population   114

A Chinese joss-house in Cooktown   115

A Chinese gambling den   115

Chinese on the Palmer track   130

A digger and a couple of packers relax in a roadside shanty   131

A canvas-walled billiard room on the field   178

Contemporary advertisement for an ore-crushing mill   179

Packhorses carrying parts of ore-crushing mills over the mountains   179

The Mulligan Highway at the Palmer River near the old site of Byerstown   194

The most substantial building left in Cooktown   194

Cooktown today   195

Cooktown's once-busy wharves have reverted to mud flats   195

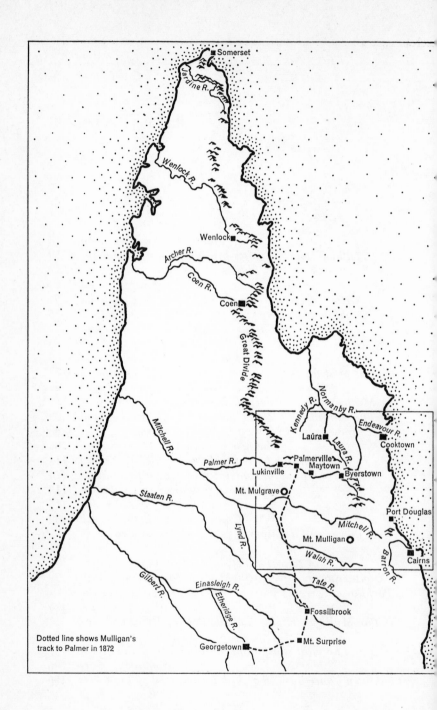

Dotted line shows Mulligan's
track to Palmer in 1872

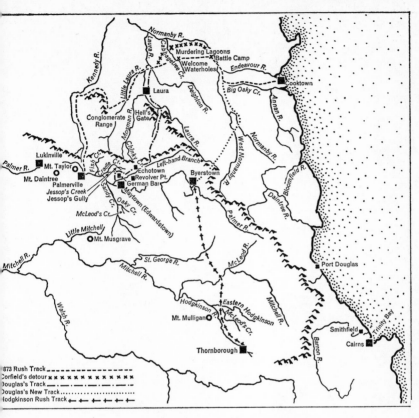

The Palmer River goldfield and surrounding district

1873 Rush Track _ _ _ _ _ _ _ _ _
Corfield's detour x x x x x x x x x
Douglas's Track _ . _ . _ . _ . _ . _ .
Douglas's New Track . . . .
Hodgkinson Rush Track ┼ ─ ┼ ─ ┼ ─ ┼ ─

Cape York Peninsula, showing the gold-rush area

1 · CANNIBAL COUNTRY

IT WAS no more than a short, hand-written notice nailed to the bark wall of a mining warden's office in north Queensland on 3rd September 1873 that started the Palmer gold rush, one of the most fantastic rushes in history. *J. V. Mulligan reports the discovery of payable gold on the Palmer River. Those interested may inspect at this office the 102 ounces he has brought back.* Those words were enough to bring thirty-five thousand men pushing through tangled jungle, across treacherous rivers, over parched mountains, and through rocky defiles that swarmed with the country's most implacable cannibals, to reach the stream that was to become the River of Gold.

Overnight a tent town sprouted on the steamy, mangrove shores of the Endeavour River, and within months it had grown to the second busiest port of Queensland. Its sole business was Palmer gold. Men and women of every race and nation jostled in its streets. Banks and stores stood cheek by jowl with shanties, brothels, and gambling dens. Its Chinese citizens outnumbered all the others put together, and in their bazaars they were predicting that Cooktown was about to become the Canton of the South.

The gravels of the Palmer, its creeks and gullies, yielded a hundred tons of gold. Men who won it easily spent it easily. Horses were shod with gold, and nuggets were wagered on flies crawling up bar-room walls and tossed to dance-hall girls as payment for Australia's first strip-tease shows. But the Palmer kept the balance by making others pay. Hundreds

1

died of starvation, of fever, of a bullet or a spear. Chinese coolies hung from trees by their pigtails for days, in batches of half a dozen or more, waiting their turn to be knocked on the head, roasted, and eaten.

Australia's most rugged frontier was pushed open by a flood of Palmer gold. It was the last of the old-style rushes, and the men who made it gradually faded away when the Palmer gold was gone. They were a race apart. Blooded in a quarter-century of prospecting and digging in the goldfields of California and Australia, they were a fiercely independent, self-reliant breed, ready to face any kind of hardship and tackle any kind of country so long as there was a gleam of gold in it. In red flannel shirts that were supposed to keep the flies away, cord trousers and top-boots to stop the fangs of the toughest snake, and wide-brimmed, floppy felt hats to keep off the sun, they would go anywhere. With a minimum of equipment—Snider rifle, axe, pick, shovel, tin dish, and billy—they had all they needed to make camp and work a claim. For food they rarely carried more than flour, tea, and sometimes sugar.

They needed all their resources on the Palmer; the Cape York Peninsula was inhospitable country. Centuries earlier, Chinese, Malays, Portuguese, Spanish, and Dutch travellers had looked at it—and wanted no part of it. Gold had been found there and, like Lasseter's reef, lost again before it could do anyone any good. The first white man to see its interior had been killed by a cannibal's spear; pioneers on its lower fringe were going broke because markets were too far away.

It was a wet country in which a man could die of thirst. Its annual rainfall ranged from less than 30 inches in the south to more than 70 in the north. On the ranges of the east coast the figure rose to 160. Half the water run-off of Queensland poured from its rivers into the Gulf of Carpentaria. But for more than half the year in the dry season those rivers were little more than strips of dry sand.

One of the few rivers that never ran dry was the Mitchell, named by Leichhardt in 1845 after his fellow explorer Sir Thomas Mitchell. Into the Mitchell ran the Palmer—the

2

River of Gold. But the Palmer's gold gleamed undetected in its gravel for a long time.

For centuries before James Cook sighted Australian shores, the crews of Chinese junks and Malay proas fished the peninsula's shores for bêche-de-mer. When they went ashore for water they left indecipherable characters carved on the durable trunks of ironwood trees—but they had no thought of gold.

A party of Portuguese bêche-de-mer fishermen, driven from Timor by the north-west monsoon, landed somewhere on the shores of the Gulf of Carpentaria. For weeks they endured a miserable existence on the inhospitable coast before the wind changed and they were able to get back to Timor. They took with them several rich samples of gold-bearing quartz. Backed by wealthy merchants they returned with a well-equipped expedition to prospect the locality. Blacks drove them off, capturing some of their number and eating them. They did not find the lost reef. It never has been found.

The Dutch heard the story, and in 1623 the exploration ship *Pera* anchored in a swamp-lined estuary. Skipper Carstensz found no gold and did not like the country, but he gave the river the name it still bears—the Staaten.

An earlier Dutch visitor, Willem Jansz, of the *Duyfken*, had his men row him up the estuary of the Wenlock River in 1606, but he had liked the country no better. The fact that an army of two hundred painted black warriors chased him out of it probably had some influence on his opinion. They are mining gold on the Wenlock today.

About a century and a half later, James Cook, coasting north in the *Endeavour*, ran on a coral reef, and, on 17th June 1770, found shelter in the mouth of a mangrove-lined river which the blacks of the district called Charco. He moored his ship against a steep bank, built a stage across to the shore, and set up camp. With the ship repaired, he named the river Endeavour and, before leaving, on 5th August, climbed Grassy Hill, a 531-foot-high granite outcrop which the blacks called Janellganell, to pick the course he would follow through the reef on his way out. The blacks

3

hurried his departure by setting fire to the dry grass and burning part of his camp.

It was not until the middle of the nineteenth century, after New South Wales (of which Queensland was still a part) had been settled, that the new colony's merchants began to think of an overland route to the north Australian coastline from which they would be right on the threshhold of the rich Eastern trading centres. Several expeditions were organized.

Ludwig Leichhardt, on his way to Port Essington, skirted across the southern butt of the peninsula in 1845. He came on the Mitchell, but failed to discover the Palmer, one of its tributaries.

On 15th September 1848 explorer Edmund Kennedy, who had struck out from Rockingham Bay on 5th June, arrived on the Palmer somewhere between the later sites of Palmerville and Maytown—right in the heart of the richest gold country. But by then he and his party were in no condition to look for gold; the blacks gave them no chance even had they wanted to. Survivors of the expedition spoke of a river with a fine, broad bed about ninety yards wide and steep banks on either side. It was easily crossed, and there was a good supply of fish in its deep pools. The starving party made camp, but they had not even settled in when high-pitched coo-ees began to echo through the bush to call the blacks to the kill.

The blacks of that stretch of the Palmer were Merkin tribesmen. In common with other tribes inhabiting that part of the peninsula, they were a well-built, virile, copper-coloured race, who had been warriors for centuries. Contact with races to the north of Australia had sharpened their wits and polished their fighting techniques. In country where an uncertain supply of wild game provided either a feast or a famine, they were all cannibals "of a particularly bad type", as one writer later put it.

"They killed and ate their own women and children, and occasionally their men," he wrote. "The older women were often killed for eating purposes like livestock. When a gin was to be killed she was taken away to a secluded spot. One man seized and crossed her hands in front of her, while

4

another hit her on the back of the head with a nulla-nulla or wooden sword. Then she was disembowelled and cut up for roasting. A woman who was unfaithful was killed and eaten. If a man fell from a tree, or was in any other way seriously injured, he was generally killed and eaten. Plenty of food to eat was the mainstay of the peninsula aboriginal's existence.

"They never ate the head of a foe. The part of a man most appreciated as food was the thigh, and of a woman, the breast, but the part most sought after was a man's kidney fat, or the kidneys themselves, which were regarded as the centre of life. They liked to carry a piece of a dead foe about with them as a trophy; it was generally rolled up in grass or leaves and carried in a basketwork dilly-bag. It was supposed to bring them good hunting—of man or smaller game."

These were the kind of natives which Kennedy, and later those who followed the Palmer gold rush, had to deal with. As it turned out, the whites were often more savage than the blacks.

The first Kennedy knew of attack was a few tentative spears dropped among his party. Unable to see the attackers, the white men fired blindly into the bush. The Merkins fired the grass and, screeching their war cry, watched the wind sweep the flames towards the explorers' camp. A fusillade scattered them, and Kennedy's men took refuge in the river whose waters were to wash over a hundred tons of gold. As soon as they thought it was safe, the weary explorers packed up and headed north. Of the thirteen men who left Rockingham Bay, three survived. Kennedy was killed by a spear within a few miles of the ship that was waiting for him at Cape York.

By the time the Government in Sydney had heard the story of Jacky Jacky, Kennedy's faithful black boy, and two survivors whom Kennedy had left on the coast south of his destination, it had lost a good deal of its interest in the northern trade route.

In 1865 the Jardine brothers, Frank and Alex, taking stock overland to Somerset, the new settlement on the extreme north of the peninsula of which their father had been made

5

superintendent, travelled closer to the west coast and found the going a little easier. Settlers showed little inclination to follow, and Somerset, once pictured as the "Singapore of Australia", languished for want of settled country at the back of it.

Queensland had become a separate colony in 1859 with sevenpence in the Treasury and an almost vacant north. Land legislation was followed by land rushes, and in the heat of competition settlers pushed north and west into land too isolated to support them. Depression threatened to strangle the new colony almost at birth. Gold could save it; and, after Government rewards had been offered, gold did save it.

In October 1867 James Nash found gold on the Mary River. A horde of twenty-five thousand diggers rushed it, the town of Gympie grew, and three and a half million ounces of gold came out of the river flats. With appetites whetted, prospectors pushed further north. Cattlemen who a few months earlier had to take whatever was offered for their stock found themselves able to set their own prices. The drays and the herds moved north.

Among the new settlers were two brothers from Victoria, William and Frank Hann, who took up Maryvale station, in the watershed of the Burdekin River. To help finance the venture they had taken as partner Richard Daintree, son of a prosperous English farmer, a geologist by profession, and a prospector by instinct. Daintree found gold on the Cape River in 1868. He found it again on the Gilbert and Percy rivers in 1869, and on the Etheridge soon after. Rushes followed, and in 1870 Ravenswood goldfield was opened, with Charters Towers following two years later.

Daintree was beginning to look further afield when the Government appointed him Queensland Agent General in London in 1872. Before leaving he predicted that gold would be found on a line between the Etheridge and the Endeavour rivers. He was right.

Influenced by Daintree's example, the Hann brothers had done some exploring on their own account. In 1872, when the Queensland Government of Arthur Hunter Palmer sponsored an expedition to ascertain, "as far north as the 14th

6

parallel of latitude, the character of the country and its mineral resources with a view to future settlement and occupation", William Hann was chosen to lead it. With him went Norman Taylor, geologist, Dr Thomas Tate, botanist, Frederick Warner, surveyor, two men named Stewart and Nation, and a black boy named Jerry. They had twenty-five pack- and saddle-horses, twenty sheep, and provisions for five months. Hann put up a prize of half a pound of tobacco for the first of the party to find gold.

They left Fossilbrook, an outstation of Mount Surprise, on 26th June 1872, crossed the Lynd River, named by Leichhardt, and then the Tate, which they named after their botanist. The next river they came to they named the Walsh, after Mr W. H. Walsh, Minister for Works, and followed it down to the Mitchell—strong-running, clear, with plenty of fish, and crocodile tracks everywhere. All along the banks were heaps of fresh mussel shells marking the recent camps of blacks. Expecting trouble at any moment, they followed the Mitchell up-stream. Several groups of blacks were seen, but none showed signs of hostility. One old woman even guided them to a native well when they needed water after turning north from the river.

About two hundred miles north of the Etheridge, Hann climbed and named Mount Daintree. He wrote: "From the summit, a large river was seen to the north about three miles from the camp which I believe to be Kennedy's Ninety Yards Wide Creek. This I have named the Palmer, after the Chief Secretary of Queensland." That afternoon they made camp on the bank of the Palmer.

Tate's diary describes the discovery of gold. "August 5th: Just before sundown Warner prospected the gully near the camp and found gold on a bed of granite. The prospects we obtained were certainly not payable and did not average more than two grains to the dish." Hann described it as light, scaly gold of a rich colour. He paid Warner his half pound of tobacco, and named the creek Warner's Gully. They followed the river up for about forty-five miles, all the way finding traces of gold, but never very much.

The party continued north. Several times black hunting

7

parties eyed them suspiciously, but did not attack. They came close to trouble when Tate brought back to camp a little black boy he had found alone in the bush. The boy was happy enough with them and gulped sweet tea with great gusto. But next day a large mob of hostile, painted warriors arrived at the camp to demand his return. No one argued about it, but even with the boy safely in their ranks many of the blacks wanted to make a fight of it. Only after a couple of shots had been fired over their heads did they disperse.

Next morning, 17th September, Stewart and Jerry were rounding up the horses when spears suddenly rained on them from two sides. They yelled at the horses, which headed for the camp at a gallop with both men after them, and two mobs of yelling blacks close behind. The noise brought the rest of the party out at the run, and a fusillade scattered the pursuers.

Several times the party was caught in the kind of swamp country that had sapped the strength of Kennedy and his men. Night after night they fought off hordes of mosquitoes while crocodiles bellowed in the mud close at hand and dingoes howled in the distant hills.

They reached the coast near the site of Cooktown on 21st September, were back on the Palmer by 28th October, and home by 12th November.

Back at Maryvale Hann wrote guardedly of gold on the Palmer. His report, published as a parliamentary paper early in 1873, said that flattering indications of a goldfield had been found, but anything in the nature of a rush was to be deprecated. He would "caution any but experienced, well-provided bushmen against coming there to prospect".

On the Etheridge goldfield, where fortunes were beginning to wane, the local newspaper published the report in full. Old diggers lapped up every word of it. A mob of cattlemen like Hann and his mates might not think they had found payable gold, but what would they know about washing paydirt. If they could find even a gleam of gold a prospector might find a fortune. In twos and threes old diggers began to disappear into the bush.

Working on the Etheridge at that time was a man by the

name of James Venture Mulligan, a fearless bushman and expert prospector who, since his arrival in Australia from County Down in Northern Ireland in 1859, had managed to be just too late at almost every gold rush from Ballarat to Gympie. He had a lot of friends on the field, and if anyone was to try out Hann's find Mulligan was the man for the job.

Mulligan left Georgetown, the centre of the Etheridge field, on 5th June 1873, with five mates: Albert Brandt, James Dowdell, David Robinson, Peter Abelsen (also known as Peter Brown), and Alexander Watson. They rode about eighty-five miles east to Mount Surprise station, followed Hann's tracks down the Lynd for a while, and then struck out through poor, rough country, to reach the Tate on 21st June. This was all new country, never before crossed by a white man. Where they crossed the Walsh River there were the tracks of blacks—thousands of them.

The party rejoined Hann's route and followed it to the Mitchell, a strong-flowing river a good six hundred yards wide, with high, scrubby banks on either side. Not far from the precipitous mass of Mount Mulgrave they found a place to cross, and from there climbed steadily up the slopes of the divide north of the river. As they topped the divide they found themselves looking out over the wild grandeur of the Palmer valley. They descended into the valley and camped on 29th June about a mile above what was soon to become the roaring gold town of Palmerville. This had brought them into the territory of the Merkins.

The blacks had watched them coming from the hilltops, and as the weary party made camp they closed in. "The first night the blacks tried to burn us out," Mulligan wrote later. "They set the grass on fire on both sides of the river and then retired to a mountain, threw stones down at us, brandished their spears at us, and showed other signs of hostility. We took precautions and burned the grass around our camp, looked after our horses and examined our firearms. After this we kept night watch."

In the morning they breakfasted well on perch caught in one of the river's deep waterholes. Then Mulligan took his prospecting dish and walked down to the river. The bed of

9

it was gravelly sand over salty rock. Choosing a large, flat rock at the edge of the water, he scraped away some of the top gravel on the upstream side of it and then scooped up the gravel and sand that lay on the rock underneath it. He dipped a little more water into the dish and ran his fingers through the rough gravel. There were some lumps of clay in it. He broke them up, dipped the dish again, and let the river wash the muddy water away. He swirled the dish around, shaking it slightly to and fro as he did so, and then lifted it slowly out of the water, tilted at an angle so the water took away the top layer of gravel with it. He picked out the larger pebbles and threw them away. Again he washed and swirled the gravel in the dish, again he let the water carry the top layer of it away. He did the same thing again and again until the dish held little more than a spoonful of sand. He was tense now, like a man who had seen something.

Very carefully this time he gave the dish one last swirl. Then he held it up to the light. Half the sand in the dish was spread out in a gleaming tail of gold. He moved the dish so his shadow fell on it. It still showed yellow. Gold! Fool's gold would gleam in the sun to fool the beginner, but only real gold was yellow in either light or shade. He scraped it with his fingers. He realized the others were watching over his shoulders, but none said a word. Here was gold, not just a colour of it, not fine dust, but good, coarse particles of water-worn gold, rather flat in shape, but with good substance in them, not scaly. If there was more like this . . .

In the first week, moving about all the time, they found more than six ounces of alluvial gold. This was the stretch of river between where Palmerville and Maytown eventually grew up.

Until now they had been working with only tin prospecting dishes to wash the gold from the gravel, but on 13th July they found a creek that looked so promising that Abelsen decided to make a cradle that would wash more gravel with less work. Looking around for suitable timber, he picked a Leichhardt tree, a large-leafed softwood, popular among the blacks for making dugout canoes because its timber was so easily worked. Abelsen chopped down the tree, cut off a couple of sections of the trunk about three and a half feet long, and split them into boards with the axe. The party's only other tools were a rasp and a hammer. Like all experienced prospectors, they carried a few nails.

Working the boards into shape with the rasp, and then nailing them together, Abelsen had soon built a sort of box, open at one end. Across the bottom were nailed two pieces of wood, rounded at the ends, so the box could be rocked like a baby's cradle. Inside he fixed a sort of slide so that any gravel dropped in the top would have to roll over it and hit the bottom at the closed end of the cradle. He wedged some sticks across the slide and covered it with an old piece of canvas so the surface had a rippled appearance. He did the same with the bottom of the box. Then he covered the top with a sieve made of a piece of sheet-iron with holes punched in it, which they had brought with them. It was a simplified sort of cradle, but it would be enough for their present purposes.

"We're ready," said Abelsen.

There was a sort of a rock bar across the creek, and they set up their cradle on it so the open end sloped slightly downward. Abelsen tipped a dish of gravel into the sieve, followed it with a couple more, and then, with Mulligan rocking the cradle at a firm, even swing, tipped a dish of water over the gravel. As another and another followed it, the muddy, sandy water poured through onto the slide, slid down to the back of the cradle, and then along the bottom and out the open end. More gravel went into the sieve, more water followed it. Abelsen raked the big pebbles out of the top and threw them away. He stopped adding gravel then, and kept pouring water until it came away clean.

"Now for it."

He lifted off the sieve and Mulligan tilted the cradle so the sun shone on the canvas-covered slide.

"Will you look at that now!"

In bands across the slide above each ripple the canvas gleamed with gold.

On 16th July they moved from Cradle Creek, as they called it, up a tributary of the Palmer they called the "Left-hand

11

Branch", and found payable gold all the way. They found it also in a tributary which they called Sandy Creek. A mile further up the river it was still plentiful.

All the time they worked the Merkin tribesmen were watching them closely, becoming more and more intrigued every day by all this searching for something in the sand. "They apparently thought it was something to eat, and as we moved further up the river, down would come the blacks and begin rooting in our abandoned holes. They put a lot of digging into it, all for no useful result to them."

For a couple of weeks the party worked in the Palmerville area. They were getting good gold, but another problem was beginning to press them. It was the usual one when a man found gold: What was he to do? The natural thing was to get down to it, work like mad, and fill his billy and anything else that would hold gold as quickly as he could. Reporting a strike brought the finder's reward, but it also, inevitably brought a rush that swamped the place and penned him in to a single claim. Discoverers of a new field had before this seen other men taking up fortunes all around them while they themselves did poorly. On the other hand, every day that a man kept quiet about a strike increased the chance of someone else tracking him and reporting the find as his own. Word soon got around if some wily old prospector disappeared for long. And Mulligan knew there were others out after the Palmer gold.

By 24th August Mulligan had decided to return to Georgetown, report the field, and come back. He had covered the ground fairly well and he thought he knew where the best spots were. "We had thirteen camps up and down the river," he wrote later, "and found gold in crevices and behind shelters. We traversed the river for nearly forty miles. We tried many gullies and ravines and found gold." They dug two holes and buried in them all the tools, surplus ammunition, and equipment they could spare, and headed back for the Etheridge. In their saddle bags they had 102 ounces of gold.

Mulligan, in whom the explorer's instinct was always at least as strong as the prospector's, took a last look at the forbidding country which he knew would soon be swarming with men in search of fortunes. "Due north," he wrote later, "the range of sandstone capping is irregularly broken into by creeks and gorges, whilst, in a parallel line south, the back of Thompson's Range is horrid to look at. Looking at the numerous bushfires and darkies' signal fires, which show so well this calm morning, the scene is terribly grand and, considered so far away in the wild bush, is a little shocking, though pleasing." His somewhat confusing description still fits the country today—harsh, monstrous, grand and awe-inspiring, unaccountably compelling.

The cliffs Mulligan saw to the north were the southern edge of the Conglomerate tableland, a great mass of sandstone resting on a thin bed of consolidated gravel or conglomerate. This conglomerate was, in places, rich in gold. The waters of Cradle Creek, the Left-hand Branch, and many other Palmer tributaries ran out from under this sandstone mass and, in doing so, brought some of the conglomerate gold with them. East and south-east of Mulligan that morning was granite country, also with gold in its gullies and in the quartz of its reefs.

At Georgetown, Mr Howard St George, mining warden on the Etheridge, listened to Mulligan's report, looked at the gold he had brought back, and tacked that notice on the bark wall of his office. *J. V. Mulligan reports the discovery of payable gold on the Palmer River. Those interested may inspect at this office the 102 ounces he has brought back.*

2 · THE RUSH

THE FIRST WORD they had in the south of payable gold on the Palmer was a telegram from Cardwell, then Queensland's most northern port. Dated 9th September 1873, it said: "Prospectors Mulligan, Brown [Abelsen], Dowdell, A. Watson, and D. Robertson [Robinson] got 102 ounces on the Palmer River which they prospected for twenty miles. They say nothing of the country outside the river. Nearly all are leaving here."

By the time the wire reached Brisbane the northern goldfields were buzzing like beehives. All over the north, men were packing their gear and heading for the Palmer. Mount Surprise station became a focal point; from there they could follow Mulligan's tracks. Horsemen, drays, packhorses, and swagmen began to string out along the barely distinguishable trail.

The size of the rush took even Mulligan by surprise. "I do wish to stop this before it grows any more," he wrote to the *Queenslander* on 10th September. "Already exaggerated accounts and too much excitement exist here. If people rush the place without rations they must perish, for there is no getting back in the wet season across the rivers which lie between. People will go there, many will get a little gold, but I believe nothing great will be got." But about the time Mulligan was writing that, a digger who had been drinking with him claimed the prospector, in expansive mood, had said, "Sure an' it's a river of gold we've found out there."

The letter to the *Queenslander* painted a different picture.

14

"The climate is hot on the Palmer, and as in other new places, we may expect sickness to be prevalent. Advise the people to wait until after the wet season. By that time the place will be better proven." It was good advice, but Mulligan had no intention of taking it himself. "A great deal of excitement prevails on the Etheridge," he wrote, "and men and drays are preparing for the road in spite of our cautions. Our party are going back to prospect more fully."

With Mulligan going straight back it was hardly likely that the others would wait. In fact he had made it clear in his letter that he knew what was going to happen when he advised that the Government should open a port on the Endeavour River, or at Weary Bay to the south of it.

Mulligan left the Etheridge on 12th September. He was followed by about a hundred men and about three hundred horses. They cut their own road as they went and reached the Palmer on 26th September. Even women and children joined in that first rush into unknown, cannibal-inhabited country.

Other miners later claimed, around their campfires, and in some of the newspapers that sprang up on the field, that they had beaten Mulligan to the Palmer. Some of them might have; it was a large field. But most of the early ones followe ' Mulligan's tracks.

By 15th September—three days after Mulligan had headed back—the Etheridge correspondent of the *Queenslander* was writing from Georgetown: "Nearly all the population of nearly four hundred have left, or are about to leave for the Palmer. Already they have chosen a name for the Palmer's first town—Eureka, meaning I have found it." A couple of days later Georgetown was a ghost town. "Claims have been thrown up, machinery is idle."

From Cardwell came news that "everyone that can is going to the Palmer rush. It is about two hundred miles from us. Anyone going now and not taking a good supply of rations will stand a good chance of starving."

From Townsville: "The *Lord Ashley* which arrives here today is said to have on board a number of diggers from the south bound for the Palmer River rush. We hope the rumour is untrue, as it is simply madness." Within days Townsville was almost deserted. The Gilbert was abandoned to the blacks. Men on the Etheridge paid fifty-six pounds a ton to have their belongings carried to the Palmer. Even recently discovered Charters Towers was denuded.

The country between Charters Towers and the Palmer was very broken, hard and dry. One miner had his mate die on the way. He strapped the body to his saddle and brought it over miles of rough country to the nearest station, where he borrowed tools to dig a grave under a tree and carve his mate's name and the date on it. He needed to borrow tools because many miners in the rush travelled without them, hoping that they would be able to buy them on the field.

It was not long before there was trouble between the diggers and the Palmer blacks. A favourite Merkin fishing spot was a big waterhole on Fish Creek, a tributary which joined the Palmer just downstream from Cradle Creek. It was also one of the first places where gold was found. A large party of tribesmen were fishing at the hole when word of the gold got round and the diggers moved in on the rock-studded, sandy banks just down-stream from it. For the rest of the day both parties went about their business, keeping a wary eye on each other, but without any trouble. Mulligan described in his reminiscences how the trouble developed.

"That evening our party and some acquaintances were having a yarn when the greatest commotion began in the camp; men tearing through the bushes, scrambling over rocks and boulders in the river, while many voices sang out, 'The blacks, the blacks!' It was, however, only a kangaroo looking for water.

"Next morning a few of the boys went up to the blacks' camp, fired some revolver shots and dispersed the blacks—in fact, spoilt their big feast. There were literally barrowloads of fish of all kinds—barramundi, cod, and bream.

"After this, hostilities commenced. Some of the boys got chased into camp next day by a mob of angry spearmen. I was one of the miners who came out of the river to defend the camp with my rifle at the ready, and I was just in time to see Bill Kelly have a very narrow escape from a spear.

16

"A party was formed that evening to find the blacks' camp and disperse them. The blacks, however, had a watch out who soon scrambled down the cliff, gave the alarm, and the whole yelling mob jumped out almost into the teeth of the miners. The spears were flying fast and furious, while the hills echoed with the roar of rifles and revolvers. Spears fell like rain—in fact, a whole forest of them was left sticking in the ground, thrown with such force that they almost brought themselves up straight."

This first encounter was typical of many that followed it. It was a win for the whites, but in the years that followed many were to pay with their lives for this kind of trigger-happy thoughtlessness which regarded the original owners of the territory as nothing more than pests to be chased out of the way.

One of the first letters from the Palmer was handed to the newspaper by a Charters Towers miner who had received it from his mate.

October 5, 1873.

MY DEAR FRED,

This is only our second day on the Palmer, consequently I cannot tell much about the place as yet. But still, from what I see and hear, I believe there will be some good gold got not far from here.

At present the blacks are very bad. It is war to the knife between the whites and them.

Parties are scattered up and down the river for miles. We have been trying in the ravines and can get a little gold anywhere, but nothing of much account—from one grain up to three to the dish.

The main camp is nine miles up the river from here. They have to camp together on account of the blacks.

I believe there will be numbers leaving before long on account of the wet season, but come what will, I shall not leave it for some time. The only thing that will kill us is rations. We will have to pack all our rations from the Etheridge, and it is a good 250 miles from here. Anyone who comes will require three good horses per man to pack rations.

Tell D—— to rest content where he is at present. If I get onto anything at all, I will write immediately to him.

17

It was the custom for miners on the field to keep their mates in other places posted on what was happening. One digger described in his reminiscences how he was working on a station when a letter from a mate on the Palmer brought him into the new rush. He describes the scramble. to get horses, pack saddles, rations, picks, shovels, and tin dishes in a bush town where everyone was getting ready to leave, and heading out onto the track.

"Outfits of all sorts, and of the strangest kinds could be seen. Here a party of foot-men tramped along with their swags rolled up on their backs, and their tin billies in their hands. There half a dozen followed in the rear of an old horse, bearing the united packs and rations of the party. Now and then a tilted cart, drawn by three or four horses, would be overtaken, containing the owner's family and effects, and followed by a few gaunt looking kangaroo dogs.

"Sometimes we passed a drove of fat cattle, or a few laden teams, all making their way towards the common focus. Occasionally well-mounted and equipped diggers, with plenty of spare horses, pushed rapidly along; and now and again a helpless looking creature, without blankets or food, and evidently depending upon what he could beg or borrow, was left behind us.

"Once or twice we came upon a couple of stalwart navvies, carrying their possessions on a hand barrow between them. On one occasion we passed a man wheeling his worldly goods in a barrow, and his nether man enveloped—for the sake of coolness and ease—in a woman's petticoat.

"All carried firearms of one sort or another, from the ancient Queen Anne musket and flintlock pistol to the latest invention in breech-loading and repeating rifles and revolvers. Everyone was animated with the desire to get to the new fields as soon as possible."

At night, according to the writer, they generally managed to camp on water, and a canvas village mushroomed as the better-off diggers settled in for the night. Every day they met diggers returning in disgust without even having washed a dish of gravel. The country was different from what they were used to. There were great, towering cliffs of sand-

James Venture Mulligan, the man who started the Palmer
River gold rush

A contemporary artist's impression of Mulligan and his mates prospecting on the Palmer

Sluicing for gold on the Palmer

stone, they said. It was not the kind of country a man found gold in. Nobody took any notice of them; the rush streamed on, and at last they reached the field.

"For a few miles before you catch sight of buildings, trees denuded of their bark for roofing purposes warn of the proximity of the main camp. Innumerable horse bells tinkle everywhere, and here and there little white tents mark temporary habitations."

There was already the beginning of a village of tents among the trees on the slope above the river. A combined public house and store stood in the centre of it. It was a single-roomed, dirt-floored affair with a rough frame of saplings, and walls and roof of messmate bark. One side was open, and the roof was extended to form a sort of veranda. Dividing the veranda from the inside was a bar made out of barrel staves and boards from brandy and gin cases. No matter how short rations were, there was always liquor on the Palmer right from the start. A hundred yards away in the bush was the killing yard where cattle were slaughtered and the meat sold on the spot. A native police detachment under a sergeant from the Etheridge were building a lock-up out of logs.

Gradually the diggers were spreading out from the township, working up the river and prospecting the gullies that ran into it. They found Sandy Creek and its tributaries, Oaky, McLeod's, Greasy Bill's, Stony, McGann's, White Horse, Sweeny's, and others. The names are of little help to anyone trying to reconstruct the story of the rush today; the same names were often given to half a dozen different creeks scattered over a couple of hundred square miles.

The country on this stretch of the Palmer was slate, and very rough to travel over. Most of the gold was coming from the beds of the creeks and from what were called the river beaches. On these stretches the gravel was stripped off for about one or two feet and there then remained about six inches or so, depending on the lay of the bedrock, of washdirt containing gold.

But although gold yields were improving, rations were getting shorter all the time. The position was made worse by bushfires between the Etheridge and the Palmer burning off the dry grass and leaving nothing for bullock and horse teams to live on. A few carriers who did get through had to break into their loads to feed their bullocks on flour and water. Before long, starving diggers on the Palmer were to be eating bullock's food—boiled grass. Some diggers tried hunting for food, but there was little game to be had, and the Merkins made it unhealthy for small parties to go far afield. In any case, the Palmer was not the kind of country a man could count on living off.

Three months earlier, Mulligan's party had lived well and come back with rations to spare. They had found the rivers teeming with perch and other fish of from four to five pounds weight. There were many wild turkeys about, and ducks were plentiful on the lagoons. Hann's party, on the other hand, about twelve months before, had been, according to Tate, "in a state of semi-starvation almost from the start, and had to subsist mainly on lizards, snakes, and white ants". Kennedy had fared even worse.

Early in October, disillusioned diggers were trooping back into Georgetown, on the Etheridge, in fairly large numbers. Lack of rations was beating them. As was always the case in a rush, the disgruntled men blamed the man who had reported the gold—Mulligan—for all their troubles. There had even been talk of lynching. Mulligan and his mates, meanwhile, had moved up the river on to the Left-hand Branch. He was supposed to be on good gold there, but only a few had enough rations to follow him.

By 20th October the Sub-Inspector of Police at Georgetown was reporting, "There are about six hundred men on the Palmer and a good many more en route for the diggings. No rations whatever are to be bought, and there are only eight tons of flour in transit by horse teams. The road is impossible for bullock drays on account of there being seventy miles of broken, slaty country. A first-class horse team was six days travelling seventeen miles. Supplies for the police have been on the road now for five weeks and are barely half way there yet."

A miner wrote to the *Queenslander* on 2nd November: "In

spite of all the caution given by the prospectors [Mulligan and his party] respecting poor gold and the probability of short supplies, many came with just as much as served them for the journey—about two weeks.

"Since then, others have come and some gone, and with the exception of a few to whom they sold their scanty supplies, all the others must either return or starve. A few hundredweight of flour which arrived was speedily bought up at two shillings a pound. A Chinese gardener has commenced planting.

"Mr Jack Edwards of the Etheridge brought in some sixty fat cattle ten days ago. He kills the last of them tomorrow and I hear there is another small lot coming."

Meat—at a price—was always the most easily obtained commodity on the Palmer. Cattle prices rose to seven pounds, to ten pounds, to thirteen pounds a head, and the time was not far off when an old, worn-out working bullock was to bring thirty pounds for butchering.

When the field was opened the farthest-out station stocked on the overland route was Mount Surprise, on Junction Creek, held by the Firths, and this was more than two hundred miles from the diggings by the nearest practicable route. A road of a sort was soon opened by diggers heading for the Palmer, drovers taking cattle to sell on the field, and carriers. It crossed the Tate, Walsh, and Mitchell rivers, and then followed up the Palmer through some of the roughest country in North Queensland. All along it blacks speared cattle, and a good many stockmen were killed.

One man out looking for strayed cattle met a number of blacks who returned his friendly greeting. As he passed, one of them threw a spear which buried itself in his back. He galloped back to the homestead in agony, but the spear was too deeply embedded to be pulled out. There followed a ride of one hundred and thirty miles for medical attention. He survived the ride, but died soon after.

As rations became scarcer on the Palmer, gold returns improved. A large part of the river bed was rocky, and across the stony spreads of it were little breaks or ripples against which the water had carried the gold. In places large quanti-

21

ties of clean gold were taken out without any washing needed. It was like picking up wheat—but they were good large grains of water-worn gold. A few were getting up to five ounces a day, and ten or twenty ounces a week was fairly common. Nuggets had been found weighing up to twenty-five ounces. Several thousands of ounces of this gold was scattered about the camp in chamois bags, in old socks, in billy-cans, and in anything else that would hold it. But there was no gold warden on the field yet. No claims were pegged, and everyone was prospecting, getting gold wherever he could. Fights over finds were frequent.

One of the early arrivals on the Left-hand Branch was a seasoned veteran of many rushes named Murdo Cameron. He had pushed up river some thirty-five miles, and on arriving at a promising spot on a Sunday evening, unpacked his horses and prepared to make camp. He took his billy down to the river for water and blinked his eyes in astonishment. Glittering amid the pebbles on the hard rock bottom was gold. The first dish he washed gave him four ounces. But it was getting late, it had been a hard day's travelling, and it was a Sunday. So far as Cameron knew, there was not another man within miles. He lit his fire, made a billy of tea, dined off the last of a damper, and slept well.

In the morning he was up early and down to the creek. Though he saw nothing unusual, he had a sudden feeling of uneasiness—a feeling that something had been disturbed since he was here last. He bent over the spot where he had filled his billy. Grains of gold still glittered on the rock bottom. He squatted on his haunches to scoop some of it up into his tin dish.

"Keep off that. I'm in possession here."

Cameron straightened up to find himself looking down the wide bore of a Colt recolver. Luckily for him, as things turned out, it was not cocked. In a blazing fury, he hurled himself straight at the man who held it. His fist connected with the other's jaw, and as the man staggered back, the revolver went flying into the river. Sitting in the water, the claim-jumper glared balefully up at Cameron and then turned his head towards the scrub that lined the creek.

"Come on boys," he roared. "There's only one man here. Come and—"

Cameron's hobnailed blucher boot caught him under the chin. Three men erupted from the bush. Cameron tugged his revolver from his belt, cocked it and levelled it.

"Right, laddies, who's next?"

The men hesitated. The revolver muzzle roamed from one to the other of them.

"Na, na, laddies, dinna be bashful."

Step by step, the men backed into the bush. Then they turned and bolted. Three shots from Cameron's revolver hurried their crashing footsteps. The man in the water was scrambling to his feet. The revolver came round to cover him.

"An noo be off," said Cameron slowly. "An if you so much as show your dirrty nose here again, I'll blow it off for ye."

Revolver Point was the name Cameron gave to the spot. In the first fortnight he took nine hundred pounds worth of gold out of it.

Half a mile downstream from Revolver Point, another rich patch was German Bar, discovered by two German brothers named Ruge.

The discoverer of McLeod's Creek was Billy McLeod, a veteran of the Gympie and Etheridge rushes. He worked among the various gullies and alluvial patches on the Palmer for a while, but, like Mulligan, he was essentially an outside prospector. He got 193 ounces of gold out of McLeod's in the first week, but he soon moved on. About three years later Mulligan met him prospecting unknown country on the Hodgkinson River.

Another "loner" was an old Gympie hand named Jessop. As soon as others began to settle near his camp he would pull down his tent and move on. He had made his way north by stages, travelling alone and taking all the lone bushman's precautions against surprise by the blacks. One trick was to build an ordinary camp and campfire, and then, under cover of darkness, sneak away and sleep somewhere else. Many a man came back to his camp next morning to find the place riddled with spears. After prospecting a tributary of Cradle

Creek which came to be called Jessop's Creek, he moved to another tributary—Jessop's Gully—and there made one of the richest strikes on the field. From a patch the size of a dining table he took about six hundred ounces of gold in a couple of days. He used the money to take a holiday, and never came back.

With hundreds of diggers muddying the water of their favourite fishing spots, the blacks became, in the language of the diggers, "very troublesome". The Palmer valley had been their hunting ground for centuries. They outnumbered the white men by hundreds to one. They were all cannibals— not, as many of the southern tribes were, for ritual purposes, but simply because, in a country where game was often scarce, they had acquired a taste for human meat.

The Palmer blacks were also less nomadic than the southern and inland tribes. They had permanent camps, always on dry ridges close to permanent water. "They build little gunyahs in the shape of a marquee to protect them-selves from the mosquitoes," wrote Mulligan. "They cover them with tea-tree bark and rope them down with straw exactly in the shape of a haystack, leaving a hole in the side, one footsquare, to get in at."

"They do not like being put off their fishing grounds on the river," wrote one of the diggers. "And they are deter-mined to keep possession of the back grounds, so they have cleared the gullies of diggers two or three times. One lad got speared in the foot, and a horse was speared in three places. He was still living, and some of the spears broken in him."

One prospector left his mates to do a little prospecting further along the Left-hand Branch. When he did not return a search was made and his tracks were followed to where he had panned in the river bed and washed several dishes of gravel. A little further on from there his tracks disappeared among those of dozens of blacks. He was never seen again.

Soon after this about thirty blacks attacked a party of pros-pectors working on one of the gullies. Even in the face of rifle fire they pressed the attack fearlessly, and though several warriors were wounded, the diggers had to run for their lives, leaving all their equipment behind. One man received a spear through the thigh. More than fifty spears were thrown in this attack. The native police came out next day and shot up a Merkin camp further up the gully. Some of the diggers' tools were recovered from it, but a lot more were missing.

In their raids the blacks always took all the iron they could lay their hands on. Though they had no idea of heating and forging it, they were very clever at converting it into weapons with patient hammering and grinding on wet sandstone. They were particularly fond of socket chisels, which they ground into razor-sharp spear heads and fitted neatly onto wooden shafts. Their own spears were made of a kind of long, straight reed, very tough, and tipped with points and barbs made of very hard wood. They poisoned these by dipping them into putrefying corpses. In the hot, often steamy climate, even ordinary scratches generally festered, and a man or animal wounded by one of these spears had little chance.

Mulligan had discovered on his return to the Palmer that the blacks had found one of his hiding places and cleaned out its supply of hoop-iron, canvas, clothing, and other articles. The hoop-iron was recovered from the top of a big tree growing in the river, together with a tent fly. Both had been covered with grass in an attempt to camouflage them.

Horseshoes were about the most valuable commodity on the field to both blacks and whites. The blacks broke them in half and pounded one end flat to make a head for a handy little tomahawk. To the whites they were literally worth their weight in gold. In the rough, slaty country of the Palmer, a shoeless horse went lame at once. If a horse died, as many did, there was always a rush to get its shoes.

With the wet getting closer and men still pouring onto the field, food became scarcer every day. Dysentery was becoming common, and several died of it. But men who were getting good gold still clung to the ground. "There is talk of a Gold Commissioner coming via the Endeavour River to make a road," one miner wrote. "The Endeavour is our only hope of getting cheap supplies here." Even as he wrote, the first contingent of diggers via the Endeavour was on the way. The Government, with hopes as high as those of the gold-seekers themselves, had lost no time.

Mulligan's report of the discovery had been telegraphed to Brisbane on 31st August 1873. On 9th September George Elphinstone Dalrymple, who had already led a number of northern exploration parties and, in 1864, established the port of Cardwell, was appointed by the Government to explore all rivers and promising inlets between Cardwell and the Endeavour River to find a suitable site for a new goldfields port.

Two cutters, the *Flying Fish* of twelve tons and the *Coquette* of ten tons, were chartered by the Government for the expedition, which consisted of thirteen white men, including Sub-Inspector Robert Johnstone of the native police, and also thirteen native troopers. There was also the master of each cutter, six seamen, and a cook.

The expedition left Cardwell and sailed out into Rockingham Bay on 20th September, and after being weather-bound for nine days, headed north. They had not gone far before they found ample evidence of the kind of reception diggers could expect at the hands of the peninsula blacks. Exploring the Johnstone River, discovered by Sub-Inspector Johnstone on an earlier trip, they were examining a huge native bora ground when more than a hundred painted warriors charged them from the scrub. The discipline and heavy fire-power of the white party broke up the attack, and the blacks retreated, leaving behind dozens of spears, shields, and the heavy, four-foot-long wooden swords for which they were famous.

On 11th October they landed again and were attacked again, this time by an army of more than two hundred. They escaped when the chief of the attackers, a man about six feet six inches tall and broad in proportion, was taken by a crocodile while swimming a creek in an attempt to take them from the rear. Nine days later a shore party was again attacked and had to shoot its way back to the boats.

"In every camp along the beach for two miles," wrote Dalrymple, "was unmistakable evidence of wholesale cannibalism; heaps of human bones and skulls were found in each camp, and in some, roasted and partly eaten bodies were found beside the fires at which they had been cooked. Lumps of half-eaten human flesh were found in the gins' dilly-bags.

These people are of most ferocious expression and are large and powerful men."

The party explored the mouths of the Moresby, Mulgrave, Daintree, and Bloomfield rivers, often delayed by bad weather and the smallness of their craft, and on the afternoon of 24th October 1873, the cutters dropped anchor near Cook's landing place in the Endeavour River. But the rush had not been able to wait for them. Next morning the Australasian Steam Navigation Company's steamer *Leichhardt* (Captain Saunders) steamed into the river at 10.30 and made fast to the mangroves in sixteen feet of water. She had on board the first batch of diggers to head for the Palmer by sea.

The *Leichhardt*, wrote Dalrymple in his report, brought "a complete Government staff of police—to be stationed at the Endeavour—of the Goldfields Department, for the new diggings, in charge of Mr Howard St George, Gold Commissioner, who until then had been Goldfield Warden at the Etheridge; and of Engineers of Roads under the able leadership of Mr A. C. Macmillan, charged on this occasion with the responsible duty of finding and making a road to the diggings. Some seventy hardy miners accompanied them, the expedition being under the immediate charge of Lieutenant Conner, R.N., of H.M. Surveying Schooner *Pearl*.

"Official correspondence," Dalrymple continued, "informed me that since my departure from the settlements, the continued good reports from the Palmer diggings and the imminence of an immediate 'rush', calculated greatly to magnify the distress and danger which it had been part of the duty of my expedition, co-operating with Mr Sellheim, to make provision for, had called forth immediate executive action to provide for all possible emergencies." Mr Sellheim had been instructed to mark a line of trees from the Palmer to Cooktown. He was later appointed goldfield warden for the Palmer in July 1874.

The *Leichhardt* had left Brisbane on 15th October with some members of the expedition on board. Macmillan and his party were taken on at Bowen; forty-six horses and about fifty diggers at Townsville; and Mr St George at Cardwell. Before even the *Leichhardt* was made fast to the muddy banks, the miners swarmed ashore. Their gear followed, and suddenly Cooktown had come into existence.

"On the day before [Friday]," wrote Dalrymple, "we had sailed into a silent, lonely, distant river mouth with thoughts going back a century to the arrival of the brave navigator, its discoverer, and his people, in knee breeches, three-cornered hats, and small swords, pigtails and silver shoe-buckles. On Saturday we were in the middle of a phase of enterprise peculiarly characteristic of the present day—of a young diggings township—men hurrying to and fro, tents rising in all directions, horses grazing and neighing for their mates, all around us—the shouts of sailors and labourers landing more horses and cargo, combined with the rattling of the donkey-engine, cranes and chains."

Dalrymple explored up the Endeavour River as far as he could, and on 31st October his whole party left in the *Leichhardt*. "The *Leichhardt* steamed out of the Endeavour, leaving a lively little seaport under her starboard quarter, gleaming with white tents and noisily busy with workmen, where a week before we found a silent wilderness," he wrote.

3 · BATTLE CAMP

FROM ITS position on the southern shore of the shallow, curving estuary at the foot of Grassy Hill, which cut it off from the sea, the new township looked north-west over the water and dark mangrove trees which fringed the mouth of the river to distant ranges of low hills. Already there were diggers lost in those hills.

Among the first of the diggers landed by the *Leichhardt* was William J. Webb, who had arrived from England as a boy in 1855. "The *Leichhardt* dumped ninety-six of us diggers, New Zealanders, Victorians, New South Welshmen, and Queenslanders, where No. 3 wharf, Cooktown, now is, in the morning of Saturday, 25th October, 1873," Webb later wrote. Every man of them, he said, was impatient to be moving. They knew there were diggers already on the field who had followed Mulligan from the Etheridge, and they were afraid all the gold would be gone before they themselves arrived.

Macmillan, who was to lead their party to the Palmer and survey the permanent road, had picked up Hann's black boy Jerry, who, it was hoped, would be able to guide them to the diggings. Most of the diggers were to travel on foot, but members of the official party were to ride. After the horses were landed, Macmillan had a look at them and decided to spell them for a few days to let them get over the effect of the voyage. The diggers roared their protest, but he stood firm.

During the following day some of the diggers decided to

29

start next morning without waiting for the official party to show them the way. They drank on it and their numbers rose to thirty. In the sober light of dawn they had dropped to five, but these were determined. So on Monday, 27th October 1873, they headed for the hills, George Batton Welch leading them.

Later that day Macmillan, St George, and Jerry climbed a hill where Jerry got his bearings from landmarks he had seen when with Hann. Next day he took them unerringly to Hann's old camp on Big Oaky Creek. As the two white men settled into camp to wait, Jerry was sent back to bring the others.

Webb, who had described their arrival at Cooktown, was a fairly experienced bushman and made comparatively light work of the trip. The new chums did not manage so well. One of them, signing himself H.H., wrote to the Cleveland Bay *Express* about his experiences on the trip, "hoping it will serve as a warning".

"The command left the Endeavour some 108 strong, about 70 of them being on foot with swags from 70 pounds to 90 pounds weight, the supposed distance being about 80 miles," he wrote. "We thought we could not overload ourselves."

Webb describes it from a more detached point of view. "Some humped swags with a pick, shovel and dish strapped to them, some pushed loaded wheelbarrows, two men who had no horse pulled a cart loaded with their food and tools."

Most of the diggers were armed with breech-loading Sniders, murderous weapons for those days, firing a bullet which made a hole four times the size of that made by a modern .303. A couple of sailors who had bolted from their ships still carried cutlasses.

A troop of native police under Sub-Inspector Dyas rode ahead of them, and in the rear came about twenty Chinese diggers. The Chinese kept as close as they could to the main party, but were not allowed to join it. A familiar sight on every Australian goldfield in those days, the Chinese had no horses or vehicles, and they carried their mining tools and food in baskets slung to a pole across their shoulders.

The first night out the party camped at a waterhole which, in rare high spirits, they called King Jerry after their guide.

Next day, heading for the camp on Big Oaky Creek, they passed a tree on which Welch, the leader of the impatient five, had cut his name, and a little farther on had their first lesson about the kind of country they were heading into. Staggering back through the scrub came the lone figure of a white man—one of the five who had gone ahead. In the last stages of exhaustion he gasped out his story. After crossing a big river, he said, the five of them topped a high range and disagreed about which direction to take. They split up, three going one way, and this man and his mate another. Later these two also parted company. None of the other four were ever seen again.

The camp on Big Oaky Creek was reached late that afternoon, and next morning they made an early start, Macmillan and Jerry leading. After two days travelling the heavily loaded new chums were already feeling the strain. H.H. wrote: "After the first day out we found we had overloaded ourselves, and many a poor fellow had to throw away his clothing in order to keep his flour. In fact the road was lined with clothing, blankets, tents, and flour." A few days later: "The men found that they could not keep up with the command, and at every camp they had to lighten their loads."

After finding a track over the coastal range, the party at last came down into the valley of the Normanby River on Monday, 3rd November. "Some blacks were shot here," wrote Webb. "I do not know why, as they had not interfered with us." But another digger, J. J. Cranley, writing later to the *Queenslander*, gave a different account of it. "When the horses were turned out, the blacks put in an appearance and attempted to drive them away," he wrote. "This led to the blacks being dispersed and the horses secured."

Next morning the mounted men found a ford about a quarter of a mile below the camp. The water was not too deep, and most of the diggers waded or swam across after the horses. Webb meanwhile had found a tree that had fallen across the river, and he and about twenty-four of the others crossed by that. Before the two parties could rejoin forces a number of blacks appeared and seemed to want to parley. They made no threatening moves, but leant their spears up against rocks and trees and stood with their arms at their sides. To Webb, at any rate, they seemed to be trying to show that they meant peace. But it was apparently another case of members of the white party seeing things differently. Macmillan either misunderstood the blacks' actions or decided to take no risks. He called the mounted men to him and led them, yelling at the top of their lungs, in a charge straight into the middle of the blacks, who snatched up their spears and ran.

Step by step, callousness, stupidity, and thoughtlessness were advancing the hostility that was to cost hundreds of white lives and lead to the extinction of whole tribes.

From the Normanby crossing the party headed north-west along the river until they came to the northern end of the range. They were not far from the spot where Hann's party had been attacked on 17th September 1872. Special care was taken in making camp that night. Saddles and other loading from the horses were stacked in a rough circle to form a barricade. Men were detailed to take turns on watch and give the alarm at the slightest sign of a blackfellow. None of them had any way of knowing that more than five hundred blacks had been following them ever since they had crossed the Normanby River.

Putting together several accounts of the affray at Battle Camp, it appears that as the diggers were settling down for the night one of them went down to the creek to fill his billy before turning in. He had been there earlier in the day and was not paying any particular attention to anything when he noticed something in the soft, sandy mud, and bent down to look closer. It was a bare footprint with the water still oozing into it. It could not have been made more than a few minutes before.

The man looked around him, and found more footprints in the mud. He followed them. They led to a patch of clear water. The sand there was a mass of footprints—hundreds of them. They must all have been made within the last quarter of an hour.

Cautiously, expecting a spear in his back at any moment, the digger straightened up and looked around him. Dusk made deceptive shadows among the stunted trees, but everything was still. Further down, a dry gully joined the creek. It could shelter a thousand blacks. Something seemed to move. He put his head down and ran for his life back to the camp.

Years later some blacks who were there that night told prospectors they had been so confident of victory that they did not even bother to conceal their presence. They outnumbered the whites by five to one and expected nothing more than an easy killing and the biggest cannibal feast of all time.

As the panting digger gasped out what he had seen, the whole camp turned out to strengthen defences. All surplus gear was stacked on the barricades. The Chinese were commandeered to chop saplings to fill the gaps in it. All fires were put out so no targets for spears would show. Double guards were posted. All that night few slept. But there was no attack.

About five o'clock next morning—5th November—they began to make preparations for moving off. It seemed that the blacks—if there had ever been any—had thought better of their plan during the night and sneaked back into the bush. Fires were blazing, billies were boiling, and some of the diggers were getting ready to round up the horses. Suddenly a dog began to bark.

"Quiet there, what's the matter with you?"

But the dog would not be quietened. To and from the barricade he rushed, barking frantically all the time. His owner tried to see where he was looking.

"There's nothing there, you silly lookin' —"

He broke off. A dark figure had slipped quietly from one bush to the shelter of another. At the same moment, out of the corner of his eye, he saw another.

"The blacks," he yelled. "Blacks. All around us."

Boiling billies were kicked over and the water hissed in the campfires as men grabbed their firearms, rushed for the barricade, and crouched down behind it. Beside them the native police boys slid up into the shelter of the saddles like snakes and found openings through which they could sight their carbines. The Chinese grabbed pick-handles, shovels, and bamboo poles, and crouched in a group of their own.

Suddenly, from all around, there came a screeching cry like thousands of parrots. From bushes and dry grass on every side sprang naked, copper-coloured figures to charge straight at the barricade.

"Hold your fire," roared the officer in charge of the police. "Hold it for the order."

The diggers crouched silent, fingers tense on triggers, as the first wave of the attack stormed up to the barricade. "The blacks attacked like soldiers," Webb wrote. "There were about forty in the first rank and as many more in reserve some distance behind." With the painted, screeching horde almost on top of them, the order came.

"Fire!"

A crashing volley rang out. Amid clouds of smoke the black ranks seemed to waver. When the smoke cleared about twenty painted bodies lay dead or writhing on the ground. As the diggers rushed to reload, the ranks that had faltered came on with a screeching yell. They were almost on the muzzles of the Sniders when the order came again.

"Fire!"

Once again the heavy bullets tore through the ranks of the myalls. Many more fell, but before the diggers could reload, the reserves charged over the bodies on the ground. Pick-handles, shovels, knives, and a couple of cutlasses whirled to ward off the spear thrusts as black and white fought hand to hand.

The native police and a few of the diggers had managed to reload. Another ragged volley crashed out. The pressure on the barricade lessened. At last the deadliness of the firearms was becoming evident to the attackers. The tight ranks broke and scattered as men threw themselves flat into the cover of the grass or ducked for the shelter of stunted trees.

But the attack was far from over. From the cover of the scrub a shower of spears were thrown into the white camp. There was a yell of pain as the barbed point of one of them

34

Cradling for gold

Crowded quarters on a ship bound for Cooktown

Cooktown at the time of the Wet in February 1874

All kinds and all races took the track

THE ROAD

JOHN 'WELLY HARD' AT IT

tore through a digger's thigh. In the long grass black bodies crawled forward as smoothly as snakes until they could see targets for their spears, which they threw in a high arc, so that there was little cover from them. But every time a black body showed itself a Snider cracked, and its bullet generally found a mark.

Even now the myalls did not realize that their men were being killed. Again and again a couple of them would run to a man who had fallen and search in vain for the spear they were sure must have hit him. When they could find none they would try to stand the dead man on his feet. They would put their fingers into the gaping wounds made by the Snider bullets and try to stop the bleeding by plugging them with grass. When they saw that the shot men did not jump up and fight again when the wounds were plugged, and saw more men falling to every volley of the Sniders, some of the attackers began to sneak quietly away. Others saw them, and suddenly all the rest of them broke from cover and ran. "They were pursued as far as a large lagoon," wrote Webb, "and all that went there stayed there."

But while the diggers had been defending themselves another detachment of the blacks had sneaked in among the trees and cut out most of the horses. The first the owners knew about it was when their slaughtering of blacks at the lagoon was interrupted by loud neighing as the remaining horses plunged wildly about the camp still in their hobbles. The blacks who had driven off the rest of the horses had them about a mile away. They were yelling and screeching at the top of their voices, and the horses, unable to gallop because of their hobbles, were rearing and plunging, half mad with fright.

Four of the best riders, Johnny Anderson, Jack the Blower, Jimmy the Poet, and a native police trooper, tore the hobbles off the four remaining horses, jumped onto them bareback, and, with horses' manes grasped in one hand and Sniders in the other, took off in pursuit. The charge was enough to demoralize blacks not used to dealing with mounted men, and one shot from the trooper's rifle, fired between his horse's ears, was enough to make them stop their yelling and bolt for cover. The horses were brought back to camp. None of them had been speared. They had been too terrified to let the blacks come within spear range.

Countless clashes with the peninsula blacks were to follow the affray at Battle Camp, as the spot came to be called, but this was the only time the myalls ever formed ranks and charged the diggers in a pitched battle. After this defeat they fell back on the familiar pattern of ambush, sneak attacks, and the picking off of stragglers and lone prospectors. Dozens of white diggers and carriers, hundreds of Chinese, and whole tribes of blacks were to die in the relentless fighting before the Palmer rush was over.

Battle Camp gave the diggers a healthy respect for their opponents. "They are a good looking race," wrote H.H., "fine, tall, and well made, many over six feet in height, and a pure copper colour. Miners going this route should not go in parties of less than eight, and then well armed with guns and rifles. Revolvers are no use as the blacks can kill with their spears at eighty feet. They always attack at the break of day, but a good watch must be kept all night. Their war whoop is the cry of the black cockatoo."

By the time the diggers had cleaned up and got away from Battle Camp the morning was well advanced. "When on the march this day, the troopers guarded the whole length of the expedition party," wrote Cranley.

About four miles out Macmillan halted them on high ground to decide what to do next. He thought they were still about seventy miles from the Palmer, and rations were running low. He told the diggers the Government party would ride on ahead as fast as they could, marking a line of trees for the rest to follow. It was a badly timed suggestion at the best, and an angry uproar followed. As most of the diggers were on foot they were certain to fall farther and farther behind, and in the end stand a good chance of being picked off by the blacks. But Macmillan would not change his plan.

With no knowledge of the track, and a mounted party and native police troopers to back the decision, there was nothing the diggers could do about it but set to and lighten their loads still further by throwing away everything but the barest necessities. Even tea, flour, and sugar were thrown away. In half an hour they were moving again. They had rounded the northern end of the range now, and were headed south-west.

Webb and the other Queenslanders—about twenty-five in all—were determined to keep up with the horses of the Government party. Some of the men towards the back began to panic, and called out after them, threatening to shoot them unless they kept together. But all through that dry, dusty day they kept the horses in sight. Several creeks were crossed— all dry. At dusk, parched and all-in, they came up to where the leaders had camped on another creek. But this one had water in it—dirty, muddy, and stagnant, but still water. They called that camp Welcome Waterholes.

Next day the official party camped on a river which Macmillan named the Deighton, after the Under-Secretary for Mines. Webb's twenty-five joined them there by sundown. The rest of the diggers were strung out along the track for miles back. "As night fell, and all night long, we heard firing miles and miles behind us," wrote Webb. "It was the stragglers trying to keep in touch with one another and with us after it became too dark to distinguish the marked tree line. They kept dropping in to the camp all through the night, the last of them only coming up next morning about seven o'clock as we were starting again."

That day, too, the Queenslanders managed to keep up with Macmillan's party. About four miles from the Deighton during the morning they came to a big river which Macmillan called the Laura after his wife, not knowing that Hann, who crossed it further up, had already called it the Hearn after his own wife. Macmillan's wife won. It is the Laura still. Four miles further on they came to the Little Laura running north, and from there they struck south-west across what later became known as the Fairview Plains.

It was hot, dry going. A man offered half a crown for a drink of water from the billy of a more provident digger, who refused. "Not on your life, mate; a man mightn't see water again for a week in this country."

Saturday morning, 8th November, saw them at the foot

of the Conglomerate Range or tableland. They battled their way to the top, crossed the tableland, and could not get down. The cliffs were perpendicular. Ahead was a deep valley about two miles wide, and then more cliffs. They had had a stiff climb and eight miles walking for nothing. There was nothing for it but to go back to where they had come up and camp at the foot of the cliffs. The last of the stragglers joined them there. "Serves yer right for bein' in such a hurry," a panting old sourdough told them.

On the Sunday they all rested while Macmillan and St George scouted on ahead. Webb and his mate Tom Lynette went foraging and, with the help of Webb's kangaroo dog, bagged a big kangaroo. "He was so heavy that it was hard work getting him back to the camp," wrote Webb, "but when we came in sight with our burden all hands ran out to welcome and help us and overwhelmed us with affection, falling over one another and almost falling on our necks. I never saw such willing and enthusiastic co-operation as there was in skinning, dressing, and cooking the meat. There was enough to let everybody in the camp—more than a hundred men—have a bit. Rations were getting very short by this time."

Next day they reached the Kennedy River and followed it up in a westerly direction for four or five miles, making camp where Emu Creek and the St George joined it. There were large numbers of blacks in the sandy river bed, but they ran off to the hills as the party came in sight, according to Webb. Cranley put it differently. "The blacks here made another effort to drive away the horses, hanging around for some time."

But Webb continues to disagree. "A lot of blacks were shot while we were at this camp," he wrote. "I do not know why, as they had not interfered with us. I saw three bodies in the water of the St George and I heard shooting while I was fishing. Some of the diggers brought two gins and three piccaninnies into the camp. The gins had in their possession a looking-glass, a razor, and the hair of a white man, besides two papers which proved to refer to the sale of a horse to a man by the name of Leahey. It was supposed that this man was one of the diggers from the Etheridge who had been killed by the blacks on the Palmer."

On Tuesday, 11th November, the party followed up the Kennedy River, which was dry. When they camped they had to dig in the sand for water, and it took the Government party most of the night to water their horses.

Next morning they continued up the river and then over the divide, coming down at about eleven o'clock off the Conglomerate tableland into the valley of a big river running from east to west—the Palmer. They crossed it and camped on the south bank. There were tracks of four horses and boots in the sand, but, apart from that, not a sign of any diggers.

The hunt for the diggings lasted nearly two more days. That afternoon Macmillan and St George climbed Hann's Mount Daintree to look around, but could see no sign of a digger. Next day St George rode twenty miles down the river without result. Macmillan tried upstream, and about twelve miles up found some diggers who showed him the township. He led the party to its destination early on the morning of 14th November.

4 · SHORT RATIONS

THE Palmer goldfield's first town was at this stage, according to Cranley, not much more than a collection of tents. "There was but one building with any pretension to stability, and that was the lock-up. This was built of saplings. But slab stores were in course of erection, and there was the inevitable shanty doing a brisk business. There was, of course, no deference paid to street alignment, each tent being fixed where and how its proprietor pleased. No claims were laid out, and no sinking was going on, each man fossicking on his own account."

The idea of calling the place Eureka had apparently been abandoned, but there still seemed some doubt about a name for it. Cranley called it Palmerston. It was not until some time later that the name Palmerville began to be used.

Only a couple of hundred diggers were working around the township at this time. The diggings on the Left-hand Branch had been opened up three days before, and most of the diggers had rushed away to try their luck there.

"On the arrival of the party," wrote Cranley, "four bullocks were killed, and in two hours there was no meat—which was sold at 9d. per pound—to be had." For the past few days rations had been very short on the track, and Webb and his mates had come down to living on a limited allowance of "bango"—boiled flour and sugar. At every stop they had gone foraging with rifle or fishing line. "Many poor fellows arrived with only 5 lb. or 6 lb. of flour on the Palmer," wrote H.H. "The road," he said, "instead of being only 85 or 90 miles, turned out to be fully 160 and most of the men stated fully 180."

St George sent back the following report: "Arrived here 14th with Macmillan and 86 diggers, all well. Good road in 120 miles from Cook's Town, Endeavour River. Natives numerous and hostile on way up. Palmer proved payable for 35 miles up from this. About 500 men now on the ground. Usual earnings about £1 per man per day, many getting much more, few or none less. Largest nugget yet found ten ounces. Believed to be the richest and most extensive goldfield ever discovered in Queensland.

"Blacks very numerous and troublesome. They have speared two men, neither fatal. Speared five horses, three dead.

"Rations very dear—fresh beef 9d. lb. and in inadequate supply, no salt or flour, three drays expected next week. Prices at drays—2s. lb. flour, 2s. lb. sugar, 7s. lb. tea, 16s. lb. tobacco, 40s. blucher boots, 2s. 6d. lb. salt, and all other things in proportion. Wages £1 per day with rations.

"Many drays on road for this from Georgetown and Townsville, but cannot get on as country is burned and almost a desert owing to drought.

"No one should on any account attempt to come here before April next. Rains will come on by Christmas when all travelling must cease. Many now here must clear out before rain as they will find it impossible to get rations. Besides, the gold now being found is all in the bed of the river and all work there must cease with first rain. Men arriving here in April will be in ample time.

"The back gullies have not, as yet, been prospected, as the blacks drive the miners in from them. Men generally healthy. Two deaths from dysentery. One medical man here.

"Macmillan starts on 18th for Cook's Town. I sent all my packhorses back for rations. Sub-Inspector Dyas goes down also with 15 packhorses, and accompanied by about 50 diggers, with 150 packhorses, all for rations. This must be the last trip this season. Two thousand ounces now in hands of diggers and storekeepers."

St George's account was cautious compared with what

some diggers had written from the field. He may have been toning things down in an effort to stem a bigger rush until after the wet, and he may have been misled by men who were quietly salting away as much gold as they could before they had to leave.

A couple of weeks later St George was reporting again: "Rations are short. The blacks have speared another man fatally, also a horse. Plenty of gold is getting, but men cannot leave the river to prospect."

As food became even scarcer, anyone who had it could ask his own price in gold dust. Webb wrote: "The only flour for sale on the field was a few bags on a 5-horse dray belonging to Ned Neil. Mrs Neil was mounted on the dray and conducted the sale of the flour at half a crown a pound. If the lady didn't like the looks of you, or found fault with your manners, or thought she could read in your eye any question as to whether the battered pannikin she measured with really held a pound of flour, you went without, and that was all about it."

With patchy storms bringing flash floods in the rivers and every day bringing the wet closer, a few carriers still managed to get through. One of them was W. H. Corfield, former station manager and gold-digger, who later was to write his reminiscences of the rush. He and his mate Billy Wilson headed out from Georgetown with two bullock wagons. At the Walsh they found the river was up, and two carriers with horse teams told them they had been waiting to cross for a fortnight.

"Horses," grunted Corfield contemptuously. He had all the bullock-driver's contempt for them. "You'd be better with bullocks."

Corfield and Wilson unhitched their bullocks and put them to grass. Then Wilson, an old bushman, rode his horse out into the river. In spite of the flood that was running the water was clear enough for him to zig-zag his way along a sandbank and reach the other bank without the water rising more than half way up his horse's belly. He rode back.

"It'll be right enough for the wagons if we put the loading up on the guard rails," he said.

All that night they worked at it, stacking the goods on the rails and lashing it there so it would be above the level of the water. In the morning they told the horse team men they were going to cross. A storm of laughter greeted them.

"You'll get washed down the river."

They came down to the bank to watch the fun. Wilson stripped off his clothes, mounted his horse, and tried the river again. It had risen about six inches during the night.

"It'll be all right," he said.

Corfield, having yoked both teams of bullocks to one wagon, likewise stripped off his boots, red flannel shirt, and moleskins, stacked them on top of his wagon load, and mounted his horse. One on either side of the combined team, the two men urged the leaders into the river.

"Come on Bawley! Up Duke!"

Two great plaited greenhide whips hissed through the air to pick their marks with unerring accuracy. Slowly the team snaked across the river, leaders slackening as they veered over to keep on the firm footing, and then taking the strain again as they could do it most effectively. The wagon lurched as one wheel struck soft sand, recovered, and moved on under the steady strain. At last the leaders were across. The team followed, and slowly the dripping wagon came clear of the water. With hardly a pause, the bullocks were unhitched and taken back to do the same with the other wagon. By the time they had it across and had unyoked the bullocks and re-packed the wagons, it was nearly dark. That night the river came down a banker and the horse teams waited where they were.

Long before they reached the Mitchell they could tell that it was up too. More than forty teams of every sort and size were camped on the bank at the crossing. There was a whole village there—men, women, and even young children. Again Wilson rode his horse into the river. He said it was fordable, and next morning his and Corfield's wagons led the way, followed this time by the others. The last thirty miles to the Palmer were easy after that.

Thanks to the other teams they had led across the Mitchell there was a sudden glut of stores on the Palmerville market, so Corfield sold his team and put up a tarpaulin store from which to sell both his and Wilson's loads in his own good time as prices began to rise again. Wilson took his team to Cooktown for another load. At that stage there was only a bridle track from the Palmer to Cooktown. It wound for 120 miles over steep, rough mountains, dangerous creek and river crossings, and parched flats choked with stunted scrub. All the way was the menace of hostile blacks.

By the time Wilson had cut a wagon track through to the settlement on the south bank of the Endeavour River it was already a town with a main street over a mile long cleared to a width of about fifty yards. There was a wharf where the *Leichhardt* had landed her first passengers, and all around the scrub was dotted with buildings. Government staff at Cooktown consisted of an acting sub-inspector of police, a police sergeant, eight constables, an acting sub-inspector of customs, and a road construction party. The population was about three hundred permanent residents, and hundreds of men were coming and going between the town and the diggings every day. Gold fever was in the air; everyone was sure he was going to make a fortune.

Galvanized iron and weatherboard buildings were already replacing the tents along the street, and rough bark and canvas shacks were scattered among the trees on the flat ground on either side of it. Speculators were buying up land, some having made quick profits on it already. All sawn timber and other building material had to be imported, mainly by schooners from Maryborough. Though Cooktown was surrounded by scrub, there was nothing that would make commercial timber other than for rough fencing. Three substantial hotels already stood out among other buildings along the street, and in the bush beside the track leading back from the Palmer a dozen or more bark shanties were each selling their own particular brand of home-concocted grog. In a new weatherboard building some distance up from the wharf the woman who was to become notorious all over the field as Palmer Kate, and a dozen enterprising young women from Brisbane and Sydney, were already doing a roaring trade with gold-laden diggers streaming in from the track.

44

Nearly everyone coming into Cooktown from the Palmer had gold. The unlucky ones, who outnumbered them by ten to one, were still on the field hoping to strike it or had headed back for the Etheridge. A man came into Cooktown if he was doing well, needed stores, and had the gold to pay for them. He also came in if he had struck it rich, and planned to go south to spend it. The pub- and the shanty-keepers were waiting for them. They could pick a man with gold at a glance, and, if he looked like passing, there was a free drink offered, "just to wish you good luck in the south, digger; you wouldn't refuse to let a man shout you a drink to that, would you?" If the digger looked like leaving after that one, there was another, "to the missus and kids", or "to the girl you've got waiting back there". Most diggers who drank to that one never got any further, and in due course headed back to the Palmer to look for more gold.

For every man leaving Cooktown for the south, ten were arriving. While Wilson was there the *Boomerang* arrived with a hundred passengers, seventy of them steerage. As the steerage accommodation of the vessel was about thirty bunks, most had not slept much since leaving Brisbane.

Many diggers were down from the goldfields to buy stores and get back among the gold as quickly as they could. Prices were reasonable compared with those quoted by St George for the goldfield. Flour was £3 a bag, compared with £20 on the field. Sugar was 6d. a pound, tea 3s. 6d., salt 3d., and drinks 6d. each. One small craft freighted on spec by a Townsville firm had no sooner berthed than she was rushed by diggers who tossed across their bags of gold in order to have a claim on the stores they needed.

Good draught horses were in demand because of the quantity of goods to be carried to the diggings. Packers were making better money than many of the diggers. Carriage from Cooktown to the Palmer was £130 for a ton of 2,000 pounds, and, on top of that, it was paid in gold at the standard Palmer rate of £3 15s. an ounce. When the carrier sent this gold to the Sydney mint, through the bank, it realized £4 7s. 6d. an ounce. Bank and shipping charges, insurance, etc., amounted

45

to 7s. 6d. an ounce, so the carriers had a clear profit of 5s. an ounce on the gold alone.

Daily, notices announced the arrival of ships with loads of new diggers for the field: s.s. *Leichhardt* arrived with 60 miners; *Lord Ashley*, with 200 men for the Palmer; *Boomerang* with 136—and so it went on day after day.

On the Palmer, with men swarming over the range and spreading out like ants, food was again scarce and the price of carriage was soaring. Corfield, with his stocks sold and no team, fretted at the profits he was missing. A packer came in one day with his team of horses, one of which had lost a shoe, making it useless for travel over the stony ridges. He wanted horseshoe nails. A carrier named Billy Yates, partly as a joke, offered to sell him five horseshoe nails for their weight in gold. The offer was accepted. The nails were placed in one scale, and enough gold to balance them in the other. The packer was getting a shilling a pound for packing goods eleven miles, and the nails were worth the price to him.

For Corfield it was the last straw. He borrowed a horse and rode out to the Mitchell where he knew a dozen or more teams were held up by the flood, some on the Etheridge side with loads for the Palmer, others on the Palmer side, empty, and on their way back for fresh supplies. None of them had thought of trying the Cooktown track.

Corfield had little trouble in buying twenty-four bullocks, two old drays, and three horses for four hundred pounds from a man who had not heard of the new rates of carriage. He came back to the Palmer with Corfield, and when he learned how prices stood he offered Corfield fifty pounds on his deal to buy the team back. Corfield refused. He then sold the two old drays to Edwin Crossland, the blacksmith, for twenty pounds and bought a new wagon for sixty pounds.

The four-wheeled wagon was a much better proposition than the old two-wheeled pole dray with which the pioneers had opened up the south. In rough country a heavily loaded dray was an unstable and murderous implement to both man and beast. Coming out of a creek with a load on, it would tip up backwards and dump the load in the water; going down hill it would bear heavily on the polers. A dray took ten bullocks to pull it, and could carry about $3\frac{1}{2}$ tons; a wagon took eighteen or twenty bullocks and carried 7 or 8 tons.

When Wilson arrived back from Cooktown he and Corfield sold the load for a clear profit of seventy pounds a ton and took both wagons back for a couple of more loads before the wet. As a sign of their prosperity they hired a Chinese cook to go with them so they could give all their attention to looking after their bullocks.

Gold yields on the Palmer, particularly on the Left-hand Branch and the creeks running into it, were improving so rapidly that miners kept on working in spite of short rations and the certainty of being isolated by the coming wet season. About the junction of what was later named Butcher's Creek and the Palmer some exceptionally rich patches of gold were struck, and here Jack Edwards put up a butcher's shop of forked posts, saplings, and bark, and opened for business with all available bullocks. Stores and shanties sprang up, and the place came to be known as Edwardstown. To be nearer the centre of things, Warden St George established a second camp there, though his headquarters remained at Palmerville.

It was from Edwardstown, on 4th December 1873, that a *Queenslander* correspondent wrote: "This creek is being worked for many miles and is turning out very well. As many as forty tents can be counted on some of the beaches. It is proving payable for twelve or fifteen miles except in places where deep waterholes occur. The prospectors [Mulligan and his mates] have had the first run of the creek and have done admirably. They only worked easy, shallow crevices. I hear of others doing well also. Some have got as much as 20, 40, and 60 ounces in a week. Almost everyone is getting gold which I never hear now reckoned in pennyweights." Many of the best patches of alluvial were in the so-called ravines—narrow gutters a few hundred feet in length, and no more than two or three feet wide.

"The present population of the whole field cannot be correctly ascertained," the correspondent went on, "but I think I might put it down as 500 or 600. A great many have come in lately, and a few of the female sex have already found their way here."

As a matter of fact, there were, by this time, quite a few unattached women on the field. They were mainly sturdy, self-reliant types, well used to making their own way. A few pimps made their appearance, but they were not popular on the field in those early, rugged days. Several were tarred and feathered and chased into the bush—to the considerable puzzlement of the watching Merkins, who must have thought the whole thing was some sort of initiation ceremony. After that, the remainder decided it was healthier to set up shanties and sell grog.

Most of the women who arrived early had previous experience of life on the goldfields. There were some tough old battlers among them, with names suited to their physical attributes and capabilities. They built their own bark huts, lived like the diggers, and in their spare time were not above taking a tin dish and fossicking for a little gold in the creeks as well as in the pockets of the diggers. There was a smattering of younger women too, but they also were something out of the ordinary run. To get to the Palmer they needed more than a nose for easily got gold. They had to have stamina, courage, and a strong streak of the pure adventurer in them.

Whatever their original intentions may have been, few of these women plied the oldest profession for long. More lasting relationships were formed, and right through the rush one could see men and women working claims together. The few white wives on the field at that time—stern, frontierswomen like Mrs Neil, concerned only with helping their husbands build a quick fortune for their families—took little notice of the other women. They had more to do.

Typical of the atmosphere of the Palmer in its early days was the diggers' attitude to the Goldfields Commissioner, Howard St George. St George was a temperate man in every sense of the word, but he saw no reason to attempt to impose his private ideas on others. The hard-living diggers christened him The Saint, and he was the best liked and most respected man on the field.

Every day food on the Palmer became scarcer. "When a dray comes in," the correspondent wrote, "its supplies last less than a day. The only things that hold out are rum and

brandy, and so long as there is a fig of tobacco or a pound
of tea on the Palmer, the shanty-keeper's stock will not get
exhausted. All this will get remedied in time. Now that payable gold has been got over a large tract of the country,
proper storekeepers will find their way here. There may be
some good reefs found eventually as there are many specimens amongst the gold." Specimens are lumps of gold-bearing quartz. This was the first hint of the rich reefs to be
found at Maytown later on.

Meanwhile the blacks were still giving trouble. "We have
had a few runs after the darkies lately up this branch. One
man got speared in three places. He is now recovering. Mr
St George, on getting intelligence, lost no time, though he
had just arrived a few days before from the new port. He
came up with two black boys and gave them a dressing.
Since then several outrages have been committed by the
blacks on the main river where there are not now many
working. Several foot-men have been chased, their swags
and rations taken from them, and a few horsemen have had
their horses speared. The blacks are also spearing all the
stray horses they can find on back creeks. They are very
numerous and gather in large mobs."

Regular thunderstorms showed the wet was close, and at
last the men who had waited began to get out. Among them
was H.H., who wrote from Cooktown: "When we started
from the Palmer there were about two hundred leaving, and
most of the others are waiting until the last moment, trying
to get all they can before the wet. As soon as the rain sets in
they will have to leave the river and try the gullies and terraces, as the Palmer has every indication of being a large
river. It is nearly two hundred yards wide, and high water
mark is fifteen feet. Of the two hundred leaving, many have
not a pound of flour; in fact, I do not know how they will get
down. There are three large rivers to cross and, if caught by
the rain, they can go neither forward nor back. Rations and
supplies are almost exhausted."

The early rains brought death with them. "Tons of dead
fish, apparently poisoned by the water, lay along the edges
of the streams." Men who drank from newly filled waterholes

49

died. "The fact is," wrote Mulligan, "that the first rains fill all the waterholes, which are more or less filled with the leaves and branches of gum trees which make the water thick and black as ink, and so poisonous that fish cannot live in it. People must use this water until the next heavy shower or two gives enough to clean out all the rubbish; then pure water is got. It is undoubtedly from this cause that at this season of the year we have so much dysentery and other sickness.

"I have seen men sickly and feverish, unable to proceed even a few miles, making their way downwards to Cooktown. Two men came to my camp last night, going to Cooktown. They were not able to put up their tent, and they got shelter with us. They could partake of no food from the effects of dysentery. They had been nine weeks on the Palmer, were able to work only three weeks, got five or six ounces of gold which they spent on medicines, and now they must leave."

If no one took pity on people like this, and helped them, said Mulligan, they died. Before long, many were dying.

5 · DEATH IN THE MUD

THE WET swept over the Palmer valley like a blanket, blotting out the mountains, hammering down in a blinding torrent that turned everything to mud. The diggers who remained—more than five hundred of them—were scattered along the river for sixty miles or more. They had even moved into the gullies and, blinded to everything by the constant glitter of gold, stacked up dirt while they waited for the wet to wash it. Now, within minutes, the dry creeks became raging torrents, and the diggers could do no more than watch helplessly as the water undermined their pay dirt and carried it away into the river. The work of weeks disappeared in minutes. The waters of the Palmer came down like a roaring tidal wave, blotting out all trace of the workings on its banks, tossing uprooted trees on its crest like corks, swallowing everything that lay in its course. Foot by foot it rose, as the helpless men watched it.

Week by week these men had put off the day they would leave the gold and head back for the coast. Now it was too late. Between them and Cooktown half a dozen raging rivers and creeks were still rising. Some of those who had left a few days earlier were caught on the track and marooned on high ground between rivers. Others were caught on flats which became quagmires overnight. The rivers, which rose quickly with rain, fell as quickly when it stopped, and in brief spells of fine weather parties of men made desperate by hunger tried to ford the swollen streams. Some of them got through,

51

but many lost their footing and were carried downstream, never to be seen again.

All along the track starving men fossicked among abandoned gear for stray bags of rotten, rain-soaked flour that had been abandoned by overladen diggers on the way out from Cooktown weeks or months before. Horses, dogs, snakes—even death adders—were eaten. Weeds were boiled up in muddy water and swallowed—Palmer River soup, they called it. The dog whose barking had given warning of the blacks' attack at Battle Camp was killed for food. His owner, who had been unable to prevent the slaughter, was offered a portion. He shook his head, staggered a few yards away and was sick. A party caught on the Normanby River ate, one by one, the horses that were carrying back their gear and gold. The gear was abandoned. If the starving diggers could have eaten the gold they would have. Women battled, starved, and died beside the men.

Dysentery and typhoid spread among the weakened diggers, and all over the field and all along the track to Cooktown they died. Often a party that stopped to bury one of its number had no sooner finished the job than another of them was dead. Beaten men staggered into Cooktown to tell their stories of the flooded Palmer and the famine. "An old donkey was made into turtle soup," wrote one. "Horseflesh was a dainty; a man who could get a bit of it was envied." "Some of them were reduced to eating horses that had been two days dead," said another. Men like Corfield, who had laid in enough food on the Palmer to see them through the wet, had to guard it with rifles day and night. Men were killing each other fighting for food.

As diggers on the field dwindled in numbers, fought among themselves, and lay dying with fever, the cannibal Merkins moved in to take revenge for the fouling of their fishing holes and a dozen unprovoked shootings. For centuries they had been in the habit of tiding themselves over the bad season with human flesh. Here was a new source of supply. Here was *talgoro*—human meat—waiting to be taken. All over the field and along the track isolated men disappeared. Few were ever heard of again. But two of them were.

52

Months later a young black girl deserted one of the tribes and was brought into Palmerville. After she had picked up enough English to make herself understood, she was asked if she knew anything about the two men, who had disappeared in the area she came from. The girl giggled happily, but at first would say nothing. After a good deal of persuasion she at last told them what had happened. The men of her tribe had surrounded the two diggers and, finding them unarmed, had closed in and grabbed them and tied them up with vines. They were kept tied up until they had been carried to the blacks' camp, and then, so they would not be able to run away, their shin and arm bones were broken by being pounded between stones. Next day one of the men was knocked on the head and roasted and eaten while his mate looked on. The following day the other man was eaten.

Among those who managed to get through to Cooktown at the last minute were Mulligan and his mates. They had stayed on the field until 16th February 1874. Mulligan described the Cooktown he found as a roaring, cosmopolitan, gold boom town, with hundreds of wood and iron buildings crowding both sides of two-mile-long Charlotte Street, which ran from the wharves out to the beginning of the Palmer road, and dotting the bush on either side of it.

New buildings were going up everywhere. A barque and two schooners, arriving with 300,000 feet of timber, sold their cargoes on the spot. Stores, banks, and licensed public houses jostled cheek by jowl with shanties, brothels, and gambling dens. Palmer Kate's establishment had grown and prospered, and a number of enterprising business men had set up "residentials" for the use of women who plied their trade in the bars, shanties, and on the muddy footpaths. A hot-blooded red-head of uncertain temper who later became notorious as Palmer Kitty was already making a name for herself singing to the customers of the Golden Nugget Hotel.

In bars all over town, hollow-eyed miners, many of them with the fever still in their bones, pulled chamois bags from their pockets and rolled bright gold nuggets on counters to illustrate arguments on the merits of the creeks and gullies where they were found. And rarely did a nugget hit the

53

counter but some hungry-eyed hard-lipped harpy came fawning on its owner to offer her affections. In saloons, hotel storerooms, and dark dives away among the trees, card sharps pulled the same tricks they had used on every goldfield since Ballarat. Wherever the lights were bright, women watched, ready to flash a silk-clad thigh or loosely laced bosom in whatever direction the gold was drifting.

The hardened diggers who were determined to take their gold home generally gathered in a few of the stores whose owners found it good business to see they were not disturbed. Some of the stores had billiard tables, and a man could while away the time until his ship left yarning or playing a quiet game of billiards or cards. These were the men who went back to the south or home to England, and built mansions with their Palmer gold. They were a very small minority.

One of these quiet card-players described how he and some of his mates were disturbed from their game one afternoon by shrill laughter rising above the drumming of the rain on the roof, and went across to the open window shutter to see what was happening.

"Here was a lady from a certain establishment, less decently dressed than one is accustomed to see in the street, and soaked to the skin by the pouring rain, running down the middle of the roadway through the mud which was inches deep. In her wake pounded a determined looking gentleman whose enthusiasm seemed to have been inflamed by the product of one of the town's numerous shanties." As the miners watched from the window, the pursuer caught his quarry, and the two of them fell together into the mud, roaring with laughter, and "went about their entertainment, and the rain pounding down on them".

"We returned to our cards," said the miner.

A total of 63 publicans' licences had been issued for Cooktown at this time, and 30 more applied for. There were 20 eating houses, 12 large stores, 20 small ones, 6 butchers, 5 bakers, 3 tinsmiths, 4 tent-makers, 6 hairdressers, and 7 blacksmiths. Figures for some of the other establishments have never been given with much exactness. One digger said the brothels outnumbered the public houses. Another said

that at night-time the main street was lit from end to end
from the kerosene lamps burning in public houses, dance
halls and gambling dens. There were few parts of the street
where a man in search of a drink or a woman had to walk
past more than two doors. There were also doctors, chemists,
watchmakers, bootmakers, saddlers, and others. Two newspapers—the Cooktown *Courier* and the Cooktown *Herald*—
were established during 1874. There were also two churches.

With the rain of the wet season pounding down in torrents,
not a day went by without a steamer pulling in at the wharf
with supplies and yet more diggers impatient to get to the
field. While men were dying by the dozen in the mud of the
Palmer track, more than two thousand new arrivals were
stamping the mud of Cooktown's long street, impatient to
get out into the country where others were starving. Dozens
of impatient men ploughed out along the track in an effort
to get through to the gold. Most came back as soon as they
saw what the country was like. Others died in the mud.

Any ship that would still float was pressed into commis-
sion for the Cooktown run—and still there were not nearly
enough. Several parties of diggers arrived in open boats which
they had sailed or rowed from Brisbane, Rockhampton, and
other ports. As well as carrying men for the diggings, every
ship brought others who had no intention of going past
Cooktown. Card sharps, pickpockets, and stand-over men,
pimps, prostitutes, and dance hall girls flocked to the new
town, until its streets and lighted buildings roared with
life—and its backyards stank with death.

Cooktown's first magistrate, Mr Thomas Hamilton, had
also acted, at first, as Sub-Collector of Customs. His first court,
held on 27th December 1873, had dealt with one case only—
the stealing of a goat from Townsville. By now there were
more serious matters needing his attention.

Arguments over cards, women, and missing gold were
settled with fists, boots, knives, broken bottles, and guns.
Not a day passed without the mud of Charlotte Street being
churned up by struggling bodies locked in deadly combat.
Police in the town were no more than a fraction of the numbers that would have been needed to keep order. Drunken

diggers were robbed in the strets in broad daylight. They were doped in sleazy bars, chloroformed in back bedrooms by women not content with the exorbitant prices they charged, and bashed over the head in backyards and left there to regain consciousness robbed even of their boots and clothing. Some died there in the mud, with the rain pouring down on their naked bodies.

The rush was attracting new chums who knew nothing of life in a gold boom town. They were easy marks, and many who came with money to buy stores soon lost every penny of it. Without even the money to pay their fares home, they swelled the ranks of Cooktown's desperate men. By the end of April 1874, there were from three thousand to four thousand men camped between Grassy Hill and the spot where the Palmer track disappeared into the scrub. Many of them were destitute.

The slackening of the wet season brought in a stream of men who had been marooned on the Palmer during the wet. Starved, broken, and disillusioned, they reported dwindling returns from the flooded creeks, famine, fever, and murder by blacks. Many had bartered their gold for any rations that could be had. Others had spent it at shanties along the way. More lost it at Cooktown.

The Palmer track, they said, was like a battlefield, with camps of sick men, the graves of the dead, and smashed and abandoned equipment of every kind. Almost every man who got back had left mates dead on the field or along the track. A miner named James Dick described seeing groups of a dozen or more graves just off the track.

By this time there were more than two thousand men in Cooktown who wanted nothing more than to go home—but they had no money to pay their passages. Vessels leaving port were rushed. Police were called, stones were thrown, and rioting became almost continuous. Early in April the s.s. *Florence Irving*, which had brought about five hundred diggers from the south on their way to the Palmer, was mobbed by twice as many more wanting to get away from it. Five hundred who had the money for their passages were already aboard. The others had no money, and there was no room for them anyway. Police, ship's officers, and agents battled them nearly all day before the ship was able to sail.

The Queensland Government, in an effort to avoid further trouble, subsidized the shipping company for passages south for hundreds of stranded men. The New South Wales Government published a warning against going to the Palmer. But still hopeful diggers arrived faster than they could be shipped away. There were said to be sixty vessels either on their way to Cooktown or about to sail from southern ports. With the rivers still up and the ground still boggy, the rush to the Palmer was on again. Each day saw men heading for the goldfields in hundreds. They died in dozens.

"The old Queenslanders stood up to the conditions best," one of the Palmer road packers recalled. "Among southerners, and particularly among men from overseas, the death toll was heavy.

"One day I was overtaken and passed by a party of five footmen. If the freshness of their complexions had not pointed them out as southerners, their black hats and extra heavy swags would assuredly have done so. One I noticed in particular was a stalwart, powerful looking fellow who walked behind the horses with me for a time. Presently he complained of a slight headache, and pushed ahead to join his mates.

"On my arrival in camp about an hour later, I found his mates engaged in filling in the grave of the poor fellow at the root of a large gum tree, where he had died immediately after his arrival in camp. For a time I could hardly realize that the man they had buried was the same man who had left me so recently. But there was his pipe which he had lit as he left me half empty, and his hat and the contents of his swag lying on the fresh mound.

"Such a scene was by no means a new thing to me, but this poor fellow's fate affected me more deeply than I can express. Not one of his companions knew even his name, nor was there anything in his swag to throw any light on his identity."

There were many unknowns who found graves along the

Palmer track. Corfield described how he once helped to bury a man whose real name nobody had ever known. "From the clothes found in his camp, it could be seen that they originally had been marked," wrote Corfield, "but the name had been cut out from each article. I found two volumes from which the names had also been cut out; these were Sheridan's Works and Cicero's Works in Latin. Many passages in the books were well marked with marginal notes in pencil, and both showed signs of being well studied."

6 · HELL'S GATE

To REACH the Palmer from Cooktown at that time, loaded wagons had to cover about 160 miles of rough, difficult country. Following the general line of Macmillan's old track, they crossed the Normanby about forty miles from Cooktown, veered south past Battle Camp and Welcome Waterholes, crossed the Laura about eighty miles from Cooktown, on over the Little Laura to the Little Kennedy which they followed up into the Conglomerate Range, and then over the divide to the Palmer valley.

With diggers spreading up the Left-hand Branch, Sub-Inspector Alexander Douglas, of the native police, who had been both teamster and drover in his time, opened up a short cut from the coast to the diggings on the branch. It turned off from the old track at the Laura, headed south, and climbed up into the Conglomerate through a desolate, rock-flanked defile which soon earned the name of Hell's Gate, and was to be the scene of more violent deaths in the few following years than all the rest of the Palmer field put together. After crossing the tableland, the track came down onto the Left-hand Branch diggings, cutting the distance from Cooktown by about sixty miles.

The Gate itself was so narrow that only packhorses and men on foot could squeeze through it. It was made to order for an ambush.

All the way from the Normanby the country between camping places was a succession of barren, hungry-looking plateaus which, as one packer put it, "would hardly feed a mosquito", and rocky passes, long, narrow defiles, and huge boulders. Winding its way through the bed of some rocky torrent, the track was often completely commanded on both sides by high ground with ample cover for attackers.

The only oasis in this wilderness was the Laura River, a rich, fertile valley where there was always a green picking on the grass. Packers and teamsters would arrive there with exhausted horses and bullocks and make camp while the animals recovered. Three days' spell on the Laura was considered equal to a week's corn feeding. In the dry season the teams would wait on the Laura until a little rain came and then push through with their supplies.

About twenty miles from the Laura along Douglas's track was an apparently impassable barrier. An old packer described what the trip over it was like.

"On near approach a huge, steep spur is seen to jut from one end, and you begin the ascent, but cannot for the life of you imagine how you are to top the louring precipice in front of you. Negotiating a succession of almost perpendicular pinches, you thread your way among huge boulders. Then, a fissure in the wall, rent apparently by some convulsion of nature, is entered, and you are within the Gates.

"A vertical wall of rock rises to about twenty feet on either hand, and there are some great blocks on the top looking as if a touch would send them down on your head. Rounding a sharp bend about midway in this passage, you ascend a succession of steps and terraces—the Devil's Staircase—and the summit is reached.

"The scene at the Gates when opposing streams of travellers meet baffles description, as there is barely sufficient room for a single person. One packhorse effectually bars the passage. The slope is pretty well littered with the remains of packhorses which have perished in the ascent. Once an unlucky animal misses his footing it is impossible for him to recover himself.

"From Hell's Gate to the Palmer watershed the road traverses an almost uninterrupted sandy level broken only by the deep gorge through which the Kennedy winds. There is an indescribable air of gloom and loneliness about this part of the track attributable to the desolate appearance of the timber, numerous detached rocks, and deep, dark gorges on either hand. This feeling is increased as the traveller occasionally passes the unburied remains of some unfortunate Chinese who has perished miserably and been abandoned by his unfeeling countrymen. It is a fitting scene for the many cannibalistic orgies which have been held in its dreary fastnesses.

"At some points the road skirts the very edge of the plateau, and from these places immense tracts of the Palmer country can be seen.

"Springs of pure, cold water occur in most of the ravines, and caves which are tenanted by the blacks in the wet weather are passed frequently. One of these I discovered by accident.

"Being overtaken by a heavy thunderstorm one evening, myself and two more packers encamped for the night at one of the springs. One of my horses being away next morning, I started to look for him. After several hours hunting, I was on the point of giving up when the single tinkle of his horse bell attracted my attention. It came from the terrace about fifty feet below the level on which I stood.

"After much trouble I found a narrow path descending the shelf which conducted me to the entrance of a large cave, and in this the missing animal had taken refuge from the March flies. The cave was formed by an enormous mass of overhanging rock, and from a crack in the innermost wall trickled a stream of water which accumulated in a rocky, round basin on the floor.

"The cave was a favourite retreat of the darkies judging by the number of broken spears and woomeras which were lying about. The ceilings and walls were adorned with paintings in red ochre representing warriors, canoes, etc.

"The cave was about 70 feet deep by some 40 feet in width, and from 4 feet to 14 feet in height. At the inner end was a large, flat rock for grinding tomahawks and bone spearheads, many of which, in a half-finished state, were lying around.

"Without waiting to make a more minute examination, I

cleared out with all expedition—having no firearms with me—lest the owners might return."

One of the first attacks in the area was on the gold escort from the Palmer. It was a strong party, consisting of Sub-Inspector Clohesy, five white and two black troopers, and accompanied by William Hann. They were carrying several thousand ounces of gold, and all were well armed.

The party was camped on the Laura, two days out from the diggings, towards the end of May 1874. They could see blackfellows' tracks everywhere; there must have been hundreds of them. One of the native troopers named Jerry pointed. "Plenty myall sit down, Mahmy," he told Clohesy. Mahmy was the usual form of address by a native trooper to his white officer.

Even though Douglas and his troopers were known to be somewhere in the locality, no risks were taken. The horses were close-hobbled for the night and a bell put on each of them. A watch was set, the evening meal was cooked and eaten and the camp settled down for the night.

It was bright moonlight and towards midnight the only sound was a snatch of conversation now and then from the tent occupied by Clohesy and Hann, and an occasional crackle from the campfire beside which the beef for next day was slowly simmering. The sentry, one of the white troopers named Egan, was stooping to put another stick on the fire when a score or more spears struck the ground all around him, scattering the fire and sending the meat bucket flying.

The screeching black cockatoo war cry of the Merkins came from the bush all round them, and suddenly spears were flying everywhere, ripping through tents, thudding into tree trunks, and zipping past the ears of the freshly aroused troopers. The sentry got a spear through the sleeve of his jacket and another through his cap. It was pure luck that no one was hit.

Clohesy's voice brought order out of the confusion. "Ready," he roared. And then, "Fire!"

The volley crashed out and the heavy Snider bullets went whistling into the shadows of the surrounding scrub. Not a blackfellow was to be seen. The shower of spears stopped on the instant.

"Load, fire," shouted Clohesy. Another volley crashed into the scrub, and again a third. The echoes died away into silence.

For ten minutes they waited with loaded rifles at the ready, but not a sound came from the scrub except the occasional note of a horse bell. Clohesy sent half the troopers to bring in the horses, and then they waited, still on the alert, until daylight. A search of the surrounding scrub showed a few spots of blood on the undergrowth and some discarded spears, but no sign of a blackfellow. Clohesy decided it was more important to get the gold through than to organize a punitive expedition, and the party packed up and took the road for Cooktown.

After this, diggers and packers began travelling in large parties for mutual protection, and from then on it was rarely that a large party of whites was attacked. But there were always men who became careless or took the risk of travelling in twos or threes—sometimes without even carrying fire-arms.

An example of what the man who became separated from his party could expect was that of a digger who remained behind at the waterhole at the foot of Hell's Gate to rest a blistered foot. After a short spell he was hurrying to over-take his mates when he came over a crest and found himself facing three painted warriors. He ducked for the cover of the nearest tree, but was hit by three spears before he made it. He pulled out the spears and threw them back at his attackers, yelling for help at the top of his voice. The blacks ran.

The digger's spear wounds were so bad that he could not move, and for several days he had to lie at the side of the track, relying for food and rough care on passing travellers who were in too much of a hurry to remain with him, and taking his chance that the myalls would not return and finish him off. When the warden heard about it he sent out two native troopers to look after the man until he was well enough to be taken back to Palmerville.

On another occasion a digger on his way back to Cooktown with a billy containing eighty ounces of gold in one hand and his boots in the other was speared in the back by a black-fellow who sprang from behind a tree. He swung round, and inadvertently raised the hand holding the boots. His attacker apparently thought the boots were some sort of firearm and went for his life. Some passing packers extracted the spear, which had penetrated about seven inches, and carried him to the nearest shanty where he recovered.

Another digger described an attack that was made while he and his party were preparing their supper:

"I took a bucket and went down to a creek for some water. On returning I heard my mate cry out, 'Look out for blacks,' and before I had time to look about me, a shower of spears whizzed about my ears.

"I immediately made tracks for the camp and found that my mate and a man he had to assist him in driving the horses were defending themselves against twelve blacks who were showering spears at them from behind some trees. Coming up from behind, I opened fire with my revolver and succeeded in dislodging the mob from their cover. I grabbed a Martini-Henry which, with the help of my friend's rifle, sent the myalls on their way.

"One man was speared in the thigh and three horses hit. One died. Not much sleep that night. Got the spear out without much loss of blood and staunched the wound with little trouble as it had penetrated only the fleshy part of the thigh.

"Met a larger party next day. Three times that day the blacks showed themselves in force, but were apparently afraid to attack the larger party.

"Next day we came up with about thirty Chinamen, all well armed, but scared out of their wits. The blacks had attacked their camp that morning, killed five of them, and carried off their boss whom they killed and ate. We later found a part of his remains, partly roasted."

Corfield, on his return to Cooktown in 1874, had made an arrangement with a Chinese storekeeper to carry for him for twelve months at fifty pounds a ton. On the trip back to Palmerville by Macmillan's old track, Corfield travelled in company with nine other teams. They crossed the Normanby and camped on the far bank. Their bullocks strayed down-river during the night, and when mustering them Corfield found the trend of the river was towards the Deighton at the spot where the old road crossed it further on. He and some of the others rode ahead to see if it was possible to cross the Deighton without having to go through the Welcome Water-holes sand—about fourteen miles of sand where the wheels often sank up to the axles. They found good, firm country, and on their way back rode their horses in single file to make a good pad for the bullocks to follow. They hitched up their teams, and the following night made camp between two lagoons. All around were beaten pads which showed that the blacks used the place regularly.

Corfield and his mate Wilson went out to see if they could shoot some of the ducks that swarmed on the lagoons. They crossed a soakage running through the sand and came into the dense scrub that fringed the lagoons. Suddenly Corfield stopped. Wilson, who was following in his tracks, had to stop too.

"What's the matter?"

Corfield's eyes were roving over the scrub, but he could see nothing.

"Don't know," he said slowly. "I can't see a thing, but I don't like the feel of the place."

"Ah, come on," said Wilson. "D'you want to feed off corn beef again tonight?"

But Corfield did not budge.

"I think we'll go back to the wagons," he said at last.

Wilson argued no further. The two of them had been to-gether long enough to appreciate each other's hunches. When they reached the wet sand they had come through, they found their bootprints almost smothered by dozens of bare-footed tracks. They had been followed, and had they not turned back would undoubtedly have been speared from the cover of the scrub.

A guard was mounted on the camp that night. The dogs barked until dawn. Corfield's wagon was on the fringe of the encampment. He let the tarpaulin down so it hung over the

65

wheels, and instead of sleeping, as he usually did, in his bunk slung across between the spokes of the rear wheels, slept on the ground under the wagon. He decided there was less likelihood of a spear catching him there.

After the convoy had crossed the Deighton, they met some teams with empty wagons coming down from the Palmer. They told the teamsters of the new road they had opened up and warned them about the blacks. When these carriers reached Cooktown they reported the new road and said they had found that the blacks had covered it over with bushes, sticks, and small trees, apparently in an effort to screen off the duck-covered lagoons which had obviously been one of their favourite hunting grounds for generations. The carriers also said they had met a German miner named Johan Strau, his wife, and little girl at the turn-off on the Normanby and advised them not to go on the new track as the blacks were bad there. The German, who had no firearms of any kind, said he was used to the blacks and would take the new track.

Corfield's party, meanwhile, on arrival at the Palmer, spread the word of the new track past the lagoons, and two miners, riding down to Cooktown with their gold, said they would go that way. Corfield warned them of the blacks. The diggers laughed. They had a revolver and three cartridges between them. That would be enough, they said.

Next word from the lagoons was when the two diggers came galloping up to a bark shanty on the Normanby where another convoy of carriers was camped. On reaching the lagoons, they said, they saw a big mob of blacks gathered round something. Suspecting trouble, they fired one of their three revolver shots and spurred their horses into the middle of them. The blacks bolted.

When the diggers reached the spot where they had been gathered, they found Strau's body under his dray, and, a little distance away, the body of his wife. A spear had been driven through her mouth and had pinned her to the ground. Her clothing had been torn off and she had been horribly outraged and mutilated before death. Both bodies were still

Camped in the bush

The approach to Hell's Gate

Almost daily, diggers had to fight for their lives on the track to the
goldfields

Diggers never knew when a shower of spears would come flying from
trees

warm. Three horses were lying dead of spear wounds. Of the little girl there was no trace.

When an armed party from the Normanby reached the spot next morning the bodies were still undisturbed. The dray had been smashed up, and most of it, including all the ironwork, was gone. Flour, sugar, and other articles were scattered over the ground. Guards were posted, a grave was dug, and the two bodies were lowered into it. Before the work was done, there was a shout from one of the guards.

"There's something moving there in the scrub."

Hot for revenge after their sickening task, every man ran for his horse. They found blacks' tracks everywhere, but not a glimpse of a blackfellow. Then they found the little girl. She was lying on her back, an ugly gash across her forehead, her stomach ripped up by a wooden knife, her eyes pecked out by the crows. She was buried with her parents.

Sub-Inspector Douglas, with a detachment of native police, tracked the raiders back across the Normanby River, came up with a tribe, and slaughtered them almost to a man. Along the trail he had found parts of the woodwork of the dray, split, broken, and sometimes partly burnt to allow the removal of every bolt, nail, and piece of ironwork.

A few of the blacks were captured. The native police had their own method of interrogating them. Two young girls aged about twelve or thirteen were chosen, and each tied to a tree a hundred yards apart. They were kept tied there, questioned and tormented by black troopers, until both told the same story, which was then presumed to be true.

Through the troopers, Douglas learned that Strau's party was camped for the night when the blacks attacked them. Strau was speared while reading a book beneath the dray, and the woman was sewing, sitting behind the wheel of the dray. The two young lubras described in blood-chilling detail all that had happened to her before she was killed. They said the blacks had intended to keep the little girl and bring her up as a member of the tribe, but two old gins had quarrelled over possession of her, and it was decided to kill her to avoid dissension.

After the police had gone, those tribesmen who had es-

67

caped came back and dug up Strau's body and took it away. It was never found.

Before that happened, Corfield, on his way to Cooktown, camped near the grave at Murdering Lagoons, as the place had been called. "That night I lay down in the centre of the bullocks when they camped after feeding, holding my loaded rifle and horse by the bridle," he wrote. "Bullocks are very sensitive to the smell of wild blacks, and will almost certainly stampede should any be about. Camping among the bullocks is considered the safest place one can find."

On both sides, after the Strau murder, the conflict between the whites and the myalls became more savage. Even those diggers and others who had once tried to make friends with them now shot all blacks on sight like vermin. The blacks retaliated. At the Laura, one digger was speared to death and another badly wounded. Johnny Hogsflesh, the mail contractor, fought off an attack on his camp, but lost his horses to the raiders.

Early in September, two packers named O'Connell and Kirby, travelling up to the Palmer with a hired man named James Flannery, camped for the night at the creek immediately under the Gates. Some of O'Connell's horses strayed during the night, and in the morning it was agreed that Kirby should go on alone while the other two looked for the missing horses. As Kirby was alone, and a more likely mark for attack, he took all the party's firearms—a rifle and a revolver.

O'Connell found his horses about an hour later, and he and Flannery loaded them, and headed up through the pass. Suddenly, as they were leading one of the pack horses through the narrowest part of the Gates, the rocks erupted with yelling, painted warriors, and spears rained down on horses and packers alike. With half a dozen spears in him, Flannery fell.

"Save yourself, Stan," he cried.

O'Connell roared at the horses, which panicked and galloped straight into the blacks, tearing their way through them. O'Connell followed before they could recover. Twenty yards up the winding defile the way was suddenly blocked by a party of Chinese coming down. Some turned and fled, others stood transfixed. Rushing at one of them who had a

68

gun, O'Connell grabbed it from his hands and ran back to where Flannery was lying. Again Flannery told him to run.

"I'm done, Stan. Save yourself."

The whole pass seemed to be swarming with painted warriors. O'Connell turned and ran for his life. As he went he looked back and saw the blacks dragging Flannery away.

This was typical of many deaths that were due to pure carelessness. An armed man who had a fair warning of attack nearly always managed to fight his way out. A prospector named McLean had a spear landed neatly at his feet. He blazed away with his Snider and the attackers ran. John Angus, a packer, was speared in the back a few miles on the Cooktown side of the Laura. He managed to draw his revolver and, with an occasional shot in their direction, keep his attackers at their distance until he reached the Laura camp.

Two white diggers arriving at Cooktown from the Palmer reported having been met on the Palmer side of Hell's Gate by five terrified Chinese running for their lives. As they were coming up through the defile, they said, two huge blackfellows had stepped from behind a rock, grabbed one of their party by the shoulders and feet, and run away with him. "When we reached the spot," said the diggers, "everything was quiet, though there were some bamboo poles and Chinamen's baskets lying about. No doubt the Chinaman made a good meal, though if he was anything like his companions he would have been in poor condition."

A killing which the diggers took far less calmly, and which stirred the conflict to new heights of savagery, was the ambushing, murder, and eating of the Macquarie brothers on the tableland just above Hell's Gate towards the end of the year. Hughey Macquarie and his younger brother Don had given up shearing in the hope of making enough by packing on the Palmer to buy themselves a farm in Tasmania, where they came from, but Don's health had not stood up to the life, and Hughey was taking him back to the coast. On the way they were pounced on from behind rocks and knocked senseless before they could put up a fight. When Hughey came round Don was dead and the blacks were getting his body ready for roasting. To make sure that Hughey gave them no trouble they hacked off his legs at the knees and left him lying in agony while they went on with the feast.

Hughey lived long enough to leave a record of what had happened. On his belt he carried a tin pannikin, and with the last of his strength, almost unconscious with agony, he found a sharp chip of rock and used it to scratch into the tin the few words that told the grim story. Then he took the pannikin off his belt and pushed it under a ledge of rock before he died. Days later a party of diggers saw the signs of the cannibal feast and, searching around, found the pannikin.

Douglas and his troopers scoured the plateau and shot every blackfellow they could find. But still the war of attrition went on.

On the Cooktown side of the Laura crossing on the evening of 18th January 1875, Bernard McAdam was boiling the billy. "There were four of us," he said later, "myself, William Peel, Ron Mitchell, and John Blair. I was setting the billy on the fire when I felt a sting in the thigh and found myself speared. It was followed by a shower of spears, one of which fastened me to the ground by my shirt sleeve.

"Mitchell and Peel were in their own tent about fifty yards from us on the bank of the river, and Blair was sitting at the door of his own tent. About the time I was struck he raced up to my tent with a spear in his back. He had only time to call out, 'Oh, my God', when he fell dead.

"We fired a good number of effective shots at them, and when the spear was drawn out of my thigh we followed them up and drove them off. They fought every inch of the ground, but we were too well armed for them."

Next morning the three white men buried Blair and moved out, not waiting even to round up horses that had galloped off during the attack.

On 7th February Alexander Mann and William Nunn were making camp at the Laura when a hail of spears landed among them. Nunn received a spear through the neck behind his ear, another through the mouth, knocking out seven teeth, and two others that made minor flesh wounds. He fell, and Mann, who was unarmed, ran for his life towards a carriers' camp about a quarter of a mile off with about fifty blacks in screeching pursuit. He had nearly reached the camp when a spear took him in the back and hurled him forward onto his face. The carriers opened fire and the attackers ran. Mann was dead when they reached him. They found Nunn still in his tent. The spears were pulled out and he recovered.

The myalls by now were regarding the white men's horses and bullocks as fair enough game to replace the native animals their coming had driven away. A party of prospectors near Palmerville had five of their horses speared one after the other without even sighting a blackfellow. Four horses belonging to a packer named Klappe were speared, skinned, and butchered at the Normanby within a few miles of the police camp. Shortly afterwards nine more belonging to a packer named McNamara were killed in the same locality. Another party returning from a rumoured gold strike on the headwaters of the Bloomfield River had two horses speared, but not fatally. Next morning one of them was dead, and the body distended and putrid, showing that the spear had been poisoned.

At the new field on the headwaters of the Palmer, a party left their camp for a few hours prospecting, and found on their return that the blacks had been and had stolen everything—tent, clothing, blankets, and rations, leaving the prospectors with only the clothes they stood in.

A shanty-keeper on the Normanby was speared and eaten. A party of diggers reported it. "The tent was riddled with spears and entirely deserted; there were free drinks for all who chose to take them."

It was about this time that another shanty-keeper on the Cooktown–Normanby stretch of the track was found hanging from his roof pole. He was supposed to have suffered delirium tremens as a result of trying to cure himself of a bout of fever with too liberal doses of his own grog.

Two carriers, John Brown and Michael Roland, sitting at their campfire not far from the Normanby camp, were disturbed by their bullocks galloping around the drays during the night. They discovered that two of their cattle were missing, and went in search of them. One of them, crouching down to look at the tracks by the light of a match, received a spear through his sleeve. The missing animals were eventually found. They had spears sticking all over them like the prickles on a porcupine.

Some men were very lucky. A digger named Michael Henry was missed from his hut on the Normanby for a few days. The native police were called out and eventually found him about ten miles away, very drunk, but quite well and happy. There were blacks' tracks all around him.

A bullock driver named John Hickey, camped on Douglas's track, lost his bullocks and went up the river in search of them. He suddenly came on a mob of blacks rounding up someone else's horses. The blacks saw Hickey at the same moment. They forgot about the horses and came charging down on him. Hickey, who had only three cartridges in his revolver, fired, and dropped the leading pursuer in his tracks. But the others came on. Hickey ran for his life, the blacks after him. His two remaining shots did nothing to check them, and by the time a carrier's campfire showed up at the opposite side of the river, he had just enough strength to yell for help and plunge into the water. The carrier dragged him out and opened up on the blacks with his Snider.

Almost daily horses and bullocks were being speared and carriers and diggers attacked. Several diggers were attacked by a large party of raiders within five miles of Cooktown.

The Chinese fared worst of all at the hands of the blacks, but raids on them received little publicity unless a white digger also was in some way involved. It was said the blacks preferred Chinese for eating purposes because their rice-fed flesh tasted better than the salty flesh of the beef-fed whites.

With the raids continuing, the Cooktown *Courier* understated the views of the diggers when it said: "Public feeling runs high on the subject of increased native police protection for the Palmer Road."

7 · GOLD FOR ALL

As soon as the wet was over, Mulligan and his old mates had left Cooktown to have another look at the field. He found men fossicking everywhere. "The whole Palmer valley had become a living mass of men, scattered all over the country," he wrote later. "There seemed to be too many people— though everyone was getting gold—and more people were coming."

The Merkins were still fighting back. While prospecting on the Palmer on 27th May the party was rushed by a strong force of painted warriors. Driven off by rifle fire, they re-formed their ranks and came on again. Again they were driven off, and again they attacked. Long grass at that part of the river afforded perfect cover for the launching of spears, and three of the party were wounded, Abelsen seriously. "I never saw blacks so determined," wrote Mulligan. The party stayed close to Edwardstown for about a fortnight while Abelsen recovered from his wound.

At that time Howard St George had his headquarters at Palmerville. Edwardstown, near the junction of the Palmer and the Left-hand Branch, was his upper camp. In July 1874, when St George was appointed police magistrate at Cooktown, and replaced on the Palmer by P. F. Sellheim as mining warden, the headquarters camp was moved up to this area because it was more central. The first inland mail to the field was established soon after.

With Abelsen recovered, Mulligan crossed the Palmer, and then Oaky Creek, a tributary of Sandy Creek, and on 13th

June camped on Pine Creek, one of the heads of the Sandy, where he found payable gold. To Mulligan "payable gold" was gold which it would pay a party, under the then-existing conditions, to stop and work. It would have to yield not less than one ounce per man per day. "All the branches on Sandy Creek are now occupied by people too late for Oaky Creek," wrote Mulligan. "They are in most cases getting good gold."

Mulligan saw "numerous good-looking reefs for gold right opposite Oaky Creek", but reef gold was no good to the Palmer men of those glutted days of the first rush. On and on the diggers pushed, always drawn by the rumour of richer ground somewhere ahead. Men were walking off claims because they were getting only four ounces of gold in a week. Good though this was, they thought they could do better.

Although they were in the tropics, the country was so high that Mulligan found his horses suffered badly from the cold. He crossed the divide to the south, and found a large tributary of the Mitchell which he named after Howard St George. The party followed the river up for a few days, finding gold all the way, but not enough to be "payable", and turned back.

They had hardly turned round when they came face to face with a party of new chums who had been dogging their tracks all the way from Sandy Creek. The word had gone round, "Mulligan can smell gold ten miles away", and these had planned to be first on the scene when a new strike was made.

On 20th July Mulligan camped on the Mitchell, prospected unsuccessfully, and returned to Palmerville on 27th July to get fresh horses. By a few miles he had missed finding the Anglo-Saxon reef, which in 1887 produced up to seventy ounces a ton at a single crushing.

All over the field new townships were growing up. When Oaky Creek was discovered in June 1874 a township grew up on the side of a steep hill and a calico street wound its way among the trees. On a patch of cleared ground Tom Leslie set up a butcher's shop on behalf of what was to become one of the Palmer's best-known partnerships—Tom Leslie,

Jack Edwards (after whom Edwardstown was named), Jack Duff, and Patrick Callaghan.

Callaghan held a few blocks of country along the Mitchell River, which he used as a depot for bullocks for sale on the diggings, and in conjunction with Leslie, Edwards, and Duff became a large buyer of cattle for the local market. The partnership made money quickly on the field, selling beef for gold. All were popular among the diggers, in spite of the money they made out of them. One partner generally travelled around buying cattle, another superintended the supply to the local butchers, and the other two attended to gold-buying, slaughtering, and the financial side of the concern. Their Oaky Creek shop was typical of those all over the field.

"It was a sight on a Sunday morning to see the crowd of diggers waiting to get beef," wrote one of the diggers. "George Bradbury [an employee] would be cutting up, and Tom Leslie in an eight by ten tent, with scales, weighing out the gold that was being paid for the beef. A man often waited four or five hours before he could get near the block to get his week's supply.

"You were not asked what amount you required. The meat was just cut off the bone and a junk placed on the scales and the weight called out—twenty or thirty pounds, whatever it might be—and dozens of voices would be heard, 'Give me that.' And so it went on till sixteen or twenty bullocks were killed and all got what they wanted, or came in on the Monday to get it. There was no salt to be had on the Palmer and they had to sun dry their meat in the daytime and smoke it at night.

"Generally they killed five or six bullocks every day, but Sunday was the big day, and packers from Cooktown would generally try to get in on that day as they knew they would be able to sell out quickly and get away again. Often when a packer came in to Oaky Creek we would go in from the gully where we were working and try to get some flour, tea, and sugar. Before the packer would sell it he would make us buy a bottle of painkiller, or something else that was not selling well, before he would part up with any flour. At one time I found myself with thirteen bottles of painkiller. I let an old 'swiper' have the lot for an ounce of gold—less than cost price—to get rid of them. The buyer could get no grog, so he liquored up on the painkiller."

Painkiller was a sort of universal remedy in the country in those days. Mulligan was a particularly strong believer in its virtues.

There were two doctors on the field at this time, both open-handed men, and very popular with the diggers. Dr Kortum, who had his tent on the north side of Oaky Creek, had served in the Prussian Army in the Franco-Prussian War. After coming to Australia he had practised at Charters Towers for a while, joining the Palmer rush from there. He later moved to Cooktown. The other, Jack Hamilton, who had his tent on the top of a ridge on the south side of the creek, was not a doctor at all, but had learnt a good deal by watching his father, who was. He was supposed to have come to Australia to avoid the consequences of having backed the losing side in some South American revolution.

"He was real good at curing the fever and 'skates', and would attend a man whether he had the gold to pay for it or not," one old digger wrote. "If you had a dose of the fever and ague—or the 'skates' as they called it on the Palmer—your mate would take you in to one or the other of the doctors, rig up your tent or fly, make a bit of a stretcher in it and leave you there. The doctor would 'find' you in food and medicine, and you paid him nine pounds a week. The food was a little rice or other soft tack when they could get it. You generally could not eat anyway. All you wanted to do was drink, preferably something sour. The cure took anything from a week to a couple of months."

Hamilton, who was eventually elected to Parliament and represented the Cook District for about twenty years, was a strong swimmer, excellent pistol and rifle shot, and a man who knew how to use his fists. The latter accomplishment often came in very handy when he was practising medicine on the Palmer.

There was a big New Zealander he had cured of the skates in a fortnight, and when the man said he had no gold and was too weak to work his claim and would pay him when he got the gold, Hamilton said, "Oh, that's all right old man", and let it go at that. Weeks went by and the man did not turn up to pay. Hamilton made some inquiries, and found the man was working a rich claim at Snider Gully, about two miles from the township. Hamilton went up to Snider Gully, found the man, and asked if he had forgotten to pay him.

"No," said the digger, "I have not, but I'm not going to pay no bloody twenty pounds. I'll give you five. If you want more, you can knock it out of me if you can."

He was a big fellow, about three stone heavier than Hamilton, but not so tall.

"Right," said the doctor. "Where will you have it, here or on the main creek?"

"The main creek will do me," said the New Zealander.

Word of the coming fight went round the field like wildfire, and when the two men peeled off on the little flat about three hundred miners were gathered to watch the fun. But it was not even a fight. In three rounds Hamilton had cut the big digger to pieces and received no more than a few punches himself. The New Zealander called "enough", and staggered down to the creek to wash. He wiped his face on his shirt and held out his hand to Hamilton. "Come on up to the tent and get your twenty pounds," he said. "You've earned it now." He paid his fee with five ounces of gold.

There was another occasion when the mate of a digger who had come down with a second dose of the skates a couple of weeks after Hamilton had pronounced him cured came marching up to the doctor's tent with the stated intention of punching Hamilton on the nose. Hamilton finished with the man he was treating and washed his hands. "Right," he said, "I'm ready for you now." The digger not only lost the fight, but was in such poor shape at the end of it that Hamilton admitted him to hospital and treated him for his injuries— and charged him twenty pounds for the treatment.

It was at the Oaky Creek rush that things started to get tense between the white diggers and the Chinese.

William Hann had arrived on the Palmer at the end of the wet with a mob of fat bullocks from Maryvale. He said

77

he had met a Chinaman on the track who told him the Chinese were coming from all the Queensland fields to the Palmer, and from southern states as well, in mobs of a hundred or more.

When St George heard about it he told two delegates of the diggers at Palmerville that if they asked him to he would turn the Chinese away, but once they were admitted to the field he would have to protect them. This was just after the new alluvial deposits had been reported on Sandy Creek and most of the white miners were heading off in that direction. They had lost interest in the old ground. "Let them come," said one. "There's plenty of gold for everyone." Another, his swag already rolled, looked without interest at the claim he was walking away from. "Let the Chows have it; it's only fit for Chinamen anyway."

That was typical of the Palmer man's attitude at the time. New gold was always brighter, and all the time good claims were being deserted on the promise of better ones somewhere else. The itchy-footed diggers had good reason later to regret their short-sightedness.

Discovery of gold in the southern states had brought Chinese diggers to Australia in hundreds. There was no White Australia Policy then. Serious riots had occurred between them and white miners at Lambing Flat and other southern fields, and the Victorian and New South Wales Governments had passed legislation restricting their entry into those colonies.

Queensland gold discoveries brought them north. There had been some incidents between them and Queensland miners, but so far no sign of widespread trouble. A lot of white diggers had a good word for them. "There are worse colonists than John Chinaman; he never lowers wages and he is a kind-hearted fellow if one is hard up for a feed," wrote the editor of the local paper on the Ravenswood field.

Reef gold like that at Charters Towers had little interest for the Chinese. They preferred to fossick for alluvial. The Palmer was made to order for them. Palmer gold was so easily won that many of the white diggers had done no more than scrape off the richest of it before pushing on to the latest gully where someone claimed he had picked up a handful or two of pure, coarse gold from some rocky pocket.

Typical of white diggers' methods on the Palmer in its early days were those of an old Scot who worked a lonely gully on his own. He washed his gold on the sluicing system by shovelling the wash dirt into a part of the gully where the water dropped about a foot onto a fairly flat, rocky bottom. The water washed away the dirt, leaving the gold in the hollows in the rock. Of course the water carried away nearly as much gold as it left behind, but the method saved a lot of hard work, and there was always plenty more gold somewhere else when this cut out.

Before the end of 1874 nearly all of Queensland's two thousand Chinese, and many more from the south, had moved up into the area around Palmerville, where only a few hundred Europeans remained. Most of the white diggers had moved on, first to Sandy Creek, then to Oaky Creek and further afield.

The old Palmer ground had rich pickings for the Chinese, who could get gold and make a living in country where a white man would starve. While a white man needed to find gold worth £3 10s. or £4 a week to "make tucker" a China-man could live comfortably on 13s. or 14s. and put away any surplus as profit.

The average Chinaman's method of working was as careful as a European's was careless. As he took out the gold-bearing wash dirt he left a channel of the stream open to provide a tail-race. The water from all the sluice-boxes ran into this tail-race, which was cleaned out and washed over again at regular intervals. Any traces of gold that were washed through the boxes the first time were recovered when the tail-race was cleaned. In the old Palmer workings the Chinese cleaned out the alluvial right down to the bare rock, and not a grain of gold remained. In dry creeks they swept the bed-rock clean and stacked the dirt until the wet brought water to wash it.

In an attempt to avoid disputes over claims, Warden St George ordered that a wall of solid ground two feet thick should be left between all the claims on the watercourses.

79

When Sandy Creek and Oaky Creek were rushed by the white diggers, a boundary line was drawn at Sandy Creek and, for a while, no Chinamen were allowed above it. A notice on a tree put it bluntly: ANY CHINAMAN FOUND FURTHER UP THIS CREEK WILL BE INSTANTLY SEIZED AND HANGED UNTIL HE IS DEAD. It was no idle threat. Though some have claimed that there were no lynchings on the Palmer, old diggers insisted that it was a fairly common sight at one time, in the more isolated camps, to see the body of a Chinaman hanging by the neck from a tree.

In a letter to the *Queenslander* that December Mulligan expressed the views of most of the miners:

"If they attempt further ingress, from what I can find, there will be a roll-up, and that at the worst season of the year, and half the police of the Colony would find enough to do with an infuriated crowd of say 3,000 or 4,000 men, armed as the miners up here are, with rifles and other weapons of offence, led on by some enthusiast as is generally the case. We are, I believe, on the eve of another Ballarat. The Chinese are an intrusion on the miner, and I do not know why the Government should allow one particular class to be pestered by them without fixing a limit.

"They are an auxiliary to other industries, but not to the miner. They make good shepherds, good farm servants, good cooks and good gardeners. But the miner, they follow up in swarms with odious filth, get the best of the gold, never give the miner the opening and chance to fall back on old ground where a man could get a little if he did not succeed in other directions.

"They never prospect any. They came here after the European had the expense, privation, and trouble of opening up the field and, with more than usual audacity, set in to work. They bought up all the provisions, were the cause of flour rising from six pounds to twenty pounds per bag, and not obtainable at one time at that. In consequence the miners had to go to Cooktown and back for supplies which the Chinese ought to have brought with them.

"Now they have got their own public houses, stores, butcher's shops, and everything amongst themselves. I believe, in their business habits, they are right enough, but some bounds must be made for them, or the consequences will be serious."

Mulligan's letter showed some of the prejudice that was typical of white diggers on the Palmer at the time. If prices went up it was because packers and storekeepers exploited the Chinese as they would not have been able to exploit the white diggers.

In any case, by the end of 1874 the Chinese had defied the notice on the tree at Sandy Creek. They were there and at Oaky Creek. All over the Palmer and along the track their blue-clad figures with burdens suspended in baskets from a pole had become a familiar sight. And every ship that sailed from Cooktown for Chinese ports took its consignment of Palmer gold.

With cannibal raids at their peak, with diggers picking gold out of the rivers and creeks by the billyful, and packers and carriers making fortunes bringing in supplies, Mulligan, still unable to settle, kept on with his exploring. It was in his blood. He could not leave unknown country alone. In one of his journals he wrote, "To me it is a great pleasure to traverse new country where no white man ever trod before. Every step discloses new scenes and fresh discoveries. The fascination is broken once I return to ground travelled over before, either by myself or by someone else."

With replenished supplies and fresh horses, he and his mates headed out from Palmerville on 6th August 1874, and four days later camped once again on Pine Creek. The place which a month ago he had found an unpeopled wilderness with gold in its gullies was now a thriving mining settlement clustered around "Tought's Butchering Establishment and Store", and known unofficially as Toughtville. All the gullies were thronged with feverishly working prospectors.

Mulligan left them to it and on 31st August reached the Mitchell, having passed within a mile or two of the most easterly point Hann had reached on foot in July 1872. Away to the south he saw the "notable landmark" sighted by Hann. Hann had turned his back on it, but Mulligan went on.

He named the river that met the Mitchell from the south

the Hodgkinson, after his friend W. O. Hodgkinson, explorer, journalist, politician, and later to be a mining warden on the Palmer. Before long Mulligan was to find gold on this river, which would make it, for a while, a rival to the Palmer.

As they rode up the river and closed in on Hann's landmark, Mulligan's mates, in spite of his protests, insisted on calling it Mount Mulligan. It is a great rugged mass of red rock, weathered by the elements over millions of years—a fitting monument to a man like Mulligan.

They found a small amount of gold on the Hodgkinson that time, but Mulligan was looking for another alluvial field like the Palmer, and he passed on disappointed. After toiling through the rugged country between the Hodgkinson and the Walsh without making any notable discoveries, the party returned to Palmerville on 21st September.

By 1st October he was away again. He named the McLeod River after Billy McLeod, the prospector, and found some "shotty gold" on the headwaters of the Palmer. A large part of the route he followed on this trip is now covered by the Mulligan Highway between Mareeba and Cooktown. From the summit of the Main Range he was struck by a magnificent panorama which today is almost unchanged. It is a wild sweep of bush and valley and ranges stretching north as far as the eye can see. Only in Mulligan's day it was dotted with the smudge of blackfellows' campfires. The party arrived back at Palmerville on 5th December.

In all four of his Palmer expeditions, Mulligan had received no help whatever from the Government. The gold he brought back from them did not pay his expenses. It is plain from his diary that he had had enough of it.

On 5th December he wrote: "This being probably my last outside trip prospecting, I may have no further occasion to write you. [His diaries were being published by the *Queenslander*.] That we have not opened up fresh goldfields beyond the Palmer is evident, yet we have assisted materially in extending the development of this field which is great enough in extent to comprise several large fields spreading from here to the Upper Palmer seventy-five miles, where we got payable prospects.

Mulligan and his party fight off a determined attack

The cannibals of the Palmer preferred Chinese food

Chinese were carried off bodily for the roasting fires

The first burial on the Hodgkinson

"Everyone on the Palmer knows that we could have kept on the inside on payable gold as well as others had we been so inclined. And now I give up exploring and prospecting for gold, finding it too expensive. I must now think of going in for something more lucrative."

Two days later he was writing again: "Thunderstorms have now set in and the rain keeps spattering the paper through the calico tent as I write. There is good grass almost everywhere. Abundant gold has been got in many gullies and ravines once not workable for want of water. There is abundance of rations on the field. Nearly all the diggers have been to Cooktown and loaded for themselves. There is, in consequence, little demand on the storekeepers at present, but when traffic stops, they will reap a good harvest."

It was clear that many had learnt a lesson from that first disastrous wet season on the Palmer. This time those who had stacked dirt had stacked it above flood level. Diggers were well supplied with rations, and so were storekeepers. This time they would keep working through the wet.

Just as the wet was setting in, Mulligan wrote to the *Queenslander* a further letter that was to open up a whole new field of operations on the Palmer and bring to light some of its richest gold deposits. Up to now Palmer gold had been all alluvial, but many rich reefs had been discovered and were lying untouched because there was no machinery to crush the quartz.

On a trip up-river to Edwardstown Mulligan was spoken to by a number of men who had reefing claims which they had stuck to while alluvial gold was being found all around them. Some were making a bare living by crushing the best of their quartz in a sort of iron mortar called a dolly. They asked Mulligan to look at their reefs and write a report on them. They felt that if he reported favourably, his opinion would carry enough weight to induce someone to bring in machinery.

"It is generally understood," wrote Mulligan in his letter, "that reefers are great blowers, and I really thought that some of what I heard was blowing. I was told of The Queen of the North, Heart's Content, and several others crushing

G

out one pound weight in a day and every day, if they liked, by dolly.

"This visit quite satisfied me of the truth of the matter, and there is no blowing about that. The reefs are very large, and in all the paddocks can be seen great blocks of quartz—two, three, and four hundredweight. In several paddocks I have tried to put my thumb on a spot without touching gold, and at the Queen of the North and several others I could scarcely do it. This gold is shotty and well diffused through the stone. No matter where a block is broken it presents the same appearance.

"Several of the claims I visited I had to examine for myself, it being Christmas Day the shareholders were out enjoying themselves at other camps or in town. I went down their shafts, looked at their paddocks and surface cuttings, and could, in nearly all instances, see a well-defined, large reef, its pretty walls easily worked, being soft, slaty sandstone. Some of the shafts are down seventy feet, carrying the same good show all the way."

Mulligan left no doubt of the impression the inspection made on him.

"I have stuck to reefing for years," he wrote, "and have been led to say I'll reef no more except I saw gold sticking out like my thumb. I think I can now almost start again, for it is nearly as prominent. I never saw better shows, not only for shareholders, but also for machines, there being such a body stone that when men know a machine is coming they can go in and rip it out.

"All the reefs working are pretty well in the same locality and within a radius of three or four miles. Good roads can be got to every claim, there being a leading spur to the river or, if they prefer it, to the Left-hand Branch.

"Hitherto the machine owners would have been mad to attempt sending machinery here at the extraordinary high price of carriage, but now that the carriage is getting lower and will continue to get cheaper for some time, there will come machinery to the place eventually, and the first in the field will reap a golden harvest."

Mulligan's letter was to have the desired effect. An engi-

neer examined the field, and within months four ore-
crushing batteries were on their way to the Palmer.

In the meantime a new gold strike was reported from the
head of the Normanby River. Sub-Inspector Douglas blazed
a new track branching off at the shanty on the Normanby
and heading almost due south. Diggers from the Palmer and
Cooktown rushed to see what gold they could get before the
wet came in earnest. Others had rushed sixty miles or so up-
river from Edwardstown to Dead Dog Creek—Mulligan's find
on the headwaters of the Palmer. This was described as a
typical Palmer field with a wide distribution of gold. It was
about twenty-five miles from the Normanby diggings—
seventy-five miles from Cooktown by Douglas's new track.
With Oaky and Sandy creeks almost deserted the Chinese
moved in. People were beginning to say there would always
be gold on the Palmer.

8 · THE ASIATIC INVASION

WHEN THE first shipments of Palmer gold reached Canton and Hong Kong in 1874—there was 3,586 ounces of it, worth £12,959—Chinese merchants began to take an interest, and before long they and their countrymen in Cooktown were organizing a mass migration to Sin Chin San—as they called Australia—the New Mountain of Gold.

Results came quickly, and soon Cooktown papers were reporting: "The arrival of the *Victoria* on 30th January [1875] with about two hundred Chinamen on board created a large amount of excitement as they filed through the main street. They seem to be quiet, inoffensive creatures, and their arrival was not looked upon with much disfavour."

Word went around that the local Chinese merchants planned to use them to pack their merchandise from Cooktown to the Palmer, and that they would then be engaged to mine gold on behalf of the Canton and Hong Kong merchants who had paid their passages to Australia. To packers and diggers alike, the coolies began to look less "inoffensive".

When word came that another vessel was about to arrive with four hundred Chinese on board it was not taken so quietly. F. W. J. Beardmore, a stock and station agent who had rented the Government's newly completed wharves and sheds, at once rode out to the Four Mile Camp on the Palmer track where Corfield and a number of other carriers were camped. He told them he intended to levy a poll-tax of a shilling a head on each Chinaman who landed, and asked the carriers to help. The carriers had a conference and decided to join him. The coolies were competing for their trade.

"Bring your ropes with you," called Beardmore as he rode away back to Cooktown.

Before the ship docked the carriers had stretched their ropes across the wharf exit and marshalled their forces to prevent any of the Chinese from leaving without paying Beardmore's tax. The coolies poured off the ship, gathered their gear, and in a chattering mob made for the exit—to find it barred by ropes and backed by a line of grim-faced carriers.

When the position was explained to the Chinese pandemonium broke out. They had no money. They had been promised work and easily won gold. The argument could have gone on for days, but the carriers ended it by confiscating the coolies' swags and locking them in the shed. The swags would be released when the tax was paid, they said. Some of the Chinese put up a fight, but they had no chance. Sailors from the ship and gathering townsmen backed the carriers. Several Chinese who escaped under the ropes were grabbed by their pigtails and dragged back, yelling their protests. The whole operation was completed without bloodshed.

After a heated discussion between Beardmore and representatives of the Chinese storekeepers, the latter paid the twenty pounds demanded by Beardmore for the release of the swags. No one challenged Beardmore's right to levy the tax, but a meeting of 250 men at the Cooktown Hotel urged an immediate ban on Chinese immigration on the ground that the Chinese were threatening to disturb the peace. No action was taken, and the Chinese continued to arrive.

A Cooktown report dated 22nd March stated: "The subject which at present is creating great excitement here is the arrival on Saturday last of two large steamers from the East, having together nearly 800 Chinamen on board. The mail steamer, *Singapore*, contributed 395 and the P. & O. steamer *Adria* the remainder. They have all landed and gone in extensively for long-handled shovels, picks, and dishes, whilst they purchased the timber in the rough and are employed making their own cradles.

"I can tell you," the writer went on, "that the arrival of

87

these Celestials is looked upon with a very unfavourable eye by the European diggers, and I should not be at all surprised if there was a row between the races.

"The customs officers here were not, in the first instance, over officious in examining the personal luggage, but when some of the larger packages came to hand an investigation took place, when, from the midst of salt fish, potted shrimps, preserved mushrooms, and other stomach fixings, there rolled out a few balls of opium. This was the signal for a general seizure, and some particularly elongated visages may be seen hovering about the wharf awaiting the overhaul."

Soon after this a meeting was held in the Chamber of Commerce Hall to "consider the desirability of preventing the influx of Chinese on the northern goldfields". One of the chief speakers was Mulligan, who moved "that this meeting views with apprehension the anticipated arrival of large numbers of Chinese on our northern goldfields and the imminent danger of serious collisions, and is of the opinion that it is desirable to bring the matter immediately under the notice of the Government". The motion was carried.

Other motions carried were "that a committee be formed with a view to concerted action in preventing by all legitimate means this Chinese immigration"; and "that a deputation wait on the Colonial Secretary with a copy of the resolutions and urge the Government to take steps to avert collisions which are inevitable should several thousand Chinese land at Cooktown".

The Cooktown *Herald* of 25th April 1875 summarized the situation: "This immigration has many features which distinguish it from any previous Mongolian rush in Colonial history. Cooktown is situated so near the great ports that empty out their surplus coolies into neighbouring countries, the facilities for reaching the gold diggings are so unusual, the expense is so comparatively slight that, apart from other considerations, it is small wonder that John Chinaman is hurrying here, with his stick and his baskets filled with pots and pans, as fast as he can.

"The whole secret of the matter is that certain Chinese merchants in Hong Kong and Canton have excited the cupidity of their countrymen by the most extravagant accounts of the Palmer. Placards are paraded in the streets announcing the astonishing fact that gold paves the highways of Cooktown, and that men pick up nuggets of gold of fabulous size at the diggings as easily as a schoolboy picks up shells on the beach.

"Is it any wonder that a fever seized the swarming population who daily vie with each other for a bare subsistence in the great Eastern ports? Chinese rushed to obtain the required equipment. Then, in stepped the Chinese merchants, charterers of steamers to El Dorado, and shippers sufficient to feed all they could induce to emigrate.

"The arrival of the steamer *Singapore* with 470 passengers, followed the same evening by the *Adria* with about 600 more, was our first intimation of the new, and certainly unexpected rush to our port." [One notices that the figures have grown since the first report of 22nd March.]

"Since then," the correspondent continued, "we have had 1,200 in the steamers *Namoa* and *Egeria*. And the *Somerset* brings tidings that we may very soon expect three steamships crowded with passengers that were laid on for Cooktown prior to the departure of the mail from Hong Kong.

"At the present time there cannot be far short of 5,000 Chinese on the goldfields and the number will shortly be double that figure. Feeling here is, with the exception of a few interested parties, decidedly hostile."

Hostile it certainly was. Daily, speakers at rowdy meetings in Cooktown streets and pubs abused the Government for allowing the influx. Riots were promised. "The men of Lambing Flat knew how to fight for their rights, and we'll show the Government we know how to fight for ours," one bearded digger with a Snider slung across his shoulder and a holstered revolver on his hip told a cheering crowd. A dozen beer mugs were raised in the air. "Good on you, Bendigo; we're with you." Bendigo responded to the encouragement. "I've shot plenty of blacks in my time," he said, "and I can just as easy shoot Chinkies too."

Everywhere, even away down in Brisbane, meetings demanded Government action to keep out the Chinese. White diggers who had often bet nuggets of gold on which of two flies would be first to take off from the bar-room wall, or tossed them on the stage to pay a dancer to take off her clothes, claimed indignantly that the Chinese were inveterate gamblers and that they were encouraging moral depravity and degrading womanhood. (There were, in fact, both white and Chinese brothels in Cooktown by this time, and many of the protesting diggers had shown a strong preference for those run by the Chinese.) Men who had followed the gleam of gold from California to Ballarat, to Gulgong, Gympie, and the Palmer, and who were ready to rush again at the first rumour of gold, said the Chinese were bad settlers who took all the gold they could get and gave the country nothing in return. Diggers who spent every ounce of gold they got at the nearest shanty on rum reinforced with laudanum and cheap plug tobacco expressed themselves as horrified that the Chinese smoked opium.

On the goldfield itself the newly arrived Chinese had settled in mainly on the old, deserted Left-hand Branch alluvial workings, but they were also reported to have opened new ground ten miles down from Palmerville. Around Revolver Point and German Bar, their main camp, there were estimated to be about five thousand of them.

Few of these newly arrived Chinese were allowed to keep the gold they won. They had signed indentures, with their families in China as security, in return for their fares to Australia, and their earnings went to their Chinese sponsors in Canton, Hong Kong, and Cooktown. Their affairs were managed by a number of Chinese tongs or secret societies, who had divided the goldfield into strictly recognized working areas. Each gang was presided over by a tong representative—a trained hatchet-man—who directed activities, arranged rations and supplies, issued a few trusted coolies with such weapons as were available, and immediately took charge of all gold that was won. A quick knife in the back was the best a coolie could expect if caught stealing gold for himself. Eventually, when his debt was paid, together with suitable interest, he was free to work on his own account. Until then, he laboured long hours, nearly naked in the scorching sun, provided with only the bare minimum needed to keep him alive.

No tents were provided for these indentured labourers. They built themselves grass huts similar to those built by the blacks, and cultivated vegetable gardens to eke out their ration of rice.

"The only person I know doing well out of John," wrote one old digger sourly, "is Jock Edwards and Co. butchers. They are killing ten bullocks a day. Edwardstown of a Saturday is like a beehive of Chinamen. It is the centre of attraction at present. All business men are rushing there with the prospect of machinery for the reefs, and Mr Sellheim, the warden, is for moving there. Together with its being on the main road for all the principal camps, it is certain to go ahead."

A packer described a camp of about four hundred Chinese on the Laura on their way to the goldfields: "Along the river's bank and on its bed scores of them were making themselves snug for the night, some carrying forks, rice bowls, and other adjuncts to the camp, while others spread leaves, grass, etc., for a bed. Here one would be feeding a litter of kittens, while another would be trying to coax a mob of ducks (domestic) to the water's edge to be caged for the night.

"Angry voices would be heard. A boss Chinaman would accuse one of his team, a nearly naked new chum, of breaking a quantity of eggs he had been carrying. Maybe the coolie would fight, rushing wildly up to his opponent brandishing both arms and occasionally aiming a flying kick at his enemy's nose. This would be dodged and returned. Both tongues would be going incessantly.

"The main body in the camp would meanwhile be clustered in lots of four or five applying chopsticks to bowls of rice. Some of the more ravenous would hold a gourd close to the mouth and literally stuff great gobbets of rice down their throats.

"It was an hour after dark before the ceaseless din ended and silence settled over their camp. But long ere sunrise in the morning they were off and, as the sun reached the treetops, many miles of the journey had been accomplished."

In those days, said the writer, one sometimes saw hundreds of Chinamen on the Palmer track, going and returning in two continuous streams. When going through Hell's Gate they blazed away constantly with any firearms they had, with the idea of scaring off the blacks. The sound of it echoed round the rocks like thunder.

About five hundred Chinese, encouraged by Cooktown merchants, formed themselves into human pack-trains to operate between Cooktown and the Palmer. Each man carried about 150 pounds in his twin baskets. To make things more difficult for the white packers and carriers with whom they were competing, they made a habit of burning off the grass along the track so horse and bullock teams would have no pasture. Retribution naturally followed. A news item stated: "Two Chinamen have been tomahawked on the Laura; it is supposed to have been the act of Europeans." Another reported: "The diggers have been playing Old Harry with the Chinamen again and two Hong Kong Johns have been killed and several wounded between the Kennedy and the Laura."

A packer looking for straying horses one morning had seen a number of hawks circling, and on investigating had found the bodies of two Chinamen lying close to the embers of an old campfire. Though the bodies showed signs of violence they were so decomposed that it was impossible to tell with what sort of weapon they had been killed. It was generally agreed that if the blacks had been responsible the bodies would have been eaten.

The blacks were, in fact, blamed for some killings, particularly of Chinese, that they never committed. "A spear sticking through a Chinaman's body was no evidence that he had been speared to death by a blackfellow," one old hand from the Palmer wrote. "Many a man was shot dead and then a barbed spear poked through the hole the bullet had made."

Occasionally someone—generally referred to as an interested party—spoke up for the Chinese. "How many white men were working at Revolver Point, German Bar, and Cradle Creek and all the ravines and gullies along the Left-hand Branch when the Chinese took possession? Not a hundred, we have found. Where the white man is, the Chinaman is not. At the best he is but a gleaner of the waifs and strays of his predecessors. It is to a certain extent true that he occupies ground that might afford a bare pittance to Europeans returning broke from the newer, far-out fields, but that calamity is of much rarer occurrence now than formerly."

In Cooktown the Chinese merchants were quietly digging in. One of them bought the Captain Cook Hotel for eight hundred pounds cash. Several large Chinese merchants in Canton and Hong Kong sent representatives to Cooktown, and large and handsome stores began to go up all over the town.

"Mongolians land in large numbers from every steamer from Hong Kong and Singapore and announce their intention of making Cooktown a second Canton," wrote the *Australasian Sketcher* correspondent. "They are genuinely surprised that the locals are not delighted at the prospect. The Chinese buy up the eligible town lots of land at high rates and quickly run up stores and open businesses.

"They also throng the roads to the Palmer diggings where long strings of them can be seen stretched out in Indian file, each man carrying his burden at the end of his bamboo pole, shuffling on with a curious jogtrot and most of them carrying on conversation with those in front or behind and making a great din with their monosyllabic chattering. Their loads consist of tinware, chests of tea, bags of flour, tents and equipage, mining tools, clothes, and all the other items of necessary equipment for mining life." The Chinese had come a long way since Mulligan complained that they brought no stores to the field, but they were still not winning the white diggers' approval.

To the cannibal blacks, the new chum Chinese were manna from heaven. Hundreds of them were ambushed, captured, and eaten at leisure in gloomy canyons like Hell's Gate, at creek crossings, and in patches of scrub along the track. The first the Chinese would know of an attack would be when innocent-looking boulders or gum-trees suddenly erupted with black figures striped with white and yellow warpaint and screeching like demons from the deepest hell.

Sometimes the Chinese were lucky. On 8th October five Chinese on the track about three miles from the Laura Crossing were surprised by about fifteen to twenty blacks who attempted to surround them. The Chinese threw down their bamboos and baskets and ran for their lives down the mountain, reaching the store at the Laura out of breath and empty handed.

The following day two white diggers coming up from the Normanby arrived at the Laura. They were told what had happened, but decided to go on. "If the blacks were ever there, they'll be gone by now," said one. Climbing the range, they found the place where the Chinese had run. All their loading—rice, tea, sugar, etc.—was scattered about, but of baskets, poles, packs, and blankets there was no sign. Seeing no blacks about, the diggers carried on. As they came to the last pitch on the hill the man in front heard his mate, who was about ten yards behind him, scream out. He turned and saw his mate lying on the ground with a spear right through him. There was not a blackfellow in sight.

The digger remained with the wounded man until some packers came up. They broke off the spear and got the man down to the shanty on the Laura. The spear, which was embedded more than fourteen inches, had entered the back close to the spine between the short ribs and was protruding from the stomach. Next day it was extracted by a man who had some experience as a hospital wardsman, and the wounded man lived.

Mining Warden Sellheim's report for that month listed further murders on the Hell's Gate road and ended: "The object was evidently the use of the bodies for food." Somewhere near the Gate there was supposed to be a large mountain cave which was given the name of the Devil's Kitchen. Rumour was that captured Chinese were taken there by the dozen and hung on trees outside by their pigtails until they were needed for killing and eating. In later years many miners looked for it, believing that some of the gold the captured Chinese would have been carrying would be found there. If the cave existed, it was never located.

Sickness also took a heavier toll among the Chinese than it had done among the white diggers. From heat, exhaustion, snakebite, and fever they dropped along the track and were left there by their countrymen to die. On 15th September a Cooktown newspaper reported: "Numbers of Chinamen are dying on the road and their countrymen systematically avoid them, even while still alive. I have seen personally a poor wretch, even within the precincts of the town, lying perfectly helpless by himself with but a few barrels to shelter him. It is a portion of their custom in such cases and the unfortunate quite accedes to the arrangement."

Soon after this a case of leprosy was reported among the Chinese on the Palmer, and there was an outcry from the white diggers about the Chinese introducing "loathsome Oriental diseases". The newspaper reported: "Mr Sellheim has taken prompt measures to prevent the spread of this disease and has ordered that such Chinamen as are not holders of business licences be confined to a separate camp on the south side of the river, as they have lately been in the habit of bringing their sick countrymen into Edwardstown and leaving them there to their fate."

But for every hundred Chinese who died more than a hundred got through to spread out along the abandoned creeks and gullies of the Palmer and its tributaries, working all day and half the night with rough cradles to pick up the rich leavings of the white prospectors who were always moving on. The men who had investigated Mulligan's report of gold on the headwaters of the Palmer had reported good yields, and diggers were flocking there. "The old fields are consequently deserted," wrote one miner, "and Chinamen are returning from the outside districts in consequence of being frightened by the niggers, and are making their way to take up the old workings of the Europeans. At Sandy Creek and on the Left-hand Branch they are working the whole bed of the river in a face to a depth of four feet and are making good gold."

An old digger later described how a prospector named Mosman crossed the divide north of Edwardstown and found rich gold in what later became known as Chinky

Creek, running into the Mosman River, which joins up with the Laura. In a few days Mosman had washed forty-five ounces. With the gold in his billy he trekked back over the divide to Cradle Creek and, at the shanty of Larry Moore, drank the lot of it.

To get money for rations to go back to his claim Mosman agreed, for sixty pounds, to show it to a party of Chinese who had been fossicking in the old Cradle Creek diggings. In the first week the Chinese cleared about a hundred ounces of gold from the creek. One of them who, unlike most of his countrymen, registered his gold, sent more than a ton of gold out through Cooktown from what came to be called Chinky Creek. There is no record of the gold won by the other Chinese in the party, but they all probably did just as well.

In due course Mosman's own claim was jumped by the Chinese while he was away on a drinking spree. When he returned to claim it protest was futile. There was not a European in sight.

The conglomerate on both north and south sides of the tableland in this area was very rich in gold, and the Chinese got nearly all of it. This layer of cemented gravel, no more than about three and a half feet thick, lay flat like a bed of coal with about eight hundred feet of sandstone above it and a slate formation below. Wherever a creek or gully exposed it, the Chinese tunnelled a hundred feet or more through the slate immediately below the conglomerate and took out the gold-bearing material by the ton. In all they took out an estimated ten thousand tons. They did so well that they cut steps in the sandstone right up the gorge of one of the creeks to the plateau above to make it easier to get their gold out. They hired unlucky white diggers to patrol the plateau to give them warning of raids by blacks, and chained savage, half-starved dogs at the entrances of their tunnels to keep intruders away. There was a rush of white diggers to the Conglomerate, but they were too late. For once the Chinese had got in first. Of the prospector named Mosman we hear no more. Could he have been the Hugh Mosman who about three years earlier had discovered the Charters Towers gold-field? It seems unlikely.

With Dead Dog Creek at the head of the Palmer the only promising new field, a new gold discovery was badly needed to relieve growing tensions. Mulligan was sounded out but he proved cagey. He pointed out that by far the greater part of the Palmer diggings had been opened up as a result of explorations by himself and his friends. What gold they themselves had won, he said, they had spent on equipping new expeditions. And while they were away, other men had been picking the eyes out of the fields they had discovered. Not one penny, Mulligan emphasized, had he received from the Government for his work.

Unable to get Mulligan's services free, the Government decided to pay for them. In 1875 he was granted five hundred pounds to equip an expedition to look for a new goldfield. He was promised a thousand pounds reward for the discovery of payable gold. The Government Surveyor, Frederick Warner, would accompany him. At last Mulligan agreed, but the move had been left a little late. Lively days were ahead for the old diggings before a new discovery by Mulligan drained off their floating population.

9 · ROBBERS AND KILLERS

By the end of 1875 the Palmer and its surrounding rivers and creeks swarmed with about fifteen thousand diggers— and ten thousand of them were Chinese. All the alluvial gold areas seemed to have been located. Most of the gold going out through Cooktown was from the Chinese working the old ground.

Trouble was brewing in every direction.

The Merkins, seeing one after another of the rivers and creeks they had fished in for generations turned into a desolation of mud and rubble, intensified their attacks on the men who were taking their livelihood away from them. They speared outlying parties whenever the chance offered, and ate their victims. With the game of the country driven away or killed off, the horses and bullocks of the diggers and carriers became their staple food. The speared horses were stripped of their shoes, and captured wagons of their ironwork, to make heads for tomahawks and spears.

Brutality on both sides increased. Killing a blackfellow meant one less man who might kill you. A double-barrelled gun and a six-chambered Colt revolver were normal equipment for a digger. "If you go for a billy of water," wrote Mulligan, "you have to take a gun with you."

White diggers who had rushed helter-skelter to and from rumoured gold strikes on the Bloomfield and Annan rivers, in the creeks of the Conglomerate Range, on the Endeavour, Normanby, and countless other creeks and gullies, found themselves beaten to the best ground by other white diggers

98

and cut off from the old ground by hordes of newly arrived Chinese. Some of them formed gangs to waylay and ambush Chinese taking their gold back to Cooktown. Sometimes they ambushed white diggers too. A newspaper announced: "A digger has been shot while passing through Hell's Gate. It is supposed to have been the act of Europeans."

Chinese pouring into the field found there was not enough gold to go round. Hungry, sick, and desperate, new arrivals fought Chinese who had been there from the start, and defended themselves bitterly against white diggers. A Chinese resisting expulsion from a claim by its original white owner was shot dead. The white digger said he had only left the claim temporarily to follow a new rush which had proved a "duffer". A Cooktown jury found the white digger fired in self-defence against assault by the Chinaman's shovel. On the field the warden appealed for additional police because of the "threatening attitude" of Chinese about the camp.

In a desperate effort to get gold from the overcrowded field some diggers cut saplings to make extra-long handles for their shovels, and waded up to their necks in deep waterholes to try the sand at the bottom of them for gold. A digger named Jerry Rohan and his two mates managed to extract more than a hundred ounces in a fortnight from the bottom of a deep waterhole in Stony Creek which they had partly pumped out. The gold was coarse and contained several pieces weighing from one to three ounces. A few white diggers who had stuck to good claims were still doing well, both on Sandy Creek and the main river. One party on the river, with thirteen men employed, had constructed a tramway and had small trucks for running the washdirt to a sluice box. They were making a good thing out of it. Cases like this, however, had become the exception.

Beaten men dragged their steps back to Cooktown to sponge on their luckier mates, to cheat and rob and become a charge on the Government which had to pay their fares back to the south to get rid of them.

"See the incoming Palmer men," wrote a correspondent of the *Australasian Sketcher* in June, "how the flesh has left their bones, how gaunt and haggard, yellow eyed and aged

H

they look. All the spring and elasticity of their constitutions has gone with the fresh red and white of their natural complexions.

"They have got gold, maybe, but they have drunk deep of the Palmer pestilence and carry with them the seeds that will ripen into disease. They have lived ten years in one.

"The last few months have been pregnant with disease and death. The disastrous rush to the Normanby and Laura opened up a fresh, fever-stricken field, and scores have only been purchasers of death when they bought their stores. The country on the heads of the rivers has been peculiarly unhealthy, and the number of sick and dying who have sought relief in hospital is exceptionally large."

Earlier in the year a Cooktown newspaper had reported seven inquests in one week on men who allegedly died of sunstroke, fever, and other causes, and numerous other deaths in hospital after short illnesses. Many cases of sunstroke or apoplexy were, the report stated, nothing more than too much grog. "We had many cases of insanity from Cooktown," the magistrate in charge of the Townsville reception house wrote, "hardly any cases at all that were not due to excessive drinking. Occasionally we had a man suffering from delirium tremens for perhaps a week."

Cooktown people were more inclined to blame the local climate for their bad health and high death-rate. "Charlotte Street, where are situated all the public offices, and where nearly all the business of the port is transacted, skirts the mangrove marsh and slimy river bank for over half a mile," the newspaper pointed out. "The humid air is very oppressive and would seem sufficient to account for a great deal more sickness than Cooktown has ever yet experienced."

Whether or not the climate caused the sickness, it certainly led, both in the town and on the goldfield, to a colossal consumption of every type of liquor. Every camp had its stack of empty bottles; in some of the older camps it covered nearly half an acre. Lonely diggers brought back a supply of their favourite brand of grog from the nearest shanty.

But there was also a humorous side. One story tells of a miner on his way back to camp after a spree, who fell down

100

a hole in the ground and woke up to find himself alongside a reef gleaming with gold. He clambered out and rushed off, yelling at the top of his voice, to tell his mates. Unfortunately he forgot to make a note of where the hole was. For years he searched for it. He tried to find it sober and he tried to find it drunk, but he never saw it again. Years later, according to the story, another man fell through the same hole. He took one look at the gold-studded reef, pegged out a claim, registered it, and made a fortune.

Out on the field where gold had been found, at every spot where two tracks joined, and at every river crossing where rising water might stop the traveller for a few days, someone had built a shanty to sell grog. Many of them were substantial structures of logs, with strong shutters, and loopholed to fight off a siege; others were of bark; and some were no more than a tent-fly over a pole tied between two trees.

The drink sold at these shanties ranged from good rum and brandy to a foul concoction of any kind of alcohol that could be got, watered down to make it spin out, and fortified with laudanum, cheap plug tobacco, and anything else that would make a half-dead miner think for a while that he was getting his money's worth. After a spree on this stuff, many became raving maniacs and ran amok, sometimes in mobs. Brawls were a daily occurrence and in the more isolated spots men were kicked to death in broad daylight and no one did anything about it.

Many of the shanties were kept by women, who sold additional services at fantastic prices to favoured customers. But more often they, like their male counterparts, would drug a digger's drink, rob him of every ounce of gold he carried, and drag him out under the nearest tree to come round in his own time. When he did, there was one drink for the road, and he was expected to get out.

If a badly treated customer made trouble for a woman shanty-keeper, there was generally some other digger or teamster about who was prepared to protect her for the sake of favours he hoped to receive. A half-starved digger, just awake from a drugged drink, was hardly a match for a tough woman with a gun anyway.

101

"Alleged and proved robberies of gold by shanty-keepers are of almost daily occurrence," reported the Cooktown *Herald* in August 1875. "An instance has just been communicated of where a couple of Oaky Creek diggers, hardworking, horny-fisted fellows, respectable, and of steady habits in a general way, knocked down the gold accumulation of many months—about fifty ounces—in a few days." With no gold to go back to, such men became desperate.

In October the paper's Edwardstown correspondent reported: "There has been a most daring robbery at the Revolver Point Butchery run by Messrs J. Edwards and Co. Fortunately Mr Edwards had been down squaring up accounts and had taken the bulk of the money with him. There was, however, silver amounting to twenty pounds locked up in the safe, which also contained valuable curios belonging to diggers valued at a hundred pounds, comprising specimens, nuggets, gold chains, and valuable papers, the whole of which, safe and all, was stolen. This robbery makes the fifth at the same place."

One robbery had an unusual sequel. A Dane named Jens Abrahams, who had won and then drunk about £1,200 worth of gold at German Bar, decided to try his luck further down river at Jessop's Gully where it was less crowded. On the afternoon of his arrival he was pottering about with the idea of getting to work next day when he came on a pocket of coarse, shotty gold to be had just for the picking-up in the little ripples of rock where years of rapid-flowing water had deposited it. In less than half an hour he had filled his billy with gold.

Being on his own, but knowing other prospectors were about, Abrahams resorted to an old miner's trick to hide his gold. Putting his miner's right, some other papers, and his comb in the billy on top of the gold, he dug a hole in the sand, buried the billy in it, lit a fire over the spot, and cooked his supper. With the embers still hot, he bedded down for the night, planning to make an early start for Cooktown in the morning. Abrahams never carried firearms, but he had a good dog and did not worry.

During the night he was twice awakened by the dog's barking, but went to sleep again. The third time the dog was barking frantically. Abrahams bounded from his bunk in time to see a man lifting his billy from its hiding place. The man with the billy ran for his life with Abrahams and the dog after him. Finding himself being overtaken, he turned suddenly and let fly with his revolver, hitting Abrahams in the leg. Unarmed as he was, Abrahams had no chance. The thief got away with the billy, which also contained his miner's right, his papers, and his comb, which, being something of a bush dandy, he always carried with him.

The sequel came a year later in Copenhagen when Mr Willman, an old Palmer man and friend of Abrahams's who was spending some of his gold on a holiday in Europe, met a Mr Kryger, whom he had known in Rockhampton in 1874.

"Did you ever happen to come across a man named Jens Abrahams?" asked Kryger.

"Yes, I knew Jens well."

"Poor old Jens," said Kryger. "Like a lot of others, he left his bones on the Palmer."

"Eh?" said Willman in surprise, "I saw him just before I left Australia; he's working at Charters Towers."

After careful descriptions to remove any doubt that they were talking about the same man, Kryger explained.

"When I was in Cooktown the police reported that they had found a man dead in the bush with a billy full of gold alongside him. From the miner's right, papers, and comb that Jens always carried, it was assumed the man was him."

The body was buried as Jens Abrahams and the death was registered in that name. What became of the billy of gold remained a mystery. Abrahams never got it back. The thief, knowing what he could expect from the rough justice of the goldfields in a case like this, had apparently kept well clear of the main track, got lost in the rugged country, and perished. It was the kind of thing that could happen easily enough. Years after the main Palmer rush was over, skeletons were to be found in the bush with bags or billies of gold beside them.

Even minor thefts on the goldfields brought rough justice if the culprit was caught and the police were not handy.

"Kangaroo courts" made up of diggers had a way of handling these matters themselves. A newspaper correspondent told how a sluice box and shovel disappeared from a claim and, after a search, was located in the camp of another miner further up the creek. "The diggers decided to handle the matter, and I was invited to be present," he wrote.

"We all donned our shooting irons and went to the spot where the box was being used. The culprits pleaded 'not guilty' but the 'judge' elected from among the diggers, after hearing evidence from both sides, convicted them. There was a big crowd of miners present, and a tough looking mob they were, and in ugly mood, as petty thefts had been almost a daily occurrence. The prisoners were sentenced to physical punishment, and this was inflicted with sticks, bamboos, fists, pick-handles, and even shovels, until justice was satisfied."

More serious offenders, such as horse thieves, often paid with their lives if they were caught by the diggers and there was no policeman handy to protect them. The best they could expect was to be driven into the bush with a howling pack of irate diggers at their heels, there to take their chances among the blacks. Others were thrown in the river, and the treatment repeated as often as they managed to climb out. Some drowned, and a few lucky ones managed to swim downstream far enough to sneak quietly away.

It was during this period on the Palmer that the man who was to become the scourge of the Chinese came into his own.

Christie Palmerston was one of the most remarkable men the north ever knew. To the diggers he became a friend in need, to the Chinese a death-dealing terror, and to the cannibal blacks a legendary figure who moved among them unmolested. He had shot blacks down in defence of white diggers, but on the other hand he had doctored and saved the lives of many who had been wounded by the bullets of the diggers' Sniders, and once he had stayed with a myall tribe for weeks to look after a sick child. He had an uncanny knack of handling the wild blacks. At a time when white and Chinese diggers alike were being killed and eaten by them,

he was always able to make friends among any tribe he chose
and recruit young bucks who would follow him anywhere.
For years he roamed the unexplored ranges with a private
army of myalls, picking up gold wherever he could find it,
defying the law whenever it suited him. But for the Chinese
he had a fanatical hatred. He raided them ruthlessly, robbed
them of their gold and stores, killed them by the dozen, and,
it was alleged, bartered those he took prisoner with the cannibal blacks knowing they would be used as food.

The first thing that is known definitely of Palmerston is
that he turned up in Rockhampton in 1870, a young man of
about twenty, with plenty of money which he set out to
spend in one of the wildest sprees the town had ever known.
Slightly built, black haired, wiry and quick as a tiger cat, he
had a partly withered left arm that he would never talk
about. One day in a pub brawl, he nearly killed a man. Before
the police could catch up with him he disappeared.

He arrived on the Palmer early in the rush, bearded, and
unkempt as a blackfellow, with a carbine slung over his
shoulder, a Colt revolver on his hip, and a small army of
half-wild myalls at his back. No one ever saw him digging
for gold, but he always seemed to have a good supply of it.
Old diggers muttered darkly that it came from miners who
had been murdered by the blacks. In Cooktown's gambling
dens he was nearly always lucky, and in the dance halls
women flocked about him.

In the rugged country between Cooktown and the goldfields, Palmerston seemed to know his way about as well as
the blacks themselves, and, with the help of his black bodyguard, he developed the uncanny knack of knowing everything that was going on in it. Several times myalls, massing
along the track to ambush diggers, found themselves mown
down by a fusillade from the Sniders of Palmerston's men.
Even the police admitted that Palmerston was worth a whole
regiment of troopers for the work he did in controlling the
blacks.

But this only made his attacks on the Chinese the more
embarrassing to them. Little though many of the police liked
it, part of their duty was to protect the Chinese. In the early

days of the rush Palmerston had organized his myalls into gangs to carry rations up from the coast. When coolies began to compete, he retaliated by raiding their pack trains with his blacks, stealing their stores to sell to the diggers himself, and, according to some of the Chinese storekeepers at any rate, paying his cannibal recruits by letting them have the Chinese prisoners as food. The blacks by then were doing so much raiding on their own account that no one could tell whether Palmerston had any part in it or not. Most of the white diggers could not have cared less anyway.

They told the story of a white woman about to give birth to a baby, left alone in an isolated shack while her husband went for help. A rising river delayed him, and when he got back with the doctor, expecting the worst, he found Palmerston's blacks camped in the bush nearby and his wife and her baby safe and well. Palmerston had arrived at the shack in time to act as midwife and had looked after the woman and her child until she recovered her strength. When she tried to thank him, he just stood up and, without saying a word, walked into the bush and disappeared. His blacks had remained to keep her supplied with everything she needed. When the husband went out to look for them, they also had vanished.

There were also stories of lost diggers, almost dead from starvation, being tracked down by Palmerston and brought back to camp. There were others he had found helpless from fever in their tents and nursed back to health. With stories like this going round, it was hardly likely that the diggers would help hunt him down for the robbery of a few Chinese.

There was nothing Palmerston seemed to enjoy better than finding a big gang of Chinese scouring the gravel in some isolated gully. With his myall mob at his heels, he would charge down on them, firing wildly, screeching the same hideous cockatoo battle cry as the blacks themselves, and, as often as not, scarcely distinguishable from them. The Chinese would scatter in panic, and while his followers pursued them Palmerston would be methodically going through their chamois leather bags for gold.

Once the Chinese set a trap for Palmerston that nearly

ended his career. They knew he was in the district, and when in due course he and his screeching band came charging down on them, they dropped their tools with more than usual haste and fled. Palmerston picked up a promising-looking bag, judged the weight of it in his hand, and unfastened the string around the top. He was about to insert his hand when the head of a death adder shot out, missing him by inches.

But it was not only Palmerston's blacks who planned their raids with care. The wild cannibals were learning fast, and in parts of the hills were establishing regular arsenals of weapons made from spoil captured from the diggers.

After a series of attacks in the Hell's Gate area, a white police sergeant and three native troopers were sent to "disperse" the attackers. Sneaking up on a camp, they surprised a party of blacks who bolted. In the camp were heaps of all kinds of material stolen from the diggers, carriers, and Chinese, and a large collection of very heavy, strong spears, all with barbed points and poisoned.

Continuing the pursuit into rough, hilly country, the sergeant and troopers had to leave their horses and continue on foot over steep ridges and ravines for about four miles, and then into heavy scrub. The blacks made a fighting retreat, frequently driving the pursuers to cover, but never showing themselves for long enough to make a target. "Piccaninnies had been left behind by the dozen," the sergeant later reported. "Their mothers simply abandoned them to their fate."

A couple of miles into the scrub, in a position that would never have been found had not the owners been tracked to it, the main camp was located. It also was deserted. In this camp an amazing assortment of raw material, partly completed, and finished weapons was found. There were lengths of hoop-iron ground into shape, sharpened, and fitted with wooden hand-grips to make a kind of cutlass or sword. There were wagon linchpins, patiently beaten out at the broad end and ground to an edge to make axes. The forehead band of a horse's bridle had been converted into an elaborate head-dress for a warrior. A number of finely made net dilly-

107

bags were filled with carefully hammered and ground metal spear-points, all poisoned, and sharp as needles. There were stacks of finished spears, all painted white, indicating that they had been used at a ceremony at which a number of different tribes had sworn an alliance to fight a common enemy. The sergeant counted them. "Must have been half a dozen tribes at least at that particular corroboree," he said.

They also found the whole body of a dead blackfellow, freshly cooked, and ready for eating.

The myalls often left children behind when pursued, and some of the police and carriers took advantage of it to provide themselves with native servants. One such was Sub-Inspector O'Connor, who had been sent with twenty-four native troopers to establish a post on the Laura for extra protection in the Hell's Gate area. His troopers were Fraser Island boys, themselves cannibals on their home ground and outstanding, even by native police standards, for their ferocity. Pursuing some black raiders one day, they saw the flash of a black skin in the bush and fired. They missed, and before they could load again a young piccaninny of about six stood up and came running towards O'Connor. They took him back to the barracks where he learnt English quickly, picked up the troopers' drill, and became a general favourite. O'Connor, who had become friendly with Corfield on the carrier's regular trips through Laura on his way to the Palmer, eventually gave the lad to Corfield, who bought him a horse of his own and took him everywhere with him.

On one of Corfield's trips, when he was camped near the Laura, one of his horses galloped back into camp with a barbed spear in his rump. Investigation showed where the blacks had killed two others—including Corfield's favourite hack—cut them up, and carried them away.

When Corfield reported it to O'Connor he found that the blacks had also killed two packers and were about to be "dispersed". In spite of heavy rain, Corfield, smarting under the loss of his hack, came too.

Over bare ridges so hard that the horses left no tracks, the native troopers followed the trail at a steady trot. Corfield turned to O'Connor.

"I don't believe they're on the tracks."

O'Connor looked at the ground.

"I can't see any," he admitted. "I'll call them back."

"Sambo," he called to the corporal. "Where track?"

Sambo pointed to a blade of grass.

"Where," asked Corfield.

"There."

Corfield got off his horse to look more closely. On the grass there was one tiny speck of blood that had not been washed off by the rain.

At last, on the bank of the Kennedy River, where it was wide and about two feet deep with a sandy bed, they came on the scene of a great feast. Among the remains Corfield found the tail and the main of his favourite hack. No tracks led from the river, so they headed down-stream with a trooper riding along each bank to watch for the place where the quarry had left it.

On the evening of the third day they saw smoke about a mile ahead. They made camp—without a fire, and without bells on their horses, for fear of detection. The moon rose about midnight, and about 2 a.m. they broke camp, leaving their horses and gear behind them. Five naked black troopers in single file were in the lead. Their only dress was a cartridge belt around their waists and their peaked uniform caps on their heads so they would be able to tell friend from foe. O'Connor, Corfield, and Sambo brought up the rear. As they came close to where they had seen the smoke the five troopers were sent out in a flanking movement while the other three waited.

Towards daylight they heard firing down-river and ran towards it. Suddenly a big blackfellow sprang up from the river. Sambo fired and the man fell into the long grass. When O'Connor, Corfield, and Sambo came up with the troopers there was not one live myall in sight, though several bodies lay crumpled on the ground. They burnt the bodies, together with all the weapons they could find, and also several dilly-bags containing the dead bodies of piccaninnies which

109

the blacks had been carrying around with them. Corfield
went with one of the troopers to where the soil at the roots
of a large gum tree had been hollowed out by the water so
as to make a sort of a cave. Without saying a word, the trooper
fired two shots into the cave.

"What are you firing at?" demanded Corfield.

"Two feller sit down there," said the trooper, hauling out
the dead bodies of two dead blackfellows.

O'Connor's troopers no doubt found that day's work good
training for future exploits. In 1878 they were lent to the
Victorian Government to help track down the Kelly gang,
and they were present at Glenrowan when Ned was taken
prisoner.

10 · ROLLICKING REEFERS

FROM BEHIND the raised window shutter of one of Edwardstown's largest bark-walled stores a long-drawn, plaintive howl like that of a dingo echoed along the stump-studded street. In the crowded bar of the nearby Diggers' Arms a couple of dozen drinkers looked up and exchanged glances.

"Mexican Jack's having a bad night," said one.

In a shack half-way between the store and the pub, a digger—unable to sleep because of the noise—was writing in his diary: "We are situated between the chief public house and the abode of a rival storekeeper, who is subject to periodical fits of intoxication, and he has just entered upon one of these paroxysms. He invariably commences by driving his wife out of doors, and tonight the poor woman is seeking a home where she can.

"He has a marvellous facility for coining strange oaths and wicked expressions. He is at present sitting with a rifle at the open window, upbraiding his wife with not having the courage to come and be shot. Occasionally he relieves his feelings by howling after the manner of a native dog. The noise from the public house on the other side is almost equally loud, though of a more varied character."

Edwardstown, by the middle of 1875, was a teeming gold town of rugged high living. There was still alluvial coming from the surrounding gullies, and some of the reefs on which Mulligan had reported were producing rich specimens. The digger whose sleep had been disturbed by Mexican Jack left the following account of it:

111

"Descending a cleared ridge, dotted all over with the stumps of trees whose trunks and branches have been used for firewood, you come in sight of a dilapidated village composed of one wide street full of tree-stumps enclosed between two rows of rickety, patched, tumbledown dwellings formed of the materials which came readiest to hand. Most have walls formed of saplings covered in with bark. Many are roofed with calico, some are composed of calico altogether, and one or two of the more pretentious are roofed with sheets of zinc which has done duty on half the goldfields of the Colony.

"A long strip of white calico on most of the buildings in the place bears, in black letters, the intimation that the miserable apology for a dwelling to which it is affixed rejoices in the sounding title of the Great Australian Hotel, or the Royal, or Empire, or some other such name, and that its owner is licensed to sell all kinds of wines and spirits, etc.

"The rest of the town is made up of general stores, a couple of butchers' shops, and a couple of horseshoeing forges built in the same style, together with a number of peculiar looking tenements."

About the latter, the writer did not go into great detail, but it was obvious that by now Edwardstown catered for more of the diggers' needs than their thirsts. During the day, according to the writer, "all hands are either in the public houses, stores, etc., or are at work in the neighbourhood. In each of the stockyards at the back of the various hotels are standing a few saddled and bridled hacks, their tucked-up bellies and sick looks betraying that they have been waiting for their owners since morning, perhaps all night.

"The rickety enclosures which surround the back kitchens and outhouses are one mass of broken bottles and sardine tins over which run large pumpkin vines, thriving luxuriantly among the filth and rubbish out of which they have sprung."

The writer also gave a fairly detached description of the bar of one of the licensed hotels. "In front of a row of brilliantly labelled and capsuled bottles and gorgeously painted kegs, a knowing-looking fellow is exerting himself to the utmost in supplying the wants of the crowd who fill his drinking shop. The few spare moments between the orders for drinks, he devotes to giving the already used nobbler tumblers a slight rinse and a hasty wipe with the corner of a much-used towel, or in adroitly pretending to undo for the first time the capsule of a bottle of Martell or Hennessy, which, in all probability, he himself has fastened on only a day or two before, after filling the empty bottle with some noxious compound of his own manufacture."

But nuggets of gold, heavy drinking, and high living in a goldfield town was not necessarily an indication that everyone was doing well. The lucky ones who had found gold came to town to spend it, to push on for the coast, or to buy stores and go back for more. For every one of them around Edwardstown at this stage there were a dozen others out in the gullies toiling for a bare sustenance.

Among the reefers, many were destitute. They had laboriously dollied the best of their quartz to get gold for tucker; the last shreds of their tattered clothing were falling off them, and their boots had gone months ago and been replaced with rough, home-made moccasins of greenhide or kangaroo skin. Their work was hot, dusty, and back-breaking.

Most of the claims were no more than shafts in the ground. Hoisting equipment generally consisted of nothing more than a windlass with a greenhide bucket operated by two miners—one at the bottom of the shaft to fill the bucket, the other at the top to wind it up. Sometimes power was provided by an old horse at the end of a whip or a whim. The whip was a simple trestle, at the top of which was a pulley over which the rope was passed. The horse was hitched to the rope, and pulled up the bucket by walking away. The whim was a sort of capstan with the horse harnessed to the pole that turned it. Timbering in the shafts was often rough and unsafe, with ladders made of saplings.

These were the claims that had been grimly retained by the owners ever since Mulligan had made his report, in expectation of the crushing machinery to come. Men had held on to these claims while rich alluvial beds all around them were yielding gold literally by the ton, and they had still clung to them when other Europeans rushed away to new strikes, and the Chinese swarmed in to clean up the white men's leavings.

And then, at last, came the news they had been waiting for. "The real red-letter day in the history of our community has at last arrived," announced the Cooktown *Herald* on 17th July 1875. "The *Blackbird* had the honour of bringing and landing the first crushing machinery for the Palmer. She brought two batteries—one, a portable, twelve-horsepower capable of driving five head of stampers. A second shipment of other machinery is on the *Mary Grant,* and a third shipment, of two crushing machines, is en route." Another machine was reported to be on its way overland to the Palmer from the now almost deserted Etheridge goldfield. By the end of the month the first of the machinery had begun its tortuous journey over the mountains from Cooktown to the goldfields by bullock wagon.

The warden, P. F. Sellheim, who had succeeded Howard St George on the Palmer, moved his headquarters up-river from Palmerville. Sellheim was an Austrian aristocrat of the old school. Scrupulously fair, conscientious and able, he had the universal respect of the diggers, but lacked some of the easygoing familiarity that had made The Saint so popular. When he set up his camp close to Jack Edwards's old butchery establishment and called the whole settlement Maytown, the diggers refused to follow his lead. Years later, when Maytown had become the capital of the whole Palmer goldfield, they still stubbornly referred to it as Edwardstown. Mulligan would never call the place Maytown.

Within a month the white population of the Edwardstown-Maytown area doubled as speculators rushed to get in on the ground floor. Substantial buildings of weatherboard and corrugated iron began to replace bark huts and canvas-roofed humpies. Rations and goods of every sort began to pour in by packers and carriers. But there were setbacks, and predicted arrival dates for the new machinery were revised again and again. It was nearly two months since the local correspondent of the Cooktown *Herald* had written: "Several bullock teams with Edwards and Co's machinery are on their way from Cooktown, and about twelve tons of

A punitive party sneaks up on a blacks' camp

A sampling of Cooktown's Chinese population

A Chinese joss-house in Cooktown

A Chinese gambling den

a Melbourne company's machinery is on the wharf at Cooktown awaiting transit."

The road from Cooktown to Maytown came through some of the roughest country in the north, and teams were encountering unprecedented difficulties in getting the heavy machinery over soft river beds, sandy flats, and steep, rugged mountains. The shortest practicable route for such a load was about 150 miles. In places the dismantled machinery had to be lowered down and then hauled up the sides of steep ravines by block and tackle. Even today deep score-marks can be seen on the rocks where the sharp, steel corners gouged out the soft sandstone. It cost more than eight hundred pounds to bring the first ore-crushing machine from Cooktown to the Palmer.

Many who had rushed to the new town in hopes of getting well-paid work got tired of waiting and headed up the river to Dead Dog Creek, where, it was said, everyone was getting at least some gold. But in spite of difficulties the machinery came a little nearer every day. Then came news that the second machine also was on its way. The struggling reefers, suddenly finding that their credit was good at the local stores, went to work with renewed energy to stack up ore for when the crushers arrived.

"The principal group of reefs, about twenty in all, are from two to four miles from Edwardstown," wrote the *Queenslander* correspondent. "The most distant of them will be within four miles of the site selected for the machines, both of which will probably be erected near the warden's quarters on the bank of the river about three miles from Edwardstown.

"The reefs on which the greatest amount of work has been done, and which are, without doubt, two of the principal mines, are the Ida and the Queen of the North. They are, by the employment of labour, quite competent to give full employment to the two machines now in transit.

"The greatest depth yet reached is 120 feet in the Queen of the North. The greatest average thickness is about two feet, carrying gold throughout. The best blocks of stone raised in the district have been obtained from the deepest levels.

I

"Messrs Edwards and Co's machine is a 10 stamper, 6 hundredweight, driven by a 12 horsepower engine, and capable of averaging 90 tons a week."

By September this machine had arrived and was being installed on the banks of the Palmer River. Crushing batteries were erected on the bank of a river whenever possible, as a good supply of water was essential for the crushing of ore. The huge bed logs which formed the foundation for the battery and the steam engine that drove it were felled farther up the river, sawn and trimmed to size, and then floated down-stream with a team of strong swimmers to guide them clear of rocks and snags.

In November, while the machine was still being assembled, the Cooktown *Herald* reported: "Maytown is rapidly assuming the proportions of a prosperous and populous township. Stores, hotels, and shops are being rapidly erected in a continuous and businesslike street, and so great is the run on this township for good business sites that one Chinese firm paid sixty pounds for a sixty-foot frontage that was already in occupation.

"Sunday is the main business day in Maytown. All the miners, Chinese and Europeans, come in from miles around to sell their gold and buy stores. The township on Sunday is more like a great fair than anything else. Already there are several good, substantial buildings and several fine, comfortable hotels."

The licensees of some of these fine, comfortable hotels were women—the kind of women who knew how to make full use of all the sidelines which the business was capable of developing. They, and then their rivals, brought pretty, coaxing barmaids, singers, dance hall girls, and others from Cooktown. Champagne began to flow in Maytown. Men coming in from a monotonous stint of dry work in a hot climate were ready for riotous relaxation—and every day more of it was provided.

"The great drawback along the road at present," the newspaper correspondent wrote, "is the absolute want of any feed, the whole country being burnt and parched. Horses and bullocks are dying. Horses are being fed on flour." The lack of

116

feed meant there were no teams available to cart the ore to the stamper, though the machine was ready to begin crushing in December, and there were more than sixteen hundred tons of ore waiting to be treated.

Christmas saw them still waiting for the rain that would let the stampers start, but the wet season was obviously close. With five European stores, about twelve Chinese stores, and nine hotels, Maytown was, in the words of one of the diggers, "rarin' to go". From all over the Palmer that Christmas the diggers poured into Maytown to celebrate. The optimism in the air was irresistible. Instead of small nuggets, as in the early days of the rush, rich quartz specimens were being shown around. The Maytown reefs were about to come into their own.

About a month earlier Harry Ahlers, of the Prince of Wales Hotel, had received a message from Walsh and Co, storekeepers of Cooktown, saying there were three horse teams that could not get loading, and could he put anything in their way. Ahlers wired back: "Load the three teams with Hennessy's Three Star Brandy." Three weeks later the loads were delivered at his hotel.

The celebration began on Christmas Eve and lasted most of the night. Christmas Day was quiet, because not many felt like moving. About the only sound to be heard was the scrape of some Chinaman's shovel in one of the nearby gullies. Boxing Day saw things moving again with sports organized by Warden Sellheim, and a race meeting. Feminine frills and parasols were paraded in Maytown's streets. With not a blade of grass to be seen for miles, the horses had been trained on anything they would eat—many on flour and water. Carefully tended Chinese gardens had been raided for greens. A few of the diggers had a little corn which they tried to keep for their own animals, but scrounging by anyone who had a horse running, or an ounce of gold to put on a horse, saw to a fairly even distribution of the corn. Considering the season, the horses came to the barrier in fairly good condition.

"Our warden acted as judge, and was most assiduous in his efforts to please all," a newspaper correspondent wrote.

117

There was, in fact, a free-for-all brawl after nearly every race.

The celebrations went on for a week, and in the middle of them the long-awaited rain began to fall. Within hours every creek and gully was running a banker. The Palmer River rose six feet overnight, causing a wild stampede by hundreds of Chinese who were camped all along its banks. "Our mailman, Mr Hogsflesh, had to come via the dray road from Palmerville on account of the river being uncrossable," the correspondent wrote. "The mail on arrival here was ferried across by the boatman, Mr Edwards, and reached the post office only two hours later than the usual time."

Sometime early in January the celebrations died down—mainly on account of liquor stocks having run out—and the town began to grope its way back to normal. Under the heading "Palmer News" the Cooktown papers published the following somewhat incongruous item: "For obscene language William Jackson was fined the sum of £9 and costs, and in another charge against him for defamation of character he was mulcted in the sum of £10 and £4 9s. costs. This individual has been brought up times without number and has paid nearly £200 for some of his offences in Palmerville." The same report mentioned that the Chinese lottery which had been strongly supported by the white diggers at Maytown had been drawn, and that no European had won any of the large prizes.

The rain brought a quick shoot of grass. Teamsters who had been camped on the Laura moved in, and quartz began to pile up ready for the crushing. The Cooktown *Herald* listed what was waiting for them.

The following are the names of the claims, the order they will crush, and the quantity of stone.

No. 3 Queen of the North	20 ton
Ada Prospecting Claim	100 ton
Caledonian	30 ton
Alliance	60 ton

Hit or Miss	30 ton
Queen of the North	150 ton
No. 1 Caledonian	30 ton

All lots look very promising indeed.

The first ore was crushed on 5th February, and the event was duly celebrated with a general dinner and toasts in an open-air booth built for the occasion. But with everyone busy digging and carting ore and the stampers settling down to a steady twenty-four-hour round-the-clock beat, the feasting and drinking was nothing to compare with the Christmas celebrations.

Before the end of the month the second crushing plant had arrived on the field and a third had been landed at Cooktown. Early results had fulfilled expectations. From the Queen of the North 110 tons of quartz had returned 915 ounces of smelted gold—$8\frac{1}{3}$ ounces per ton.

After each of those early crushings the owners would get a wooden washtub and fill it up with champagne and carry it around the town ladling out liberal helpings with a quart-pot. Anyone who was slow in draining it had his head dipped in the tub.

The Chinese by now had almost undisputed possession of the old alluvial workings and were cleaning them out with a thoroughness that left not a grain of gold behind. The days of the white digger on the alluvial seemed to be finished.

"By their system of work," wrote a newspaper correspondent, "they take everything on a face instead of only working the most likely spots as the Europeans do. Their perseverence is naturally rewarded in an essentially patchy diggings, with an occasional lucky find.

"Men who return here after being absent a few months actually do not recognize the places where they formerly worked and where they depended on again getting a little gold. The Chinese have rooted up every gully and ravine that the white man had only pot-holed, carrying everything before them like a swarm of locusts.

"Nearly every digger with a horse or two is pushing outside to the Mitchell watershed and other places, and many would leave the district and go south if they had the means of doing so.

"There is an impression on the field that at least three-quarters of the gold got falls to the lot of the Chinamen. European diggers are distributed in camps of five, ten, and twenty all over the old workings, but there is at present no settled camp anywhere. The only people really doing well are the packers and carriers."

Carriers were making such good money at that time that one was offered a thousand pounds for each of his three teams and refused it. Many of them, like Corfield, were former station managers. Former squatters, inspectors of police, Navy men, and all kinds were swinging the bullock whip in those days for the sake of the good money to be made. There were some characters among them too.

Big Bill Doherty, an all-round expert with either bullocks or horses, claimed to have been the first man to drive a team from Cooktown to the Palmer. "King of the Road", he called himself, and he had defended the title with his fists in most of the pubs in Cooktown and on the field.

A colourful character named George Kersley, when drinking—which was whenever the chance offered—was in the habit of threatening to shoot himself and leave his teams to whoever he happened to be drinking with. He had made the threat so often that no one took any notice of it. One day when he was drinking with Doherty he made the usual threat. As usual, no one took any notice of it. Before anyone could stop him, he snatched up his rifle which was leaning against the bar and blew his brains out.

Another carrier by the name of George Hawkins was fond of women and had a wife who did not trust him. As she generally travelled with him, George got into the habit of writing letters to himself saying he was urgently needed somewhere else to help a sick mate, give urgently needed support at a meeting, or something equally important. He thus managed to live a fairly full life—until someone told his wife what was going on and she put a stop to it.

Most packers and carriers, high prices aside, were strictly

120

honest in their dealings with the diggers—except, of course, where the Chinese were concerned. The story was told of how, during one wet season when few carriers were travelling and local supplies of liquor were running low, a Chinese store-keeper named Ah Pan, with an eye to a good profit, gave a packer named Jumping George five pounds to go down to the coast and bring him back two gallons of rum, promising him another five pounds if he brought it back within a week. Jumping George had to swim several creeks, but within a week was back with a two-gallon keg of rum. Ah Pan pulled out the bung and sampled the rum. He found it good and handed the promised five pounds to Jumping George, who left fairly hurriedly. Ah Pan smiled happily at the customers who surged up to the counter. He half-filled a glass—and the rum stopped pouring. He shook the keg. There was still plenty in it. He took a long, thin knife, jabbed it into the bung hole to clear the blockage, and tried again. Out gushed a strong stream of muddy Palmer River water. Jumping George had tacked a circle of canvas inside around the bung-hole, filled this compartment with rum, and the rest of the keg with water.

This being the type of story that appealed to the diggers, it spread rapidly, and at least half a dozen versions of it were circulating in the north before the rush was over, and that muddy water was alleged to have come from almost every river from the Burdekin to the Jardine, right at the tip of the peninsula.

During the wet, Corfield was bringing up three wagons from Cooktown when he was caught in flooded country beyond the Normanby River. By double-banking the teams and working in the rain he and his partner managed to keep moving until they reached an ant-hill flat which was so boggy that the bullocks sank to their bellies in it. They had passed two teams camped on the edge of the flat, but Corfield and his drivers decided to push on. They spent three days cutting saplings and making a "corduroy" across which they sledged their twelve tons of loading. It was a risky job, as they were carrying dynamite. The detonators had been inserted in fifty-pound bags of flour.

While they were sweating at the job, the camped teamsters frequently rode past and called out encouragement. "That's right boys; make a good road for us." None of them offered to help. Corfield and his men fumed silently and kept on working. Before they were done Sub-Inspector O'Connor arrived from the Laura with some of his troopers and gave them a hand.

On the third day, by the time they had got the last of their wagons through and reloaded them, it was dark. As he puffed at his after-dinner pipe, Corfield looked across at the distant flicker of the campfire of the carriers who had refused to help them.

"It'd serve them right if we took up those saplings and burnt them," he said.

The others looked up and grinned.

"That's it," said one.

The idea caught on, and most of that night, dog tired though they were, they and O'Connor's troopers toiled in drizzling rain to take up every stick on the road they had made and stack them for burning. The logs were wet, and it was quite a job getting them alight, but they succeeded at last, and spent the rest of the night drying themselves out around the roaring flames.

Next morning, as they were yoking up to move on, the owner of the other teams rode up in a tearing rage.

"What right have you got to destroy the road?" he demanded.

"There's plenty more saplings if you want to cut 'em," said Corfield, as he rode after his wagons.

The blacks were still making life dangerous for all who used the Palmer track.

A packer was making his campfire at one of the Palmer crossings when three spears hit the ground beside him. He fired in the direction they came from, saddled up, and went for his life.

On another occasion a packer was lying on the grass beside

122

his campfire with a handful of tea, waiting for his billy to boil, when he heard something, and turned to see about half a dozen blacks about twenty yards away getting ready to launch their spears. Having no rifle, he jumped to his feet and ran towards a party of Chinese porters who were camped about fifty yards away. The Chinese ran for their lives, leaving their packs, a couple of ancient guns, and their half-cooked dinner behind them. The packer drove off the blacks with the Chinamen's guns, helped himself to a Chinese meal, and returned to his own camp.

During that wet season the Government sent a man with a boat to the Laura River to ferry stranded travellers across. But not many were travelling and the boatman was alone a good deal. The blacks speared and ate him.

11 · HANG MULLIGAN!

WHILE THE teams were toiling to bring Maytown's first stamper over the ranges, the Dead Dog Creek rush was steadily gaining momentum. New arrivals scattered up and down the upper reaches of the Palmer and into the back gullies. Most of them did well on good alluvial with plenty of water to wash it.

At the first crossing of the Palmer on the newly opened road from the coast to Maytown, a little over fifty miles south-west of Cooktown and a mile or two down-river from the spot where the Mulligan Highway from Mareeba to Cooktown now crosses it, a big camp had grown up on the high river bank. Johnny Byers and Billy Little—already well-known on the Palmer as Greasy Bill—had opened a butcher's shop there, and the place had begun to be called Byerstown after the former. They were killing six to eight bullocks a week from the start, and before long their establishment was surrounded by three bark hotels, twice as many unlicensed shanties, about ten stores of various kinds, a Chinese doctor, and a Chinese gardener.

On 30th November 1875 Mining Warden Coward had moved his camp there from the Normanby, finding it more central for the area under his control. No place had improved so rapidly in the past two months, he wrote. His main complaint was the amount of drinking that went on. The police did nothing to control it, he said, and on Sunday, when the diggers all came to town to buy supplies, drays drove round the streets selling grog to them.

Mulligan, meanwhile, was laying the foundations for the biggest rush since the beginning. His Government-sponsored expedition had left Cooktown on 29th April 1875. The party consisted of Mulligan, his old mates Peter Abelsen and James Dowdell; Frederick Warner, the Government Surveyor; William Harvey; Jack Moran; and a black boy named Charlie. They had twenty-two horses.

They followed the track to the Byerstown diggings, struck south across the mountains to the junction of the Mitchell and Hodgkinson rivers, and on 16th May followed up the Hodgkinson through very rough country to what was later called the Granite Range. Mulligan made east for a gap in the range, which in most places drops sheer to flat forest country north-west of the present site of Mareeba, and came down onto good grazing country near the source of the Mitchell.

On 24th May the party struck the Barron River, mistook it for the Mitchell, and followed it up until they came to dark, impenetrable jungle. After trying vainly to get through it, they skirted to the west of it until, on 3rd June, they found a native track which they followed through the jungle-choked hills.

While they were camped on the edge of the jungle, Jack Moran, looking for lost horses, wandered a little farther east to the crest of the coastal rampart, and saw the sea spread out below him. He made his way down to the beach to somewhere not far from the site of Port Douglas, thus becoming the first white man to cross the range to the coast. He was not looking for a port at the time, but he was to remember the trip later.

The party eventually returned to Cooktown on 23rd September 1875. No gold had been found, and the five hundred pounds granted by the Government was spent. But Mulligan had been bitten again by the exploring bug. Waiting in Cooktown only long enough to make sure that the Government would advance no more money, he dug deep into his own pocket once again and on 23rd October headed back to the Hodgkinson. With him went Abelsen and Warner.

Before leaving, Warner had written a terse note to the

Minister of Works saying he had no funds to get back to Brisbane, no paper and instruments with which to make a chart of the expedition just completed, and that he was going with Mulligan on his new trip. Newspapers and diggers alike bitterly criticized the Government for its parsimonious attitude.

Cooktown at that time, scarred by a great fire which on 4th September had begun in the Gympie Hotel and destroyed a large part of its main business block, was entering on its unhealthiest summer ever. Dwindling alluvial returns and hordes of Chinese on the Palmer had brought white diggers crowding back to town to live it up or scrounge a living while they waited for something to turn up. Wet, muggy weather, swarms of mosquitoes from the mangrove flats, and insanitary conditions in white and Chinese camps all around the town brought an epidemic of dysentery. The police station became a hospital, and before long the police chief himself, Inspector Clohesy, his assistant, and four constables were among the patients.

"Everyone whom you meet abroad is ill, whilst many more of the people are too hopelessly ill to leave their homes," wrote the Cooktown correspondent of the *Queenslander* on 29th January 1876. "The hardiest veterans are succumbing to this unhealthful time. The police station is literally a fever ward."

At the height of the epidemic good alluvial gold was found at Emu Creek, about thirty miles south-east of Byerstown. The inevitable rush followed. On 29th January the correspondent wrote: "Mr Warden Coward came into Cooktown with samples from the new rush. He exhibited some forty ounces of gold and explained the simple conditions under which it was obtained. A complete confirmation of the prevailing rumour was forthwith established. The effect of it was the visible and more cheerful aspects of our commercial men. Teamsters, carriers, and packers improved the occasion by raising the price of carriage. Our reserves of sickly diggers trooped away noiselessly."

The new rush brought additional prosperity to Byerstown, which grew rapidly. The overflow from it fell back on Byers-

126

town's back gullies. The Chinese poured in until all along the track from Byerstown to Emu Creek they could be seen fossicking—a sure sign that there was alluvial gold to be had. Some of the old miners used to say that the presence of Chinamen brought the cannibals the same way as a dog in the water will bring sharks. Whether they were right or not, raids in the area certainly increased. Chinese were kidnapped by the blacks by the dozen and taken away to be eaten at leisure. Horses were speared at night and, being too heavy to carry, butchered on the spot.

Mulligan, meanwhile, was deep in the jungle. In his diary of the trip he wrote that from the time they left Cooktown on 23rd October until they arrived back at Byerstown more than four months later they had seen almost the whole of the Hodgkinson River and its branches. With the wet season setting in, Mulligan, Abelsen, and Warner crossed the Mitchell River on 11th January, and between there and the Hodgkinson "got a tolerable show of gold". During the next fortnight they found more on the eastern and western branches of the Hodgkinson and in the surrounding gullies.

Mulligan had no idea at this time that his party was not the only one in that part of the country. There was, in fact, another party consisting of William McLeod, Robert Sefton, Hugh Kennedy, and W. Williams. On 26th January Mulligan wrote in his diary: "Hugh Kennedy and W. Williams, who are out with McLeod's party, were camped one mile distant from us, but we did not know it. Hearing horse bells, Abelsen went out to see if he knew them, and in the twilight Kennedy, taking Abelsen to be a blackfellow about to spear the horses, fired at him from about eighty yards. In another instant Williams would have drawn his trigger also had not Abelsen sung out. From our camp I replied to their shot and then Warner and I went out to see whom we had so near us in that great wilderness. We found Kennedy, Williams, and Abelsen in mutual congratulations. Kennedy is a dead shot and Abelsen can only thank Providence and the darkness of the evening for his life. Neither of the parties expected to meet the other in this unexplored country in the wet."

They continued prospecting, and their luck held.

127

"February 7th: Heavy rain continues. . . . Have found several quartz reefs showing gold in the stone freely. The alluvial is payable in places, but very patchy."

"February 19th: The weather has now settled and we shift Palmer-ward, having got a little gold and seen several reefs which present a payable appearance."

"February 21st: Came up to McLeod and party's camp in the evening and stopped, the creeks being up. Getting payable gold in the ravines."

"March 5th: There having been no rain for ten days we think the Mitchell is low enough to cross; we propose going to Cooktown. The grass, being trodden down and dry about the camp, caught fire and, being carried by a strong breeze, our tent, with all our clothes, blankets, rations—in fact everything save a few useful papers and cartridges—were destroyed. McLeod's party supplied us with all necessities and we arranged to go to Cooktown with them and report the field."

It was agreed that Mulligan and his party should return to Cooktown and report the new field as "a payable goldfield for reefing". All were to share the reward. On their way to Cooktown Mulligan, Abelsen, and Warner called at Byerstown to get fresh horses and supplies before reporting the find. They had not been there for long, however, before Warden Coward guessed there was something in the wind. "He was very kind and off-handed with us," wrote Mulligan later, "so we made up our minds to tell him under promise that he would not report it until we got to Cooktown. But he did not keep his promise. Two days later, on entering Cooktown, we met runners with papers crying out, 'A New Goldfield Discovered'." The very night Mulligan had confided in him Coward had sent a constable to Cooktown with the news.

Coward had never been popular with the miners, and when this story got around among the old-timers it was the last straw. One complaint after another was made about him until the Government gladly accepted his resignation and brought W. R. O. Hill from the Etheridge to replace him in April 1876.

Mulligan, on his arrival in Cooktown, took out prospecting areas on reefs for himself, Moran, McLeod, and the others. They all insisted that the Hodgkinson was a reefing field, suitable only for experienced reef miners with enough money to keep them until the quartz was dug and machinery brought in. The alluvial, said Mulligan, was "fit only for Chinese". But with the smell of gold in the air, no one was in the mood to believe it. Within a day of Coward letting out word of the new field, a large party of Byerstown diggers had headed out for the Hodgkinson without waiting even for anyone to show them the way. Before leaving they had bought up every particle of stores to be had.

On 23rd March a wire was sent from Cooktown reading: "Mulligan and party arrived at Cooktown last night. They have discovered a new goldfield and brought in splendid samples of gold. Likely to turn out a large and rich field. Good alluvial and rich reefs have been found. It is higher up than any of the present diggings and said to be on the Hodgkinson River about 160 [later given as 135] miles from Cooktown. There is a good road for drays to the diggings. None of Mulligan's party will disclose the whereabouts of the field until they have made their own arrangements for horses and rations. That another rush to the Palmer will be an immediate consequence of the exciting news there can be no doubt, and it is to be hoped that the new field will be sufficiently extensive to afford remunerative employment to the thousands of diggers, Europeans and Chinese, that will soon be congregated there. There will naturally be a perfect stampede of miners to the new El Dorado."

After a report like that there could hardly fail to be a stampede. Mulligan and others later claimed that the message had been inspired by local storekeepers and other business men who stood to make a profit out of a rush whether there was gold at the end of it or not.

Mulligan's report was much more restrained and, as it turned out, an exact forecast: "The field will be one of the largest reefing districts in the Colonies, but, regarding the alluvial, there is not a field on which I believe there will be more disappointments."

129

A newspaper correspondent seized on the optimistic part of the prediction: "Cooktown, 27th March: There is great excitement here respecting Mulligan's new discovery and, from all I can learn, I believe it will be the richest quartz reefing district ever known."

All over the old Palmer diggings white diggers were moving out for the Hodgkinson—and, following established custom, the Chinese were shifting camp and occupying the deserted ground almost before its original occupants were out of sight. Even Maytown reefers who had stuck to their claims since the start packed up and left. Every ship that arrived in Cooktown was packed with men on their way to the Hodgkinson. The steamer *Blackbird*, calling at Townsville on her return trip south, was mobbed by about six hundred diggers willing to pay the captain almost anything if he would turn the ship around and take them back to Cooktown. He refused. Men set off for the Hodgkinson on foot, and for Cooktown in almost anything that would float. Several parties left in rowing boats.

Mulligan was showing signs of being fed up. To the *Queenslander* he wrote: "Parties who have arrived at Cooktown these last two days inform me that the miners and others are mustering in hundreds at Byerstown to accompany me out to the new field. I do not wish to be rushed by 400 or 500 people with twice as many horses who will not lose sight of me, as it was with me as I was coming to the Palmer, and if I am not deputed to mark a road, I might see the Hodgkinson without ever touching Palmer waters, overland from Cooktown." He was prevailed on, however, to lead the way, for two hundred pounds subscribed by the people of Cooktown, who were later reimbursed by the Government.

The *Queenslander*, taking its lead from Mulligan, had warned in an editorial that there were enough men already on the field to work out all the gold on the Hodgkinson, even if the rosiest stories were true. But the rush was greater even than the original rush to the Palmer. Every ship that berthed in Cooktown from the south was packed with men, and by the time Mulligan left Cooktown on 30th March he was trailed by

Chinese on the Palmer
track

A digger and a couple of packers
relax in a roadside shanty

a motley army of hundreds. Hundreds more were only days behind them.

The *Queenslander* correspondent arrived in Cooktown by the steamer *Blackbird* only a few hours after Mulligan had left. She carried 125 diggers and 45 horses. Every inch of deck space was packed. Most of the new arrivals took the road immediately, trying to catch up with Mulligan's party.

Mulligan had blazed the trees to mark a dray road, but it was far from the easy track some of the reports had claimed. It was through country as rough as any on the Palmer, and swarming with blacks. Within a mile of the Normanby township a couple of weeks before, a packer named James McNamara, on going to round up his thirteen horses in the morning, found seven speared to death, three others with spears sticking in them, and the place where another had been killed, skinned and cut up. Blood on the ground showed where the meat had been carried away.

Striking south from Byerstown, the gold rushers camped on Blackfellow's Creek, a "field of bones" where the skeletons of a whole tribe of blacks who had been killed a month or so earlier in a retaliatory raid lay bleaching in the sun. From a spot only a few hundred yards away a Chinaman had recently been taken bodily from the midst of a party of his countrymen by a mob of hungry blacks, cooked almost alive, and feasted on only a mile or two further on in the bush.

The wet season was late ending that year, and when the diggers reached the Mitchell it was running a banker. Mulligan, knowing the river could rise or fall six feet or more in the wet season, was inclined to wait, but the impatient gold-seekers would have none of it.

"The scene," wrote the newspaper correspondent, "was indescribably exciting and ludicrous, and in all its details perhaps unparalleled in Queensland goldfield history. Imagine a confused multitude of men, mostly in a state of nudity, of horses and mules, and here and there the headgear of a woman. The atmosphere was charged with lusty vociferations in choice terms of bullock-drivers' vocabularies, with gesticulating, yelling, and whip-cracking to urge through the current the poor, heavily packed animals. Others crawled

131

K

their uncertain way over logs and rocks in imminent danger of their lives, had hairbreadth escapes, and lost swags innumerable. One man was unhorsed and carried down-stream, but fortunately was a strong swimmer.

"We were more fortunate than a gentleman from Cooktown whom we met. In swimming his horse, he had his clothing strapped before him and every stitch carried away by the current. He came to land half drowned and in a most pitiable state of nakedness.

"Further on, a sickening odour of decomposed blackfellows indicated the whereabouts of a recent brush between earlier diggers and a party of blacks. All along the route men in search of missing horses were common, armed with rifles and revolvers and corrugated with cartridges. From one camp a man went to look for his horse and did not return. A day or two afterward, a digger was speared in the head by a blackfellow. Some ineffective shooting was done on a mob of his brethren by way of retaliation.

"It is surprising the number of white-headed, worn-out, decrepit old men bending under a swag, and in many cases with broken boots and tattered clothes, sometimes completely knocked up, met with and overtaken at this early stage of the rush in a part of the country so utterly unsuited to any but the most robust. Men who, destitute of almost everything, can adapt themselves to almost any circumstances. It would appear as though many of these old veterans had waited for just one more chance, and that this rush appeared to present that chance, which they had seized eagerly and recklessly."

Three others caught the writer's attention. "These consisted of a powerfully built Amazonian female carrying a heavy swag strapped New Zealand fashion, followed by a couple of herculean gentlemen of colour, evidently her companions, all happy in the speedy prospect of the termination of their journey."

A few weeks behind Mulligan more than two thousand diggers rushing from the Palmer to the new field were stopped by the Mitchell River rising still higher. They banked up at Byerstown and ran riot there, raiding shanty-keepers' stocks of liquor when their money ran out, robbing Chinese, and threatening the lives of any who got in their way.

One night, after the camp seemed to have settled down, a shrill scream echoed through the hills, which started all the dogs barking and brought Warden Hill bounding from his bed. Roaring for his police boys to follow him, he floundered from tent to tent until at last he found a woman, still young and attractive, lying on the ground in a small tent with her right arm chopped off above the elbow. Rough surgery saved the woman's life, but the man she accused of having chopped off her arm in a jealous rage was never seen on the field again.

In an effort to get rid of the mob of idle miners, Hill and his chief orderly, Bill Norris, undertook to swim the flooded Mitchell, have a look at the new field, and bring back a report on it within three days. Hill spent two days riding about the Hodgkinson and came back to report. "The alluvial is no good. There are no large finds and very few are making tucker. The alluvial rush must be stopped if possible or starvation and more serious results must ensue. The reefs are really good." On the strength of this, some of the men headed back down river for Maytown, but many more refused to believe it and waited until they could cross the river.

"Hundreds of diggers from the Palmer side are reported to have reached the Hodgkinson River, and the old diggings appear to have been abandoned to the Chinese," the correspondent wrote. From Cooktown also they were pouring in. "Thousands came looking for alluvial gold," wrote Mulligan. "And that, too, without tools or rations. Many went back, while many stayed. Plenty remained to pilfer and steal specimens from the few claims that were working."

With neither warden nor police on the field, "kangaroo courts" administered justice in their own way. The correspondent reported one of them: "The first case of lynch law occurred on Wednesday last when a man was flogged and his property confiscated and he was driven from the diggings for stealing a digger's horse. The proceedings were

133

conducted in regular form, with a jury of twelve to try the case, the prisoner being allowed the right of appeal to sixty respectable diggers. The offence was clearly proved and it was considered necessary to make an example of the offender." An example it certainly was. With no horse or rations, and more than a hundred miles of rough country between him and the coast, it was close to a death sentence.

Mining operations, because of the lack of a warden, were, to say the least of it, confused. Irate diggers claimed that Warden Hill, on his brief visit from Byerstown, had granted a large number of reef protection areas which, having been secured, did not need to be worked. The names of the same men appeared on several different reefs, the diggers claimed, and this meant that a few men had some of the best ground tied up, while others could not get ground to work on.

Like every rush, this one had attracted large numbers of loafers who knew nothing of mining, and had come to the field without either rations or equipment, in the hope of scrounging enough of both from better-equipped or more lucky diggers to enable them to pick up a little easy gold for themselves. But here there was no easy gold. Most of the genuine alluvial diggers were headed back for the Palmer, and there were few to scrounge from.

Rich specimens began to disappear from the ore heaps, several suspected thieves were driven into the bush, and the remainder looked around for someone to blame for their misfortune. Mulligan became their target for no better reason than the fact that he had discovered the field. Groups of dead-beats gathered and muttered about lynching. Any incident would have been enough to spark off trouble.

Mulligan's old mate, Billy McLeod, roaming restlessly over the field as usual, discovered some alluvial on a tributary of the Eastern Hodgkinson which soon became known as McLeod's Creek. A small rush followed. The correspondent reported: "There was a great clearing out of diggers yesterday and last night, and the exodus is still going on, to a reported new rush down the Hodgkinson twenty-five miles north-west of here, where a few parties are stated to be getting a little gold. It is supposed that between 600 and 700 diggers have started, and the butcher is following the crowd with a mob of cattle."

Without rations, equipment, money, or much taste for hard work, the dead-beats were talking about the new rush when Mulligan returned from one of his trips to Cooktown. The mob surged about him, asking to be shown the way to McLeod's Creek. What they really wanted was someone from whom they could get free rations and equipment. Mulligan at first agreed to take them, but when he found there was a well-beaten track to the strike he refused and, not mincing his words even by goldfield standards, told the whole mob what he thought of them. At once they turned ugly and milled about Mulligan's horse.

"Lynch him! Hang him!"

As the yelling mob pressed closer, Mulligan unslung his rifle and levelled it in the direction of a man who was reaching towards his horse's bridle.

"First man that lays a hand on my horse will get a bullet through it," he announced calmly, but loud enough for everyone in the crowd to hear.

The man jumped away hastily; but further back, in the comparative safety of the crowd, others were more vocal.

"Lynch him! Haul him off his horse!"

Mulligan swung his rifle towards the group that was making most noise.

"And the first man that tries to lay a hand on me, I'll drop in his tracks," he said.

He took advantage of the uneasy silence to go on.

"I've been among blacks when the spears were flying," he said. "I had to shoot a few men in self-defence. If you force me to it, I'll shoot some more in self-defence today."

"There's others here can shoot as well as you, Mulligan," called one.

Mulligan's rifle came round until it pointed straight at his chest.

"Try it," he invited. "Half a dozen will die before me."

That quietened the ringleaders, and the fickle temper of the mob changed. A score of hats were tossed into the air. "We're with you, Jim." A ragged cheer went up. The change of mood was lucky for all concerned. Later Mulligan was to write: "I would have done all I said. I had a rifle in my hands, my revolver on my hip, and a horse that I could depend on under me. It behoved me to act determined, and that rowdy mob could see it." He did not blame most of the miners for the incident. "Very few decent miners took part in those threats," he said, "but they could not help being in the crowd."

Soon after this, on the track to Cooktown, some miners pelted Mulligan's packhorses with stones. He charged at them and they scattered into the bush.

In Cooktown things were the same. Everyone who had ignored Mulligan's warning that it was not an alluvial field now blamed Mulligan for his misfortunes. Mulligan wrote: "I happened to be in Dinny Callaghan's pub in Cooktown one day. There was a crowd in the bar, and one fellow was blowing about what he would do with Mulligan if he met him. I asked him did he know Mulligan. He said no. I cautioned him to be careful, as Mulligan was dangerous. He stopped his blowing.

"Another day I was buying a rope and other things at John Walsh's store in Cooktown. A mob gathered outside, and some of the shop hands wanted me to sneak out by the back to dodge them. I refused, and carried the rope through the crowd. 'This is the rope they are going to hang Mulligan with,' I told them. Some of them pointed at me and said, 'That's him.' They opened a passage and let me pass."

Mobs began to roam Cooktown from pub to pub saying what they were going to do with Mulligan if they caught him. In an effort to clear the air, Howard St George, now police magistrate at Cooktown, arranged for Mulligan to address a meeting at Mayhew's pub. The meeting was rowdy, but Mulligan made his points.

"All I said to the Press was warning diggers that it was only a reefing field," he told them. "I never encouraged miners to come."

He spoke long and forcibly. St George backed him up by reading extracts from newspaper reports. What Mulligan did not know at the time was that St George had packed the meeting with special constables appointed for the occasion. He was taking no chances.

"Many expected that some damage would be done to the stores, blaming them also for encouraging the rush," Mulligan wrote, "but there was not, and on the whole people were satisfied with the result of the meeting. Soon after this Mr St George asked me to cease wearing my revolver in my belt through Cooktown."

COOKTOWN by now was a flourishing seaport. Ships lay in the bay waiting for wharf space, while overseas vessels stood off and lightered their cargoes ashore. Horses were simply tipped over the side and made to swim for it, taking their chances with the crocodiles which were fairly plentiful. Only Brisbane had a greater volume of trade than Cooktown, but Cooktown's was the more varied. London, Bremen, and San Francisco, Hong Kong, Canton, and Singapore poured their goods into the boom town. All along Charlotte Street, leading out from the wharves to the goldfields beyond the mountains, shops and hotels, bawdy houses and bazaars jostled for place with Government offices, banks, and warehouses.

Miners arriving empty-handed could, if they had the money, equip themselves better here—and their wives too, if they had them—than anywhere else in Australia. There were the plain, old-style stores where a man could buy a useful hat—felt or cabbage-tree—or trousers of tweed, moleskin, or drill. Blucher boots were 6s. 6d. a pair and elastic-sides slightly dearer. There were stores large, spacious, and tastefully laid out to appeal to the feminine eye with calicoes—white or grey—velvets, velveteens, satins, muslins, and fancy dress materials. There were small places with the personal touch like Jimmy Dick's "Little Wonder Store" near the police barracks, featuring millinery, haberdashery, and all kinds of things from ladies' elastic-sided boots at seven shillings a pair to lamp-glasses at sixpence each. And there were great, sprawling stores that a man could pull up his

138

dray in front of and load it with anything that a goldfield might need. Blacksmith's bellows and anvils, Old Colonial rum, whiskies, brandies, ales, and porters were part of their normal stock, as were detonators, blasting powder, and cartridges, horseshoe nails, Snider rifles and Colt revolvers, tea, sugar, and flour. English stores sold Chinese tea; Chinese stores sold Birmingham hardware.

Jack Leslie, of the Edwards, Leslie, Callaghan, and Duff partnership, had opened up a butchery and been followed soon after by two other Palmer pioneers, Baird and McNeill. Both shops advertised themselves as "shipping and family butchers—prime beef, 3d. and 4d. per lb.".

The streets—dusty in the dry season and inches deep in mud in the wet—were an ants'-nest of activity. More than 250 horse teams, as many bullock teams, and twice as many pack teams were working the road over the mountains to Byerstown, Maytown, and the Hodgkinson. Cobb and Co coaches ran a regular passenger service through Byerstown to Maytown. From daylight until dark a maze of wagons, drays, buggies, and pack teams sorted themselves out amid shouts and curses and streamed up Charlotte Street to disappear into the ranges. Beside them, between them, all around them, sworn at, kicked at, lashed at with whips, shuffled the hordes of cane-hatted, loin-clothed Chinese coolies, each with a pole across his shoulders and dangling loads on the ends of it. Every day ships from Eastern ports brought more of them. They were pouring out over the Palmer country in a never-ending stream.

In June 1876 the *Queenslander* correspondent wrote: "While at Byerstown, where the tracks to the Hodgkinson and the different parts of the Palmer diverge, I saw hundreds of Chinamen, mostly new chums, arriving and passing through to distribute themselves over the various branches of the Palmer every day. In the course of two days upwards of six hundred of these people passed through, mostly from Hong Kong, Canton, and Amoy.

"They trudged jauntily along in Indian file with their quaint cane hats up to three feet in diameter, their scant habiliments, and bare or moccasined feet, carrying on their

139

bamboos pondrous loads of provisions and tools and household goods sufficient to crush into the earth the most sturdy of our own countrymen.

"One, perhaps, would be freighted with rice only—100 or 150 pounds of it—while another carried some half-dozen iron buckets and a cradle at one end of his bamboo balanced with a dozen sheet-iron hopper plates and a gun that might have seen service in the American revolutionary war at the other end. Others again groaned under perfect donkey-loads of picks and shovels and dishes and tents and utensils of all kinds together with innumerable sundries packed in their own neatly constructed wickerwork baskets and fixed to their long bamboos in every conceivable fashion in order to arrive at a just equilibrium.

"But for a short cotton garment around the loins, a considerable portion of these new arrivals were in a state of absolute nudity as they pushed past on their way under a sweltering sun. Their heads only were well protected.

"It is in this almost naked state that they may even now be seen working in the gullies—in some places as thick as ants—some cradling, some carrying the dirt in baskets on the universal bamboo, and others again, picking and shovelling and filling. So they carry everything before them like locusts, leaving nothing behind."

In 1876 and again the following year more than 50,000 ounces of gold valued at £200,000 went out through Cooktown to China by official channels alone. The amount that was smuggled out without payment of customs duty can only be guessed at, but it must have been much more.

Though many Chinese diggers made fortunes during these peak years that followed the Chinese seizure of most of the old alluvial diggings, by far the greater proportion of the gold that was won still found its way into the pockets of their sponsors, the wealthy Chinese merchants of Canton, Hong Kong, and Cooktown. It is no wonder that these Chinese tycoons were by now able to buy up some of Cooktown's best land and many of its most prosperous businesses. European diggers who had won fortunes in gold and lost them in shanties, pubs, brothels, and gambling dens claimed sourly that the wealthy Chinese—Mandarin Chinese, they called them—owned more than half of Cooktown. A number of large stores owned by Chinese were burnt to the ground. Disgruntled diggers were blamed.

The many Europeans who, by one means or another, had managed to get their hands on a good share of Palmer gold without ever going further afield than Cooktown were not sympathetic. The Chinese were bringing trade and prosperity to the town, and everyone was benefiting, they said. If the white diggers liked to squander their gold, they had only themselves to blame. But it was hard for a digger to hold on to his gold. On the goldfield itself there were 97 pubs and 163 brothels, 35 of which were Chinese. In Cooktown he could lose his money even more easily.

As he came down out of the mountains, dusty, dry, half-starved, with months of hard, monotonous work behind him, Cooktown beckoned with ninty-four licensed hotels, with as many brothels, with gambling dens, opium halls, dance halls, and good-time girls ready to entice and please him and strip off an apparently endless array of clothing at the rate of one nugget per garment. Many a digger saw his gold gone before the last garment was shed and found a bouncer called to show him the door.

But gone was the murky squalor of those early boom days; gone, from the main street at least, the poison-dealing grog shops and the hard-lipped harpies. Darkness now saw the two miles of Charlotte Street a blaze of light from square-framed kerosene lights and many-coloured Chinese lanterns.

At French Charley's, almost opposite the A.S.N. Company wharf, champagne always flowed freely; bare-shouldered beauties in silks and satins served in the bar, shared tables in the saloon, danced the can-can, and later, if a man's money held out, took him upstairs. M. Charles Bouel was probably one of the greatest rogues who ever dodged the guillotine, but he was a man of such polish, such taste, and such unbounded enthusiasm that, on the whole, France's loss was Cooktown's gain. There was no better food to be had in Cooktown—or probably in Australia in those days—than at French Charley's. His liquor was the best, his bar and his

141

saloon the most sumptuously furnished, and his girls the gayest and most shapely.

It was said that Charley hand-picked his girls in Sydney and Melbourne and then coached them in all the accents and mannerisms of the French so his place would have the right atmosphere. One disillusioned digger complained bitterly that a pretty young redhead who had coaxed him seductively in soft French accents under the subdued lights of an alcove one night when he was spending freely had cursed him roundly in the language of the Sydney waterfront next morning in Charlotte Street.

Few who took their gold with them to French Charley's came away with it, but most did take away memories to draw on in the long, dusty days ahead as they replenished their fortunes digging quartz at Maytown or on the Hodgkinson. Even when a digger's gold was gone, Charley was still prepared to help him. By signing a few papers, the digger could—if Charley had reason to believe he was on good gold—have all the credit he needed to finish his spree and equip himself for his next foray into the field. There were men who said Charley had hundreds of men working for him like that.

But with all his faults, Charley was something of a dreamer. Sometimes in the small hours of the morning, when all his girls were sleeping, and the crowd in the bar had begun to thin out, he would bring out a bottle of cognac. Then he would expound, to a few of his cronies, a plan he had for the white colonization of New Guinea on a scale that would re-create the lost glories of Louisiana, with white sugar-planters living the gracious life in a society supported by the cheap labour of tamed head-hunters.

A little further up the street was Harry Poole's Sovereign Hotel, a more robust sort of place than Charley's, patronized by those who liked hard liquor and a bit of healthy horse-play. For a distance half-way up the main staircase of the Sovereign you could see the indentations of horseshoes in the wood. They were made when Sub-Inspector Townsend, of the native police, galloped his black stallion in pursuit of

Harry Poole after Harry had asked him to take the vicious brute out of the bar while there were ladies drinking there.

Townsend, who had shot his share of myalls with the rest of them, was fond of animals and always insisted that they be properly treated. He had three fine hounds which he had named Jesus Christ, Holy Ghost, and Virgin Mary. They all ate and lived on the same scale as Townsend, who never stinted himself. When they died of old age and good living, he had a fence built round each grave and a headstone placed on each with the words "Sacred to the memory of ———" followed by the dog's name.

Mining Warden W. R. O. Hill, of Byerstown, who saw a good deal of Townsend after the latter replaced O'Connor at the Laura, described him as a "good hearted, fool-to-himself sort of fellow". The judgement, coming from Hill, was a generous one. Hill himself was a hard-working, God-fearing man who occupied what little spare time he allowed himself with playing an organ he had bought for the local church and organizing a Sunday school for the children of Byerstown, whose main Sunday pastime until then had been "shootin' 'roos".

Another of Cooktown's popular haunts was the Steam Packet Hotel, recently owned by a former bêche-de-mer fisherman and smuggler named Bill Smith. It was patronized by the crews of visiting ships, by new arrivals, and by men looking for a passage south with their gold. Bill had sold the hotel to go into business with a mule team packing stores to the Hodgkinson, where enough gold was being got by dollying the best quartz to make packing stores there a paying proposition.

There were times when there was a fight going on in front of half the ninety-four pubs in Cooktown. Bets, arguments, libels, and rivalries were generally settled on the spot, and licensees were always ready for them. "Right boys, leave your guns on the bar," was the familiar call as things became too heated, and that was the signal for the contestants to down drinks, hitch up their belts, and troop out into the street to settle it. On one occasion a jealous Chinese husband waived the rules: "Cooktown, 30th December: Last Sunday a

143

Chinaman, a publican here, and a European had a dispute which ended in shots being exchanged. The quarrel arose about Mrs Sea Wah, the Chinaman's wife."

The outcome of this dispute was not, unfortunately, reported. Wild shooting was a fairly common occurrence as drink-warmed men settled bets on who could first knock out some light further down the street, or tried out a new weapon in the backyard of a hotel. Occasionally some citizen refused to settle matters in goldfields fashion and had recourse to the law. In January 1876 the Cooktown *Herald* reported: "The perpetrator of a disgraceful assault on the editor of the Cooktown *Herald* has been sentenced to eighteen months' imprisonment."

But all this was only one aspect of Cooktown life. Turning out of Charlotte Street towards the river, one came suddenly into what might have been Canton or Hong Kong. This was Chinatown, a town within a town, an exotic world all of its own, a series of narrow, covered alleys like a great bazaar. Chinatown blazed with the colours of lanterns and banners and goods laid out for sale in countless stalls—blue, gold, and scarlet embroidered silks and brocades cascaded beside fruit stalls with pyramids of yellow oranges, red apples and golden nectarines, red and white fish-shaped lollies filled big glass jars, snakes of jointed bamboo wriggled and struck at passers by, and toy monkeys looped on sticks. There was ginger in willow-patterned jars and in jars with scarlet dragons on them, there were fire crackers, brocade slippers, and unknown mysteries of the Orient gleaming under the light of many-coloured lanterns.

In one stall a Chinese sold lottery tickets, in another pieces of sugar-cane. Here a Chinese herbalist carried on his trade, there a barber. Doorways invited with a blaze of burnished brass, polished ivory and scarlet and black lacquer. From dim interiors, shaded by painted screens and curtains of beaded bamboo drifted the unmistakable smell of opium.

And moving everywhere through the colourful maze, often almost indistinguishable from it, was John Chinaman himself, loose robed, pigtailed and skull-capped, now thrusting forward his wares, praising their virtues, haggling, bickering

144

with neighbours, or bowing over his folded hands. Some watched quietly near the doors of gambling dens or Houses of Heavenly Bliss to screen those who entered; some furtively proffered strange Eastern drugs.

On higher ground, further back from the river, stood the larger Chinese stores and the restaurants with their piles of rice, dragon-painted porcelain, chopsticks, shark fin soup, old eggs, and delicacies unknown. Closer to the wharves were dives and hotels like Sea Wah's, which served as depots for Chinese going to and coming from the Palmer, and handled a good part of the town's smuggled opium.

About 2,500 Chinese lived in and around Cooktown, most of them in Chinatown, the rest on market gardens or on sampans in the harbour. The latter provided the town with nearly all its fish. Many of the larger fish were dried and then carried inland by coolies to sell at high prices in the gold-field towns. The smaller ones were hawked around the streets in baskets on the ends of the usual bamboo poles. More Chinese than Europeans lived in Cooktown in the boom days. The European population totalled about two thousand permanent residents.

But there was yet another side of life in Cooktown. Above the chattering blaze of Chinatown, above the roaring pubs, brothels, and gambling dens, the Government officials, bank officers, and some of the more prosperous business men and their families formed an exclusive set of their own. From the high ground around Grassy Hill, aloof from the high-pitched squeals and lusty laughter of Charlotte Street, came the more sedate tones of their piano recitals, formal dances, and sentimental songs. Nothing is left now of their passing but some tumbledown remains of the stone walls with which they shut out the raw doings of the diggers, and the foundations of their once-comfortable homes. In their heyday their entertainments were lavish.

When the new Customs House was opened, the Sub-Collector of Customs, Mr Bartley Fahey, gave a ball that was remembered for years. The weather was warm, and tons of ice, especially made for the occasion, was brought by boat from Townsville and stacked along the walls and in a great mound in the centre of the hall. It had been covered with tropical flowers, ferns and wild orchids. Chinese lanterns, flags, and banners by the dozen hung from the ceiling.

Bartley Fahey, a fine horseman, useful in a boat, and later a member of the Legislative Council, was a very popular man—except among some of the Chinese, whose smuggling activities he did a lot to limit.

One of the favourite stories in Grassy Hill circles was told by Fahey's second in command, Mr J. W. Knight, a man who was fond of his food and not afraid to experiment. All the Chinese were very fond of eggs, and as the local production was limited, Chinese merchants imported large quantities from China, encased in well-salted clay, and landed in quite edible condition—from a Chinese point of view at any rate. One day Knight decided he would like to try some, and helped himself to a couple from a case that had been opened for inspection.

"I'll have these for breakfast," he told the Chinese importer.

The merchant protested politely. That was not a number one case, he explained. He would open another case so that so gracious and important an official should have the best eggs, not eggs that were imported for coolies. He protested just a little too much. Knight had another look at the eggs and, pretending to be clumsy, dropped one. From the broken shell there oozed, not egg yolk, but a thick treacly substance—opium.

It was Knight, also, who solved another customs problem. Every Chinese who died in a foreign land wanted his remains eventually to rest in China. So, in due course, the relatives of every Chinese who died on the Palmer—if they could afford it—had his bones dug up and shipped home to China in a large earthenware jar. They were farewelled with great ceremony amid the clash of gongs and the roll of joss-house drums. The first shipment of dead Chinese set a poser for the Customs Department. Their export list made no provision for human bones. Knight scratched his head for a while and then entered the shipment in official records—"Specimens of natural history, three cases". That became the formula for all dead Chinamen. When the earthenware jars were examined by customs no one felt like pulling out the bones to look for contraband. The result of this was that many a jar left for China containing more gold dust than bones.

Gold brought a better price in China than in Australia, and quite a few of the diggers who complained so bitterly about Chinese competition were by now selling their own gold to Chinese buyers at a price slightly above the £3 17s. an ounce which had been fixed as the local price by a gentlemen's agreement between the Bank of Australasia, the Bank of New South Wales, and the Queensland National Bank.

One man who had never compromised in his hatred of the Chinese was Christie Palmerston. His depredations never slackened. Influential Chinese of Cooktown and the goldfields never ceased to lay complaints about him, and the police were regularly out looking for him—ostensibly—for one outrage or another committed against Chinamen. Warrants for his arrest were issued regularly, but there is no record of any of them ever having been executed. There was always some grateful digger to tip Palmerston off, or to put the police on a false scent to enable Palmerston to escape. Once a digger who was sheltering him kept a pursuing police constable in conversation while Palmerston sneaked out the back door, round to where the constable's horse was tethered, and rode away on it.

Every so often, no matter whether the police were looking for him or not, Palmerston would come into Cooktown for a spree. Always inclined to the dramatic, he generally rode in dressed in an old cabbage-tree hat, goggles, and shabby overcoat which the romantically inclined claimed still bore the label of one of London's Bond Street tailors. The disguise deceived no one, but the police were never known to interfere while Christie was being welcomed and fêted in every bar in town.

The gay ladies of Charlotte Street found Palmerston irresistible. It was said in those days that it cost a good-sized nugget and a fight to have Palmer Kate for the night—but she was Christie's for the asking. As a gambler, his luck was equally good. Losers claimed he cheated, but none dare challenge him to his face, or follow him into the bush where he camped at night, surrounded by his black bodyguard.

The fact that he would disappear into the mountains for months at a time, and that he always seemed to have gold, led to a rumour that he and his blacks were working a secret claim. A party of disgruntled prospectors decided to track him back to it and, the first time his back was turned, jump it. Day after day, at a safe distance, they followed Palmerston and his blacks up through rugged mountain country and deep gorges. They pushed through vermin-infested jungle, wallowed through swamps, and were nearly driven mad by leeches and mosquitoes. Food ran short, and they went on half rations. The only thing that kept them going was the sight of Palmerston's tracks in front of them. But every day the going got worse, and every way they looked there were more mountains.

At last they found themselves on the top of the Conglo-merate tableland, and stopped by a sheer precipice in front of them. They looked round for any trace of Palmerston. There was none. He had laid a blind trail, doubled back, and was probably miles away. Weeks later the would-be claim-jumpers staggered back into Cooktown. They were lucky to have got out of it with their lives.

It was generally believed that Palmerston had discovered a path across the mountains that he never revealed to any-one. Time after time while police were following him he would vanish from under their eyes. Those who said the police were not trying may have been right. There were worse men loose on the Palmer than Christie. His favourite hideout was a small hollow in rough country to the south of Cooktown which had come to be known as Christie's Pocket. No one else knew how to get into it. There he had grass for his horse, water, and a safe shelter to take it easy for as long as he liked.

So confident was he of help from the average digger that he took it for granted. A man who had been a boy on the Palmer recalled how a bearded rider had reined his horse beside his parents' wagon, said good day, and got straight down to business: "I'm Christie Palmerston. I'd like you to get a few things for me at Byerstown. Bring them out when you are on the way back. Here's a list and money to pay for them—cartridges, tea, sugar, matches, tobacco, flour, soap, and other goods. Say nothing about seeing me. I'll be here to meet you."

"He rode away singing," the writer recalled. "And a fine voice he had too. The song, I recollect, was 'Afton Water'."

Some said Palmerston got his singing voice from a famous Italian opera singer who they claimed was his mother. Whether this was true or not, all who knew him agreed that Palmerston, though often morose in his manner, was always ready to sing. "Afton Water" was one of his favourites when in Cooktown, while on the track many a digger's first hint that Palmerston was about was the sound of Christie's rather high-pitched voice raised in a popular song of the day called "The Girl with the Pretty Little High Heeled Boots".

Though he could mix easily with anybody he chose and fight at the drop of a hat, he had an innate aloofness that always kept him on the outer fringe of the wilder types of goldfield ribaldry. His normal company was his own, and his normal place the bush where he and his wild followers blended with their surroundings like the trees.

In spite of the volume of traffic then passing daily over the Palmer track the myalls had by no means been beaten, as many, misled by Cooktown's crowds into a false sense of security, still regularly found to their cost. A returning digger was speared within sight of the town. Straying horses were regularly cut out, butchered and eaten.

Two men who ought to have known better—Captain Sykes, the harbour-master, and Mr W. J. Hartley, a local merchant—decided to spend one Sunday towing in a large cedar log lying on Sandy Beach, to the north of the town. They had left their boat afloat and were jacking up the log to get a towing rope under it when a shower of spears scored hits on both of them and wounded Sykes badly. Hartley managed to get out his revolver and blazed away until the attackers ran. He then broke off both the spears, hauled Sykes into the boat, and rowed seven miles back to Cooktown.

149

A punitive party took the boat back and, leaving a lad in it to keep it off the sand and pick them up quickly if they had to run for it, scouted around. They found the blacks' camp, lunched off some of the food they found cooked there —taking something of a risk, one might think—and burnt down the blacks' sapling and tea-tree-bark huts. They recovered Sykes's and Hartley's boots which they had left behind when making their escape.

A week later Sub-Inspector O'Connor and his black troopers—recently replaced on the Laura by Townsend and his troop—found thirty-one blacks bathing on a small beach not far from where Sykes and Hartley had been attacked. According to O'Connor "all but three were accounted for".

This slaughter of blacks who may or may not have been to blame for the attack was typical of dozens of incidents that occurred on the Palmer, but being closer to town it brought some criticism. The usual excuse was given: "It was impossible to identify the blacks actually involved in the attack, and after a lesson such as this, this particular area will, in future, be safe for white men." Warden Hill, in spite of his interest in church matters, subscribed to this view. "Life was never safe," he wrote, "and the only wise thing to do on seeing a black was to shoot, and shoot straight, otherwise he would certainly spear you. I had several very narrow escapes."

There were some strange tales about the blacks circulating in the bars and drawing rooms of Cooktown in those days. A digger from the Hodgkinson described how his camp had been raided by a mob of blacks whose leader had blonde hair and skin as light as a white man's, in spite of having it striped with war-paint like the rest of the myalls. This white blackfellow had shouted orders and directed his men, and only the fact that there were four well-armed diggers in the camp enabled them to come through the attack with their lives. Other diggers reported having had glimpses of this same white blackfellow.

Christie Palmerston, one night after he had drunk more brandy than usual, produced from his pocket a bundle of white woman's golden tresses a couple of feet long. He said he had found them in a black gin's dilly-bag. Men recalled the killing of Strau and his wife and the kidnapping of their baby daughter and her death because the gins fought over her. It was well known that not only white men, but women and children too had been kidnapped by the myalls since the rush began. Many diggers reported having seen white women living with the blacks, naked and unkempt as the black gins themselves, but certainly white women. Some rescue attempts had been made, but so far none had been successful. One of these women had been seen several times in the thick jungle to the east of the Hodgkinson field, but none had been able to get near her.

Another white woman had been seen regularly with the blacks around the headwaters of the Normanby, to the north of Byerstown. The diggers called her the Normanby Woman. Several years later this woman was captured by a police party. She could not understand English, and had obviously been with the blacks long before the Palmer rush started. She pined in captivity, and died soon after her capture.

A sea captain reported having seen a white woman with the blacks at Cape Grenville, near the tip of the peninsula. As the blacks hurried her out of sight into the jungle she waved to the ship's party. They searched, but never found her.

All along the coast north of Cooktown were many old wrecks, some of which were never identified. Survivors must have come ashore, and a few, apparently, were not eaten. Most of them were.

Four men named Callaghan, Thompson, Perrett, and Lynch, who had spent three months trekking more than a thousand miles across country from Port Essington, on the west side of the Gulf of Carpentaria, to join the Hodgkinson rush, reported that they had struck the coast well north of Cooktown and followed it down. They said they had seen several wrecks on the beach; one, apparently, that of a vessel of four hundred tons or more. It had been broken up by the blacks, presumably to get the iron, and the sand was strewn with scraps of copper sheeting, apparently from its bottom. The party had fought off several attacks by the blacks, and in one of the blacks' camps they had found the remains of white people who had obviously been cooked and eaten, and some shreds of clothing—some of it women's clothing.

A blackfellow, caught on a punitive expedition, was said to have made a secret Masonic sign just as he was about to be shot, and later told his astonished captor that it had been taught him by a red-haired white man who had been washed ashore on an overturned boat, and whose life he had saved.

When men began talking there seemed to be no end of such stories. Though Cooktown had become a roaring metropolis, it was still almost surrounded by unknown jungle in which anything could happen.

13 · MURDER ON THE REEFS

ON THE Hodgkinson, where rocks and dead trees still bore notices reading "To Hell with Mulligan", and drawings of him hanging by the neck at the end of a rope, most of the miners were fuming with frustration. The Government had sent neither mining warden nor police to the field. Nor had a mail service been established. Many of the best reefs were tied up by men who were not working them, and a miner had to travel more than a hundred miles over rough country to register a claim or take out a miner's right.

On 26th May 1876 the *Queenslander* correspondent wrote: "The idea seems to be that, because the alluvial is of no account, the whole field is the same, or, at any rate, not worthy of any special attention on the part of the Government. The 600 or 700 men now here, the majority of whom are good miners anxious to test the reefs, are kept week after week in idleness for want of some officer to lay off claims and set men right as to certain rulings which no one can understand or believe."

The discontent found expression in fights, brawls, and drunken sprees lasting for days. Robbery and murder became common. A digger was found in the bush with a bullet through him, another with his skull smashed.

In June the Cooktown *Herald* reported: "Only last week the shanty-keeper Lindsay received a sentence of ten years' hard labour for murdering the woman with whom he was associated, and now another crime, even more revolting, has

153

been brought to light in the neighbourhood of the clearance on the Hodgkinson.

"A man named Lovett and a woman named Curley had been living and working together at McLeod's Creek. The woman did her fossicking with the dish or digging work of any other kind regularly as a man. When fortune favoured them with a nugget or a few pennyweights patch, a drunken orgy was the inevitable result.

"A fortnight back, in addition to whatever else she might have possessed, the unfortunate woman had in her possession a 26 dwt. piece of gold. Both she and Lovett had been drinking. When last seen alive she was accompanying another man into the bush.

"The discovery of her body in an advanced stage of decomposition and with one arm chopped off, apparently with a tomahawk, was made last week by a man in search of his horses about a mile from the nearest tents.

"There were no police to refer the matter to, but Dr Hamilton, a J.P., was only fourteen miles away, and to him information was sent. The doctor, having sworn in a couple of special constables, arrested Lovett—who had apparently made no attempt to get away—on suspicion of having committed the murder.

"He was covered with blood and made no resistance or denial of the charge. The man with whom the woman was last seen has not yet turned up."

The chopped-off arm did not pass unnoticed, and some diggers, remembering the recent case at Byerstown, muttered darkly that the wrong man had been blamed.

As week after week passed with nothing done by the Government, men who had rushed to the Hodgkinson from the Palmer headed back to the Palmer again—only to find the ground they had abandoned taken by the Chinese. They had not the money to dig in and develop reef claims, and they would die rather than work for wages. Some of them did die. Others drifted back to Cooktown to scrounge and sponge until some new strike should come to send them rushing again.

By March 1876 good crushings from the Maytown reefs were beginning to attract back the experienced reefers as well. On 4th June Warden Sellheim reported: "The white population has been largely increased by disappointed diggers returning from the Hodgkinson, and numerous prospecting areas have been granted to them. During the month I have laid off fourteen new lines of reefs and re-laid off one line that had been abandoned. Many numbers on these lines have been taken up. In every instance good gold is visible in the stone, and once machinery is placed at the disposal of the reefers the yield of gold from this field will be equal to former years.

Competition for good reefing claims became a scramble, and many fell in the struggle. There was the McAuley family —father, mother, and three sons, Jack, Hugh, and Andy— who all worked the claim together and split the gold five ways. They found the Alexandra Reef and had taken eight thousand pounds worth of gold out of it when their claim was jumped. The legal battle that followed was one of the big cases in Queensland mining history. The McAuleys lost their case in the Mining Warden's Court, and lost an appeal to the District Court at Bowen and the Supreme Court at Brisbane. They then appealed to the Privy Council in England—and won. But by then their gold winnings were all gone in legal fees. When they got the mine back it was flooded with water. They had no money for an engine and pump and the claim they had fought so hard to hold was abandoned.

While the European miners were developing the reefs, the Chinese, still pushing in steadily, had taken over all the old ground and, foot by foot, were putting every shovelful of it through their sluice-boxes. As well as pushing up into the headwaters around Byerstown, they spread south to the Mitchell, north up over the Conglomerate tableland down into its countless creeks and gullies. They had even tunnelled underneath it to get at the consolidated, gold-bearing gravel under the sandstone. They had edged their way west down-river from Palmerville where the alluvial was almost as fine as dust but still in sufficient quantity to make it worth their while mining it.

Chinese gold was pouring out through Cooktown from all over the Palmer field, but there were so many digging it that most made no more than tucker. With insufficient alluvial to go round, outnumbered European fossickers who a couple of years earlier had chased the Chinese away from the best ground now found the tables turned on them. "Complaints are made," wrote a correspondent, "that the Chinese neglect the regulations requiring them to peg out their claims, but they are in strong force and will not allow their ground to be jumped with impunity. It is alleged that they purposely neglect to peg out their ground because their actual boundaries shall not be known, and any stranger—European—attempting to take possession of an unpegged piece of ground, as he is legally entitled to do, is at once over-powered and driven off by the Chinese."

Numbers made the Chinese so daring that even the cannibals found they could no longer pick them off with impunity. On the Left-hand Branch a party of Chinese were sluicing for gold in the bed of the river when they were rushed by blacks who had been hiding in the scrub near by. With spears falling all around them, the Chinese bolted for their hut—a substantial, slab-walled structure with a bark roof—and slammed and bolted the door. They had a rifle and a couple of old muzzle-loading shotguns between them and, poking these through the cracks between the slabs, they blazed away. The blacks rushed in close and tried to skewer them on spears poked through the same cracks. The Chinese, when their supply of shot ran out, loaded the guns with nails, gravel, and anything else they could lay their hands on.

While the shooting was going on, two of the blacks climbed up on the roof. The bark caved in, and they fell in on the Chinamen who jumped on them with knives and literally carved them to pieces. The two men's screams so unnerved the attackers that they bolted, leaving a couple of badly wounded men for the Chinese to pick off at leisure. As proof of their victory, the Chinese cut off the ears of their victims, pickled them, and brought them into the township in a jar.

The first issue of a Maytown newspaper, the *Golden Age*, was published on 29th July. Its proprietor, as might have been expected, was John Edwards. Soon the *Golden Age* was reporting: "Now that there is a certainty of having machinery in a few weeks at Cradle Creek and Revolver Point, great excitement has evinced amongst the miners who are all heavily engaged in getting up stone pending the advent of the crushing machines. By the time they are erected, thousands of tons of quartz will be at grass. The quality of the stone is much superior to any seen before and the reefs are improving as they go down."

Sellheim had recently laid off a new township, Echotown, two miles above Revolver Point on the Left-hand Branch at a spot where the steep slopes opposite sent back an echo. In no time the place was a cluster of miners' tents and bark huts with the usual shanty on the slope of a handy gully. A crushing plant was brought in by a Mr Binnie to handle the ore from its reefs. His son, J. H. Binnie, who spent six years on the field as a boy, left an account of life as it was on the Palmer in those days.

When the boy, aged six, with his mother and eight-year-old sister arrived at Cooktown early in 1876 to join Binnie on the field, the coach to Maytown was booked for a couple of months ahead. Binnie, busy with the peak ore-crushing period, had not been expecting them until later and had made no arrangements.

After three weeks, Mrs Binnie managed to arrange transport by a four-ton, nine-horse dray loaded with groceries, general mechandise, and several kegs of brandy and cases of whisky and wine. The teamster's wife went with them, and they had two half-wild black boys and a black girl aged about twelve.

At the Normanby they were held up by floodwaters, and the teamster, who until then had contented himself with a daily pannikin from the brandy cask which he kept topping up with water, now rode off to a shanty about twenty miles away and did not show up again for a week. Every night the terrified women huddled together with a revolver, while the two black boys painted themselves with ochre and danced and sang until nearly dawn. On the slopes across the river they could see the campfires of myalls.

In due course the teamster returned from his spree and the river fell enough for them to get the team and dray across it. But it was still the tail end of the wet season and there was hardly a day that the dray was not bogged. Sometimes another carrier was handy to hitch his bullocks in front of theirs to pull them through. When there was none, the dray had to be unloaded, pulled clear, and loaded up again.

One night they camped about a hundred yards from the infamous Murdering Lagoons where Strau and his wife and child had been killed. The teamster gave the twelve-year-old black girl a billy and told her to get water. She screamed with terror and refused to go. The teamster flogged her with his whip until she dropped, ignoring the protests of the two women.

A few nights after this, the two half-wild blacks had an exceptionally loud sing-song. When they quietened just before dawn the teamster became suspicious and, on looking for them, found they were gone. He saddled his best horse and caught up with them in rough country about seven miles from the camp. They had apparently intended to join the mob of blacks who had dogged the dray all the way from the Normanby. He shot them both.

The going was so boggy and rough that it took the dray three months to cover eighty miles. Then they met a man with horses who had been sent by Binnie to bring his family the rest of the way. From then on Mrs Binnie rode side-saddle with her six-year-old on her lap over mountain tracks, flooded river crossings and sweltering plains. It was the first time she had ever been on a horse. Heat, flies, mosquitoes, and snakes were with them all the way. Waterholes were scarce on the long stretches between flooded rivers, and when they reached one shortly after a few teams of bullocks had watered, there was still nothing but to fill the waterbags and be thankful.

Though there were plenty of women and children on the field by this time, and three families with young children at Echotown, the Binnie family found life fairly rugged. They lived in a bark-walled, tin-roofed house on the slope over-looking the river. The slope was so steep that one side of the roof almost touched the ground, and snakes—venomous varieties up to six feet long and carpet snakes more than three times that—found it convenient to slide across onto the rafters from which they sometimes dangled to explore the prospects of a meal. Death adders were common amongst the rocks outside. The children always went bare-footed, and somehow were never bitten. Chief victims of the snakes were Mrs Binnie's fowls, which disappeared nearly as quickly as she could replenish stocks from the Chinese carriers, who brought them from Cooktown in their baskets for sale on the goldfield at about fifteen shillings each. The Chinese also brought in hundreds of kittens which they sold for ten shillings each. Before long the field was swarming with cats.

The myalls were never far away. One day, needing his horse for a rush trip to Cooktown, Binnie sent a man to the river flats about a mile from the town where the horses usually grazed. All the man found were the bones and the hooves of two horses. They had been butchered on the spot and the meat carried away. No other horses being available, Binnie decided to walk. It was about 120 miles to Cooktown, but he calculated that by cutting across some of the steep ranges instead of following the road he could shorten it. He left early in the morning carrying a small bag of food and a billy-can. He was totally unarmed, considering firearms and ammunition too heavy to carry. Without even a compass, he travelled as much as possible at night and had some sleep in the daytime to dodge the blacks. He swam three rivers with his clothes and boots strapped on his head, and on one occasion reached the top of a ridge at night and almost walked into a blacks' camp before he saw their fires on the other side. He made the trip in five days. Bushmen said he was mad to have tried it.

While working at a saw at the Echotown battery, Binnie's right hand slipped against the revolving blade which ripped off his first three fingers. There were twelve men in the machine house at the time, but not one of them knew what to do. Binnie got a pair of pliers, pulled out the splinters of shattered bone with them, and then stitched each finger with his left hand. The doctor at Maytown was on a drinking spree and could not help. The weather was very hot and the wounds began to fester. Binnie lay in bed for three days with his arm suspended in a sling at arm's length out of the bed with cold water dripping on it night and day to prevent inflammation. Within a month he was working again.

There was no dentist in the district, so, with all the family suffering from toothache, Binnie made a pair of forceps and tried them out by extracting three of his own teeth. Then he took out some for Mrs Binnie and the children. He was also the boat-builder and coffin-maker, sawing his own timber and supplying coffins free of charge to all who needed them.

Most of the Echotown mines were worked only to the depth that ore could be hauled up by windlass—about a hundred feet. The country was so rough that the quartz had to be brought to the battery on pack-horses. Some of it came ten miles along a narrow bush track in the side of a steep mountain slope. It was not easy country to work in, and as the Hodgkinson began to come into production and attract experienced reefers, Echotown was one of the first fields on the Palmer to feel the pinch.

Things had begun to change for the better on the Hodgkinson from 24th June when Howard St George, now magistrate at Cooktown, was transferred to the new field for two months to put things in order. Diggers who remembered The Saint from his early days on the Palmer hailed his coming. "The appointment is, without doubt, the very best that could have been made," the local correspondent of the *Queenslander* wrote.

Mulligan had tided himself over the hard times by opening the Hodgkinson field's first store, a substantial bark structure, in which St George now set up a temporary office and began to sort out the mess. He recommended the appointment of an experienced warden permanently, and reported: "The facilities for erecting quartz-crushing machinery are good, there being ample water and suitable timber. Mr Douglas with his detachment of native police is now stationed here and, by continuously patrolling the neighbourhood, has prevented outrages by the blacks."

Within a month of St George's arrival, the *Queenslander* correspondent was writing: "There are now on the field 1,500 to 2,000 people. Rich reefs are daily being opened, and the majority of miners are satisfied with their claims. There is not now so much dishonesty as at first, the loafers having pretty well cleared out. People can now leave their tools on their claims, and stealing specimens from the heaps of quartz has ceased."

On 26th August: "A man named William Fanning, from County Kilkenny, died of inflammation of the lungs after giving his will duly made. This gave rise to the necessity of having a cemetery laid off." A published sketch of the burial was one of the first pictures of the Hodgkinson that the outside had seen.

There was, nevertheless, a feeling of confidence and optimism in the air. Several stamping machines were on the way and the postal service had come at last. The camp at Mulligan's store was called Thornborough after the Postmaster-General.

A building boom followed, although the Government still showed a good deal of reluctance to spend money in the area. Mulligan's store was used as court-house, and prisoners were kept chained to a tree, causing the correspondent to express some sympathy for the police who had to sit up in the open on the cold nights then being experienced on the tableland to prevent marauding blacks from taking the prisoners for food.

Apart from the lack of such minor amenities, the main problem remaining was the isolation of the place, and the long, expensive haul of supplies overland from Cooktown. Some of the miners had remembered Jack Moran's trip down to the sea when Mulligan first discovered the Hodgkinson, and several parties had been out looking for a track over the jungle-covered, razorback ranges that barred the way. Among them was Bill Smith, former bêche-de-mer fisherman, hotel-keeper, and mule-driver. Hard drinking, hard swearing, and still in his prime, he had become a well-known character on

161

the Hodgkinson, where nobody ever called him anything but Old Bill. With him on his expedition had gone Jack Cardnow, a mate from his bêche-de-mer days, and John Doyle, one of the best-known bushmen in the north at that time.

On 8th July 1876, a Saturday afternoon meeting of about five hundred miners was held outside Mulligan's store to discuss the position. Warden St George presided, sitting on a pile of logs. Old Bill, who in his bêche-de-mer days had covered the whole coastline from Bowen to north of Cooktown, told them about a deep creek that ran into Captain Cook's Trinity Bay. It would make an ideal landing for stores, he said, and he was sure he could find a track down to it. The cheering diggers passed around the hat and put in two hundred pounds to equip an expedition for Old Bill and his two mates to find a track. They set out and reached the edge of the rain forest at a stream later named Grove Creek, and then had to turn back for lack of supplies.

Another meeting on 21st August subscribed funds for Old Bill to go back to Cooktown and down the coast to attack the range from the sea. Coming ashore at his old landing place in the creek—Smith's Landing—Old Bill, with two men named Stewart and Lipton and two black boys, followed a blackfellows' path up the range, reached his old camp at Grove Creek on 15th August, and arrived at Thornborough on 21st September. They told him there that a Government-sponsored expedition led by Sub-Inspector Douglas of Hell's Gate fame, together with Government Surveyor Frederick Warner and his brother Charles Warner, had left four days earlier to look for a track. A party of impatient diggers led by "Greasy" Bill Little had followed them. Douglas, taking a different route from Old Bill, reached the coast on 23rd September to be welcomed by Sub-Inspector Johnstone, Sub-Inspector Townsend, and a party of native troopers who had been sent from Cardwell by police cutter to meet them.

The combined party cut a track back up the mountains. On the banks of a river they passed on the way they saw tracks Bill Smith's hobnailed boots had made there on 19th September. At Grove Creek they met Little's party of diggers and brought them back to the little opening they had cut in the dense wall of jungle at the crest of the range. Through it Greasy Bill looked out on the flat country about a thousand feet below, and the sea beyond it. He looked at the almost perpendicular drop at his feet.

"This what you call a track?" he demanded. "Why, you'd have to put a breechin' on a crow to get him down there."

Nevertheless they did get down, and Douglas named the river where they had seen Bill Smith's footprints the Barron, "after T. H. Barron, clerk in the office of the Commissioner of Police".

Back at Thornborough the happy diggers were cleaning up the last of the brandy and gin in honour of Old Bill. Two of Douglas's troopers who arrived on lathered horses with news of the Sub-Inspector's success were received with raucous laughter. As soon as the last of the liquor was drunk another meeting was called so Old Bill could tell them his plans. The newspaper correspondent quoted him in full:

"Well here I am, and I understand you want to know what I know about the new port that is to be if we are to have a good, short, easy road to these diggings; and I can tell you all about it. For two or three years I was bêche-de-mering along the coast, and there's a nice little creek north of Cape Grafton where I put in for firewood. We had to go some distance up it and found plenty depth of water; in fact, while shipping the wood the kanakas could step from the banks onto the vessel and you couldn't touch the bottom with a sixteen-foot oar, and as to the depth at the bar or entrance, I can't say, but I know my craft drew six feet six inches and I waited for no tides, so you can take what you like out of that.

"When I was down there the other day I recognized the place again, and that is where the new road will go to. I believe it will make a good harbour with a good road to it not more than seventy miles in length."

When Old Bill headed back along his track to the coast he was followed, according to the *Queenslander* correspondent, by about 160 men, all singing, in the highest of spirits, and convinced that they were on their way to a fortune in some shape or other, though of what kind they had not the

163

least idea, except that they had heard there were business sites at Trinity Bay "to be had for the sitting down upon".

Behind them at Thornborough, life was still lively.

"Mexican Jack, alias John Akinnon, is remanded for further trial on Monday by Mr St George for horse-stealing. I think he will probably get a change of climate at Rockhampton."

It was reported that "a party of prospectors were interrupted in their camp by a shower of spears. They scattered for the shelter of the trees. One of them drew a revolver but it misfired. While he was snapping it a spear took him through the leg and he fell. A blackfellow rushed forward with nulla raised for the kill, but a bullet dropped him dead alongside his intended victim. Four more died before the blacks retreated. Part of the spear had to be cut off before it could be pulled through the wounded man's leg. Barbs at its point prevented its being pulled out the way it entered.

"Next morning four of the whites left the camp armed with a gun, a rifle, and a half axe. About four miles out they found the blacks in camp busily engaged in fitting barbs on spear shafts, apparently for a fresh attack. The man with the revolver circled round to the other side of them and attacked. The blacks fled towards the other members of the party who opened fire and attacked with the axe, and so dispersed them."

More raids by the blacks followed this. Taking advantage of the absence of the native police at Trinity Bay, they speared and butchered horses regularly, and several diggers were wounded. The erection of telegraph lines to the goldfields had provided them with a new source of material for weapons. Poles were scaled and miles of wire stolen to make spear points. Porcelain insulators also were taken, to be broken up and patiently chipped into knives.

Grog continued to take its toll. "Abraham Gibson, father of John D. Gibson, storekeeper, was brought into Cooktown tonight as a prisoner committed for trial on a charge of murder of Frank Norris, an employee. It appears that Gibson had been drinking heavily, and, no further supply of spirits being obtainable, some persons gave him a dose of laudanum and it sent him mad. He slept partially, but suddenly awoke and thought the stores were being robbed. The first person he met was Frank Norris whom he thought was a robber, and stabbed him fatally." Gibson was eventually acquitted on the ground of insanity at the time.

"Another man has been found dead on the Hodgkinson twelve miles from McLeod's. The dead body was much wounded in the head," reported the Cooktown *Herald*.

In Maytown the *Golden Age* took a patronizing tone: "We are informed that a man arrived in town on Thursday last from the Hodgkinson and reported that a person named Brian McSweeny was shot dead the other day. It appears he was engaged by Mr Purdie to look after some cattle and a dispute arose between McSweeny and others. A man has been taken up on suspicion.

"There is also a rumour of a woman having poisoned her husband and a man having been stabbed through the heart. Altogether, society seems to be rather unsettled in that part of the Colony."

Unsettled or not, the Hodgkinson was growing every day. All over the field roaring camps with hundreds of tents, bough sheds, and bark huts were springing up to become towns like Woodville, Wellesley, Waterford, Stuart Town, Union Camp, and Kingsborough. Thornborough soon became the capital of a large community. Men like Mulligan, Dr Hamilton, Johnny Byers, and Bill Little—anyone with capital, in fact—were buying shares in the most promising reefs. Experienced reef miners now were deserting Maytown for the rich reefs of the Hodgkinson.

Echotown was almost deserted, and Binnie found supplies of quartz dropping to a point where his machine was not paying its way. He decided to move it to the Lone Star lease in the Conglomerate Range about seven miles away. It had to be hauled, piece by piece, by bullock teams along a rough track in the side of the mountain with an almost sheer drop on one side and a wall of rock on the other. On arrival at the new location it had to be lowered with block and tackle into a deep gully where there would be enough water to keep

165

it supplied. The earnings of months were paid out to packers before Binnie once again got up steam for the stampers.

After six months' crushing, the Lone Star lease also was abandoned as its owners headed for the Hodgkinson. Binnie was left with his machine stranded in the deep, isolated gorge. As he prepared to dismantle it for moving once again, two miners, who worked a small reef about two miles along the side of the mountain and relied on the battery to crush their three or four tons of quartz occasionally, arrived and announced that if any attempt was made to move the machine they would wreck it. The plant had to be guarded day and night until it could be moved. The two miners had no choice but to abandon their claim after having toiled for months to develop it. Packing their quartz fifteen miles to Maytown would not have paid. Before they left they blew up their mine with dynamite.

Binnie set up his battery at German Bar, now dominated by Chinese working the old alluvial ground, but supporting a growing number of white reef miners. The Chinese butcher killed a bullock every Sunday morning at daybreak, and most of the miners and all the children came along to see the half-wild beast yarded. Though meat was cheaper now than in the early days of the rush, the Chinese themselves ate very little of it. They were, however, getting hold of most of the businesses, butchers' shops among them. The only Europeans holding their own against them were Edwards and Co. Most of the Chinese butchers' shops were supplied with meat from one or other of the various cattle runs which the Old Firm had acquired on the fringe of the goldfield. If a Chinese butcher tried to buy his cattle more cheaply from anyone else, Edwards and Co would start a shop in opposition and cut prices until the Chinese was forced out of business.

In the early days of the rush the Chinese had mostly worked their claims individually—one man rocking a cradle —but with the coming of large numbers of indentured coolies, large parties were now sluicing. This took a great deal of water and, once the wet was over, water brought a high price. One of the sluicing parties paid Binnie fifty pounds for the right to bail water out of a big waterhole in the river for which Binnie held a water-right licence. As it was impossible to drain this hole by gravitation, the Chinese cut a drain along the river bank and bucketed the water into it. They worked in shifts, twenty-four hours a day for several weeks, and they got enough gold out of the nearly dry river-bed to make the back-breaking work a paying proposition.

While Binnie was spending his earnings moving ten tons or so of machinery around the gorges of the Palmer, the miners on the Hodgkinson were complaining that the owners of the newly arrived stampers were having things all their own way. The Hodgkinson reefs were easy to get at, and many of them were very rich, but carting and crushing costs were far too high, they said. In addition to this, the machinery being brought in was old, out of date, and badly handled. Fine gold from the stampers was being washed away for lack of proper equipment to catch it, they said, and the machine owners could not care less.

Mulligan, with shares in a number of reefs, and in several machines, owner of Thornborough's main store, a capitalist for the first and last time in his life, was not sympathetic. "The fact of it was," he wrote later, "that the golden stone was too easily got and was as easily spent in a ludicrous way. There were too many of the wrong sort of miners getting backers. The majority of them were only alluvial miners, and hundreds not miners at all and did not understand reefing.

"A very large number drew their money every week from the business people who had backed them or the owners of the claims, who themselves had not time to go and see how their claims were looking. Some of these miners would come into town on a Saturday morning and remain in until Sunday night or Monday morning, go out to their work on Monday, and be sick until after Tuesday. They might possibly do two or three days work in a week."

When Mr William Mowbray arrived on the Hodgkinson as warden on 26th August 1876, he reported that the reefs were improving as they went down. In spite of mismanagement, rich new finds were constantly spreading the field wider and keeping a steady stream of ore flowing into the stampers. On 8th October the Thornborough correspondent reported: "Last week at the Band of Freedom claim, while drilling into the reef, the drill was clogged and, on being examined, showed gold. Hammers and gads soon got out two hundredweight of quartz which, on being broken, showed a piece of gold estimated to tip the scale at forty pounds at the very least. All through the week they have been getting small nuggets of gold through the stone." Before the wet season set in there were eight crushing machines on the field. The Explorer, one of the reward claims granted to Mulligan and party, was yielding six and a half ounces of gold to the ton of quartz.

The smell of gold brought a new stream of migrants along the road from Cooktown. Dance halls, brothels, and gambling dens nudged in between the hotels, shanties, and stores. A jockey club was formed and race meetings were organized. The Chinese, though not allowed to mine the reefs, moved into the gullies to look for alluvial or settled on the fringes of the towns to start market gardens. Others began building hotels and stores—better buildings than those of the Europeans. Miners began to bring their wives and families in increasing numbers, and Thornborough, particularly, developed a lively social life.

Then, as all the best of the Hodgkinson reef claims were taken up, the pendulum began to swing back again. Sellheim reported the overflow of the reefers trooping back to the Palmer. Several reefs had been opened in the Byerstown area and a stamper brought in. There was still gold to be had, literally for the picking up, on the Palmer.

Hill recalled how a European miner came into his office at Byerstown one morning for a miner's right. Next day he came back and asked if he could put a bag in Hill's safe. "It's a few specimens I got yesterday in about three hours," he explained. The man told Hill he walked up a gully looking for his horses and found that one of them had kicked over a large stone to disclose a whole nest of nuggets. Hill weighed them—179 ounces, 3 pennyweight. "They were lovely to look at, all waterworn and of the most fantastic shapes," wrote Hill. "One beauty was exactly $13\frac{1}{2}$ ounces."

The whole countryside was bustling like an ants'-nest. And pouring into it, filling every gully, washing every inch of gravel, pushing out from its fringes, came the toiling, wide-hatted Chinese. "The amount of gold obtained by them was enormous, and thousands of ounces of gold were taken back to China privately," wrote Hill. "One of the Boss Chinamen told me he sent home at least one thousand ounces a month for some considerable time, and I believe him."

14 · THE CHINESE PANIC

THE EARLY months of 1876 saw the Chinese pouring into the Palmer by the thousand, and, among the white community, fears of the consequences came in some cases close to hysteria. "It is no longer a question of repelling a coming invasion," summed up the Cooktown *Herald* in May, "so much as to defend, not alone our hearths and homes, but our very lives against the invaders who swarm around us. The danger is imminent and deadly, and unless the most strenuous measures be at once taken, it may be that ere long, one of the most disastrous and bloody chapters in Australian history will have to be recorded."

Mining wardens were reporting from all over the field an epidemic of robberies, murders, and other crimes committed by starving Chinese who could find no gold, and they were warning of worse to come when the dry season saw an expected twenty thousand Chinese on the field, and the alluvial unworkable for lack of water.

"A gentleman who arrived in town yesterday from the Palmer informs us," said the Cooktown *Herald*, "that the district is overrun with destitute Chinese in a state of starvation, wandering here and there, unable to obtain the necessaries of life, and that they are committing wholesale robberies for bare sustenance. He states that he would not be at all surprised if Cooktown were visited by a few thousand of these starving men. As they are all armed, what resistance could a few of us make?"

Every ship from the East brought its quota of Chinese. In

an effort to stem the tide, the quarantine regulations were being strictly enforced. In April a batch of 553 coolies arrived at Cooktown by the steamer *Bowen* and were at once placed in quarantine down the coast on Fitzroy Island for sixteen days. A few days later they were joined by almost as many more from the s.s. *Normanby*.

They were still there when the s.s. *Galley of Lorne* arrived from Hong Kong, and her master, Captain McDonald, reported that the 1,050 Chinese he had on board refused to land on Fitzroy Island, claiming with some justification that there was no accommodation there for them. They pointed out that there were not even tents for them to sleep in. The weather was wet and squally. There was no doctor stationed there, and sickness, starvation, and death for many would be almost inevitable.

The captain, who had been having trouble with them throughout the voyage, wanted to be rid of them. He threatened to put them ashore on the beach on the north bank of the Endeavour River, where a few steamers had landed Chinese in the past. He got up anchor and moved into the river. He was promptly boarded by the water police who threatened prosecution for breach of the quarantine regulations. The captain said if he did not get rid of the Chinese he would have to arm his European passengers in self-defence.

After hot words had been exchanged at considerable length, the authorities said the law would be enforced, and Captain McDonald sailed for Fitzroy Island. The Chinese rioted, police boarded the ship, searched them for firearms, and forcibly landed them. It was still raining. No sooner were the Chinese ashore than they rioted again and demanded to be taken to the mainland immediately. Many of them, in spite of having been searched, produced revolvers. All that night the crackle of small arms echoed around the island.

There were now about two thousand Chinese on Fitzroy. The s.s. *Killarney* was expected daily with another thousand. Another report said that a further three thousand Chinese were waiting at Hong Kong to get berths to Cooktown.

The Mayor of Cooktown received instructions from the

Government to take any necessary action to see the quarantine regulations were complied with.

"Cooktown, 1st May: Captain McDonald of the *Galley of Lorne* has been fined twenty pounds for a breach of harbour regulations."

"Cooktown, 2nd May: Captain McDonald of the *Galley of Lorne* was fined again today the sum of twenty pounds for breach of the quarantine laws through not hoisting the yellow flag. The steamer left for Hong Kong this afternoon with 150 returning Chinese and 1,250 ounces of gold."

Newspapers suggested that in view of the extraordinary conditions prevailing a warship should be stationed at Cooktown to help enforce the regulations, because of the open acts of defiance that had been reported. Soon after this the Queensland gunboat *Paluma* made her appearance in Cooktown "on exercises".

As their quarantine period expired, two thousand Chinese flocked ashore from Fitzroy and headed inland to join the hordes on the goldfield. At Byerstown, on the direct route from Cooktown to the Palmer, Warden Hill was taking the brunt of it. The *Queenslander* correspondent reported: "Chinese being released from quarantine are arriving in such numbers at Byerstown that Mr Warden Hill has his work to do to see that they all take out miners' rights."

Warden Sellheim, from Maytown, warned that with too many Chinese already on the field, the last of the alluvial gold being rapidly cleaned out, and more Chinese arriving, destitution and starvation were inevitable. "Some measure should be taken to check this Chinese immigration if only for the sake of the immigrants themselves," he wrote. A few days later a Chinese digger found a 72-ounce nugget of gold at Jessop's Creek. His newly arrived countrymen jostled around him in hundreds.

The Chinese had monopolized the whole of the alluvial ground, and already had a tight grip on the whole of the Palmer's business life. Chinese stores were everywhere. There were Chinese butchers, Chinese banks, gambling dens, and opium hells. At strategically situated spots there were several large encampments of Chinese prostitutes. In an editorial the

Queenslander complained: "No European is permitted to work in any mine in any part of the Chinese Empire, nor are any business men, outside of certain prescribed areas. If one should attempt to travel through the country, he would certainly be murdered. Yet at this very time, a Chinese population are occupying a hundred miles of alluvial workings in the bed of the Palmer and its tributaries to the exclusion of our own countrymen, by whose enterprise and hard work this Colony has been founded and our goldfields discovered and developed."

With more Chinese arriving daily, and every foot of gold-bearing ground taken, the inevitable soon began to happen.

"Byerstown: There has been a fearful murder committed in Doughboy Creek, six miles beyond Byerstown, in a store kept by a man named Towhey.

"Thomas Green, an employee, was found stabbed in sixteen places, in face, mouth, ear, head, and chest. The body was dragged face on the ground for forty yards. Pools of blood were found at the entrance of the store. There were tracks of Chinese outside and inside. Goods were stolen and turned upside down. The victim's pockets were rifled and all money was taken. The warden and police went out. An inquest was held and a verdict of wilful murder returned. Placards have been posted offering fifty pounds reward for information. Great indignation is felt here. Chinese are starving, and robbing all around."

A few days later, near the scene of the murder, Johnny Hogsflesh opened fire on a Chinese who was trying to lead off all the mail contractor's packhorses.

"They are still coming, and we know a ship is on the way with another thousand," the Cooktown *Herald* complained. "What is to be done with these, we know not."

Sellheim reported: "The want of water begins to be felt heavily. In a month or so the bulk of the Chinese will have to fall back on the main watercourses where earnings will be trifling. Crime is becoming very prevalent among the Chinese, and I have thought it my duty to bring under the notice of the Colonial Secretary the absolute necessity of the employment of some Chinese detectives."

173

From Byerstown, Warden Hill reported: "The great influx of new chum Chinamen will, unless checked, cause want, misery, and consequently crime in this district. All the alluvial diggings are now comparatively poor, and it is as much as Chinamen can do to make a living which would be nearly starvation to Europeans. Should the Chinamen be allowed to flock into this district in such numbers, I must again ask you to take into consideration the necessity of augmenting my staff to enable me, in case of some emergency, to prevent a recurrence of murder and robbery."

The Cooktown *Herald* was less restrained: "Any day an army of famishing wretches, numbering many thousands, desperate and armed, may march on Cooktown, and in what position are we to repel it."

News items constantly fanned the flames.

"May 18th: Gregory, Beach, Palmer, and Flynn, packers, when looking for horses, were assaulted and knocked down by the Chinese and robbed of ninety-two pounds."

"May 18th: Duff, a butcher, when making up his cash in the shop, was daringly robbed by a Chinese of a bag containing sixty pounds."

"May 22nd: A highway robbery by Chinese is reported on the Palmer."

Hill attributed a large part of the crime among the Chinese to the activities of the proprietors of illicit Chinese gambling dens. He claimed they fleeced their countrymen right down to their last pennyweight of gold and left them no choice but to turn to crime to keep themselves alive. He raided their dens regularly and made dangerous enemies. "It was funny after a big haul," he wrote, "to see the native troopers lugging sometimes six or eight Chinkies in each hand, holding them by their pigtails."

In one such raid, Hill and eighteen troopers took more than sixty prisoners. Hill had grabbed the proprietor of the den, diving across the table to get at him. The lights went out and Hill and his prisoner went down together with the gaming table on top of them. Hill received a kick on the ankle which disabled him for a month, but the following morning hobbled into his court to fine his prisoner fifty pounds and each of the men caught in his den ten pounds. All the fines were paid, Hill reported. One dark night soon after this a bullet whined through Hill's camp, narrowly missing him.

In the midst of the turmoil on the field, one old digger found a way to collect a little revenue from the Chinese on his own account. With an old chequebook containing a hundred forms, he took up a position on the track and issued the first hundred new chum Chinese who came along with what he assured them were miners' rights at ten shillings a time.

But in spite of its lighter moments, the situation was becoming explosive. The *Golden Age* reported: "A few days ago the men on top at the different claims in the neighbourhood of the Captain Cook reef were taken by surprise on the appearance of a Celestial in European garb with a tomahawk and pegs in hand marking off an abandoned shaft. On being questioned, John, in very plain English, expressed his determination to try his luck as a quartz miner, and was on the point of boldly asserting his right when the limb of an iron-bark tree and a rope were very significantly brought to his attention. John, thinking discretion the better part of valour, decamped in hot haste to lay his complaint before the warden. As that functionary was absent, we are unable to ascertain what move the would-be reefer is next likely to take."

In due course Sellheim reported: "A couple of Chinese have spoken to me about applying for a reef, but I am glad to say they have acted on my advice and desisted. I have explained to them their perfect right of application, but also considered it prudent to point out the probable consequences of their action."

Early in June "thirty Chinamen stuck up ten of their own countrymen fourteen miles on the Cooktown side of Byerstown and, after severely ill-treating them, robbed them of any valuables they could lay their hands on and decamped".

Later that month Sellheim gave figures which showed the extent to which the Chinese had come to outnumber Europeans on the goldfield. "The population of the Palmer consists of 1,400 Europeans and 17,000 Chinese scattered over an area of 2,000 square miles," he wrote. "On the Hodgkinson there are 4,500 Europeans and 300 Chinese. Figures for the principal camps on the Palmer are: Maytown 900 Europeans and 300 Chinese, Palmerville 12 Europeans and 600 Chinese, Jessop's Creek 6 Europeans and 1,000 Chinese, Stony Creek 16 Europeans and 1,200 Chinese, Byerstown 16 Europeans and 800 Chinese, Uhrstown 10 Europeans and 600 Chinese." Only on the Hodgkinson and at Maytown—the two principal reef-mining areas—were there more Europeans than Chinese. In some of the old alluvial areas the few European diggers who had stuck to good claims were outnumbered by Chinese two hundred to one.

From Byerstown, Hill, with a staff consisting of a clerk of petty sessions to handle the bulk of the office work, such as issuing miners' rights, registering claims, and so on, together with three white orderlies and three black trackers, reported that during May "no less than 1,541 Chinese have been made to take out miners' rights, the money having been collected under great difficulty. Not a single Chinaman came freely with it." Hill often rounded up and arrested mobs of 100 to 150 Chinese who claimed they did not have ten shillings for a miner's right. He carried on his packhorse a long, light chain—a marching chain—with 75 pairs of handcuffs attached, thus providing accommodation for 150 prisoners. Whenever he made camp the chain was locked around a tree. The chained prisoners had to carry their swags back to his headquarters with them, and there the swags were confiscated and held until the fees were paid.

On these patrols, said Hill, he and his men had to be on the alert all the time. Knives were often drawn on them when a Chinese camp was entered, and sometimes a rescue was attempted. They were often out in the ranges struggling through rough country in sweltering heat for two or three weeks at a stretch. He and his white assistants were rarely free from fever, said Hill. Shivering spells alternated with raging fever which generally made him delirious. At times he had to lie down in the dust for an hour or so, guarded by his native troopers, before he could go on.

In June, with 2,300 newly arrived Chinese on their way from Cooktown to the Palmer, Sellheim reported that a mob of new arrivals had jumped the claims of other Chinese. Many Chinese now arriving on the goldfield, he said, had come from Macao and other coastal ports, and a good proportion were probably pirates. "Inspired with some degree of boldness by the vast extent to which they are in excess of the European population," he wrote, "they are becoming very dangerous, even to officials. They gather in large numbers, resist the enforcement of the goldfields regulations, and threaten with their lives all who approach them. Their disarmament has become a necessity, but it is not possible to carry it out with the force the wardens have at present on the field, and scarcely possible to maintain order."

A correspondent wrote: "I don't think there are ten diggers within a radius of fifty miles of Byerstown who have not been robbed by the Chinese of something—generally tucker or firearms. Any parliamentary action that will exclude them from the Colony will be hailed with delight."

In Cooktown the Chinese business men were gradually taking over. With the Chinese population on the goldfield approaching twenty thousand and cargoes pouring in from China to keep them supplied, European packers and carriers found it more profitable to work for the Chinese. "Some of the largest carriers are engaged for months, and consequently European business is at a standstill," the Cooktown *Herald* reported. "Although plenty of orders are on hand from the Hodgkinson and the old Palmer centres like Maytown, carriers cannot be had, and goods are lying in the stores."

At Byerstown, Hill was fighting a losing battle. He reported that during June, 2,400 Chinese had left Cooktown for the Palmer and he had taken every precaution to see, as far as possible, that all who passed through his territory had paid for their licences. But up to the end of the month he had been able to catch only 877.

"It matters not whether I camp thirty miles on the road or keep watch day and night at the crossing, the Chinese are getting so knowing that directly I get the first mob they send express messengers back in the night, ten or even twenty miles, and get old chums to escort their newly arrived countrymen through the bush and so avoid paying the licences."

177

There is no doubt that Hill's patrols at this critical time did a great deal towards preventing the situation from getting completely out of hand. During the nineteen months he worked on the Palmer, he recalled, his collections from the Chinese for miners' rights and business licences alone amounted to £5,707. It was hard, rough work, every minute of it.

All over the goldfield at this time it was considered necessary to keep somebody in the camp day and night to prevent pilfering. When a thief was caught retribution was dramatic.

Two European diggers who had struck a good patch of alluvial not far from Maytown were packing up to go back to Cooktown with it when they found that about half their gold dust had gone from the chamois leather bag in which they kept it. They spread the word among other white diggers, and, on searches being made, it was soon discovered that others had lost gold too. Suspicion fell on a Chinese storekeeper named Ah Joy.

Next morning half a dozen diggers who had lost gold called at the store. They were all tough men, and very indignant. Ah Joy denied all knowledge of their gold. They could search his shop if they liked, not a grain of gold would they find except a few pennyweight he had received for purchases that morning. The diggers had already started searching anyway. Every box, sack, and cask in the place was closely examined. Rice was tipped out on the floor, stacks of clothing were scattered. One man had helped himself to a shovel and was digging up the ground where it seemed recently to have been disturbed. But there was no sign of the missing gold. They tore Ah Joy's clothes off him. They found nothing. There was nowhere they had not searched. A big digger named Joe the Blower, fists on hips, glared at the still protesting Ah Joy.

"A man ought to belt the daylights out of you for giving us all this trouble," he said. He seemed likely to do it, when another of the diggers pointed to four huge German sausages hanging from the rafters of the bark roof.

"I could use one of those," he said.

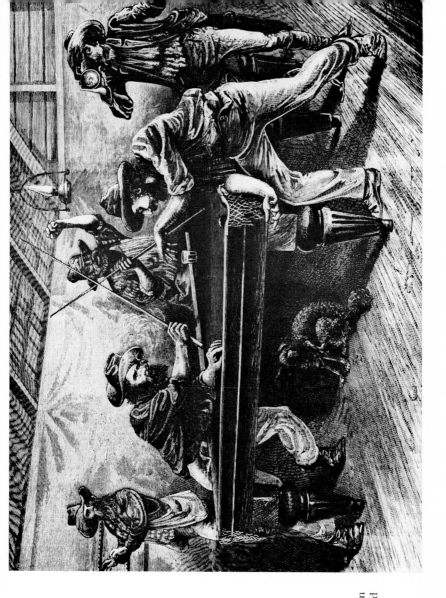

A canvas-walled billiard room on the field

Contemporary advertisement for the type of ten-stamper, ore-crushing mill used at Maytown and on the Hodgkinson

The smaller parts of ore-crushing mills were carried over the mountains on packhorses

They brought a box to stand on and cut down the sausages. "Hey, feel the weight of this one. Did you ever know a sausage as heavy as that?"

They slung the sausage on the counter and Joe the Blower whipped a Bowie knife out of his belt and split open the skin. Out poured pure gold dust.

"Seize the Chinaman!"

But Ah Joy had slipped out during the excitement. They searched the camp, and then saddled horses and scoured the surrounding bush. They found him at last, still naked, crouching under a bush. They sliced off his pigtail, tied his hands behind his back with it, and ran him back to the camp. They stood him on a bucket with his back to a tree, nailed his ears firmly to the trunk, and then kicked away the bucket. He was still nailed there next morning when the police came to collect him.

The Chinese method of dealing with thieves was hardly less drastic. Young Binnie described having once gone into a Chinese store at Revolver Point and seen a Chinaman strung up to the ridge pole by one wrist and one ankle.

From Maytown on 13th August Warden Coward, who since his transfer from Byerstown had been stationed up-river at a section of the field called The Springs, wired to the Mines Office: "My camp at The Springs has been stuck up and robbed by Chinamen during my absence on duty. Two hundred pounds in cash was taken from the safe and the safe itself smashed to atoms. My orderly was nearly killed. The robbers came prepared with ropes and tools. The orderly was lashed head to one post and feet to another. His hands were tied behind his back, a rope placed around his neck, and a bag pulled over his head.

"On receiving intelligence of what had occurred, I returned to the camp, got tracks of Chinamen, and took measures of their footmarks. I then went to Stony Creek and arrested one Chinaman answering the description, and found four spots of blood on his feet. Also arrested another who, I think, was the instigator. I came to Maytown late last night.

"Before the Chinamen left my camp they told the orderly

179

they would shoot me on their next visit, a threat which they have frequently made before. I return to camp tomorrow."

After this attack, arrangements were made to place the native police at the service of the wardens on the Palmer when needed. Still the robberies continued.

"Byerstown, 29th August: A butcher named Jimmy Weston was shot at and seriously wounded in the back shortly after leaving his shop on the Left-hand Branch when taking his gold to another shop. After going a short distance he saw some Chinamen in the track with firearms. Thinking something was crooked, he rode back and told a European storekeeper they were lying in wait to shoot him and collar the plunder. He then took another track, but John Pigtail was not to be so easily baffled. This time Jimmy saw no one until he was shot. His horse bolting probably saved him. He reached town exhausted from loss of blood and the twenty-mile ride."

Six Chinese, more imaginative than the rest, blackened their faces to look like blackfellows and held up several parties of Chinese packers between Cooktown and the Normanby. They reaped a fair haul of gold dust.

A public meeting in Chinatown petitioned the Government for more police protection. About a year previously the Chinese merchants of Cooktown had offered to subscribe a thousand pounds towards the establishment of a Chinese police force. The Government, understandably, had shown no enthusiasm for the idea.

In one respect at least, Sellheim's gloomy predictions for the Palmer proved wrong. The exceptionally dry season which he had expected would see thousands of Chinese destitute because of lack of water to work the alluvial proved a blessing in disguise. The drying up of the Palmer River itself uncovered virgin ground usually covered with too much water to be workable. All along its course the Chinese flocked into the river bed to work the new ground. Many who might have starved in a good season did very well in the dry one. On many of the creeks also, newly bared ground yielded well. Where there was no water at all, tons of paydirt were stacked above the usual water-level to be put through the sluices when the rains came.

The European reefers, on the other hand, had been brought to a standstill. With most of the stampers left high and dry, and the whole countryside reduced to bare rock with not a trace of feed for carriers' horses or bullocks, the quartz piled up at the mines and many of the miners stopped digging it. In a few cases coolies were employed to carry the quartz to the machines. For short distances they did the work for less than the teamsters usually charged. Some talked about making more use of them as beasts of burden. It would be one way of putting to profit the teeming hordes who roamed the field.

But though few realized it yet, the end of the Chinese panic was near. The warnings and protests had taken effect. A thousand miles away in Brisbane, legislation had already been passed that was to turn the tide. Before long many who had cursed the Chinese would be complaining that the north would be ruined because they were being driven away.

15 · GOLDEN HORSESHOES

OVER the razorback divide east of the Hodgkinson, diggers, packers, explorers, and speculators were meanwhile shaping events which, though outside the Palmer River's watershed, were to play a large part in shaping its future. At the foot of the ranges three new towns—Smithfield, Port Douglas, and Cairns—were pushing up to battle with Cooktown for a lion's share of the golden harvest. Smithfield was to become famous as the town where horses were shod with gold, as the "wickedest town in Australia", and, after a short, hectic life, was to perish—for its sins, many said—in a tremendous flood. Port Douglas was to flourish for a few years as a boom-time port for the gold and the newly opened tin-mines of the interior, and then die back to a ghost town. Cairns was to flourish and see even the foreshores of roaring Cooktown revert to the mangroves.

The 160 men who followed Old Bill out of Thornborough on 27th September 1876 arrived at Trinity Bay three days later, to be joined before dark by a smaller party, led by Warden Mowbray and including Mulligan and Johnny Byers, who had left the day after Old Bill and had come down by Douglas's track.

According to the Townsville correspondent who went with them, they had a rough trip. "We descended sheer down the range about half a mile, and after considerable swearing, slipping and blowing, emerged suddenly on a splendid flowing stream, the Barron, where it receives Stony Creek with mountains and scrub on both sides. If this was the dray

182

track of Douglas, and Bill Smith's was no better, the blacks could have Trinity Bay, we decided."

But there was no chance of Trinity Bay being left to the blacks. Word of the new track had no sooner reached Cooktown than merchants began to bale up their stores and publicans to pack their liquor to make a quick sale at the new settlement. Every available vessel was chartered. Within a week the s.s. *Leichhardt,* which only three years before had landed the first diggers on the muddy shores of the Endeavour River, had tied up at Old Bill's landing in Smith's Creek, and several sizeable vessels and a swarm of small craft had dropped anchor or found moorings wherever they could. The *Porpoise* had arrived from Townsville with Commissioner J. P. Sharkey and an official party to survey the new town and name it Cairns after the Governor of Queensland.

The official party set up camp at the entrance to the inlet at what later became Lower Abbott Street; the men from the Hodgkinson clustered around Smith's Landing. Already Cairns was a canvas town of more than three hundred men, women, and children. It had three stores, a public house, and about a dozen canvas and bark grog shanties.

The diggers paid Old Bill the three hundred pounds reward they had subscribed for the discovery of a route to the coast, but they never liked Trinity Bay. Its shores were mangrove-choked and muddy, and there was no fresh water or feed for their horses. They were still growling about it when William Bairstow Ingham, who had explored the inlet earlier, arrived back in the bay with his stern-wheel paddle-steamer *Louisa.* He took Sub-Inspector Johnstone and his troopers up the Barron River about eight miles, as far as the rocky rapids where the overland party had originally reached it. The police party scrambled ashore over the rocks, pushed through the scrub, and made camp on flat ground. Here was both good feed and water for any number of horses. They either ignored or did not notice the tufts of flood debris hanging high in the trees.

While the town of Cairns was being laboriously hacked out of the mangroves on the shores of Trinity Bay, packers found that by having their stores sent by boat to the rapids they could save about twenty miles of winding around boggy, mangrove creeks, and could then load about 180 pounds on each horse and go straight through to Thornborough—about seventy miles—by Old Bill's track. Soon there was a big camp at the rapids, and a liberal sprinkling of grog shanties to cater for its needs. By the end of November—two months after the first miners reached Trinity Bay—the camp at the rapids was a bigger township than Cairns. Packers had begun to call it Smith's Camp after Old Bill, or sometimes Smithville or Smithfield.

A special correspondent of the Brisbane *Courier* wrote:

"The New Township, Barron River, Trinity Bay, 29th November [1876]. I concluded my last communication from Cairns by stating that Mr Surveyor Warner proposed going up-river the following day to lay out this township.

"We started at 10 a.m. on 22nd November on board the steam tender *Fitzroy*, lately purchased by Mr Ingham. Mr Howard St George, Police Magistrate and Warden, was a passenger. We proceeded up-stream to Bill Smith's camp and, having taken that now celebrated citizen on board, the party returned about a mile down-stream to a place where the river bank was higher than anywhere else for the ceremony of christening the new township.

"Mr St George, with a few neatly eulogistic sentences complimenting Mr Smith, gave the name Smithfield to the new township. Smith's health and the prosperity of the new town was drunk in copious glasses of champagne and schnapps."

Next day Surveyor Warner went to work.

"There are two landings about five chains apart," the correspondent continued, "and a reserve two chains wide has been laid off along the river bank from which the two main streets, starting opposite the landings, run for ten chains through thick scrub abounding in good timber for building purposes to a pocket of open forest land. After crossing this, the track enters another belt of scrub beyond which is a large extent of good, well-grassed country where great numbers of horses are running.

"The road party who, for some time past, have been cutting through the scrub up the spur along which the proposed

184

dray track will be made have not yet reached the level country beyond the range. During the week about eighty horses have come down via the existing pack track."

Though a great deal of work and about fourteen thousand pounds were put into the proposed dray road, it never became more than a track for packhorses. Thick scrub had to be cut through all the way up the range, cuttings made, and rivers and creeks crossed. In the wet season it was often blocked until floodwaters subsided. Carriage rates were high because of the hard work and risk on the steep, narrow track. Many a packhorse and mule lost its footing and crashed hundreds of feet to its death. In spite of all the difficulties, a great deal of heavy mining machinery was packed over the range by this route before the track finally went out of use. The heaviest single item ever taken by one horse was a four-hundredweight wheel for a stamping battery.

Smithfield was a thriving settlement from the start, far bigger and richer than the number of its permanent population would indicate. It was a wide open town right in the middle of the gold route, but it was sufficiently isolated, both from the teeming goldfields and from the coastal ports, for all inhibitions to be cast to the winds. Within a month it was the Las Vegas of the goldfields—a town where money was plentiful and was spent with a lavishness that was often fantastic.

Old Bill himself was one of the first to see the possibilities of the place. He built a hotel there and called it the Beehive—a name it quickly earned—and before long a wife whom few had heard about joined him there. Ingham's steamers and many smaller vessels came up to the landing daily to discharge full cargoes. Palmer Kitty came up the river in one of the paddle-steamers, summed up the prospects, and hired a team of Chinese workmen to build her a house of entertainment. Stores, banks, gambling dens, and shanties sprang up as fast as the cedar that lined the Barron Gorge could be felled and sawn.

Johnny Byers, of Byers and Little, came down from Thornborough with two packers and twenty-six packhorses and opened a depot there. Robert Jackson Craig, of Craig and

185

Co, established a store at one of the landings, and Mr Nolan, of Cardwell, a rival store at the other. Craig was young, pushful, and an experienced bushman; he also owned a couple of small trading vessels, one or the other of which was generally tied up at his jetty, bringing in stores or taking out gold and sawn red cedar.

Though the official foundation ceremony had been performed some weeks before, Christmas Eve 1876 saw the beginning of an unofficial christening of the new town which was wilder by far than anything even the Palmer had ever seen before. The *Louisa* tied up at the landing with a full cargo of champagne; Craig's boat brought another, and from Christmas until well into the New Year no one was sober. Miners poured champagne into wooden tubs which they carried round the streets, dishing out drinks by the quart-pot and ordering every man and beast they met to drink. Even horses and dogs were drunk. Every loafer from Cairns was there to drink his fill, and, as word of the celebration spread, parties of expectant diggers came trooping down the track from the Hodgkinson and the Palmer, and small boats brought pilgrims from Cooktown.

As the good-time girls gathered for the feast, Kitty and a few special friends met them at the landing with a proposition. They could come in with her, or they could take an involuntary plunge into the river, on whose banks, just around the bend from the town, crocodiles could be seen basking. Kitty's establishment grew in size and prosperity.

Old Bill flourished with his town, becoming daily more flamboyant, though some said he spent more time drinking his liquor than selling it. One day he reined his horse at the blacksmith's forge owned by Edwin Crossland, one of those who had followed him down the range on his first trip from the Palmer, and threw two solid gold ingots at the blacksmith's feet.

"Make 'em into shoes for me horse, Ed," he said.

Crossland protested, but Old Bill insisted. He stood there while the shoes were shaped. He had Crossland turn them up at the sides and beat them out so they covered the whole of his horse's hooves. Then he mounted and galloped away up the street with the golden horseshoes glinting in the sun. Several diggers down from the Hodgkinson followed Old Bill's example, but the novelty did not last long. After a day or two the golden horseshoes were removed and, more often than not, traded at the Beehive or Kitty's for things more urgently needed.

On 3rd March 1877 a cyclone gave a hint of the fate that was eventually to overtake Smithfield. The Barron came roaring down in flood and the whole town was inundated. Though most were able to reach high ground in time, several men were never seen again. Goods worth hundreds of pounds were lost.

Within a week of the floodwaters falling the town was roaring on its way again as though nothing had happened. Sudden death and the threat of it were already too familiar to occupy anyone's mind for long at Smithfield, and the months that followed were to make them more so. Bendigo Jack was shot and robbed on the fringes of the town, George the Greek was speared by blacks, Frank the Austrian was murdered by an escaped convict whom he had befriended, Jimmy the Poet was stabbed in a brawl, Ah Moy went to sleep on the river bank and disappeared, his pigtail later being recovered from the belly of a crocodile. A crocodile also accounted for a cordial manufacturer named Matthews. He also had chosen his sleeping spot badly. A policeman named Michael Dwyer was found in the bush suffering from a gunshot wound and died without regaining consciousness.

Still the Hodgkinson gold poured down the mountain in a steady stream, golden horseshoes flashed in the sun, and champagne bubbles sparkled in the candlelight of Kitty's parlour. Fists flew at the drop of a hat or the flash of a pair of lace-trimmed knickers. Several men who had died of a bullet were described as having been "shot by accident".

The climax came with a suddenness that stunned Smithfield into a semblance of sobriety from which it never wholly recovered. Robert Craig and Old Bill were killed in a shooting incident.

There are several conflicting accounts of how Craig and Old Bill met their deaths. It was well known that Old Bill had been drinking so steadily that most of the Beehive's profits had found their way into other hands, and soon it was rumoured that he was in financial difficulties. His main creditor was Craig, and it is generally acknowledged that about a week before the incident Craig had stopped his credit. One account has it that Old Bill and Craig shot it out in the town's main street, and that as Craig dropped dead, Bill turned his gun on himself.

The report of the inquest which was held next day tells a story which, in spite of its official tone, has something of the flavour of a story that has been toned down for the sake of the memories and the families of two men who, in their different ways, were well respected and liked. The inquest, before Mr W. Mowbray, P.M., on 27th December, found that Robert Jackson Craig, 34, storekeeper, was shot and killed by William Smith, about 45 or 50, publican, in McDonald Street, Smithfield, about 3 p.m. on 26th December 1878, and that Smith then turned his revolver on himself, inflicting a wound of which he died about fifteen minutes later.

Constable James H. Norris gave evidence that about 3 p.m. he heard several revolver shots, saw Craig running across the street, and immediately afterwards saw him lying in his own doorway.

"I went over to Smith's public house on the opposite side of the street and saw Smith lying on his back under the veranda. There was blood on his shirt. He stretched out his hand and said: 'Will anyone hold me up?' Another man and myself took him by the hands and raised him up to a sitting posture. A few minutes after he seemed to get very weak. He said: 'Oh, I am done.' He died in about fifteen minutes in the place where he was lying.

"I found the mark of a bullet about two inches under his right breast. There was only a small quantity of blood on his shirt. There were marks of powder on it too.

"I examined the inside of the dining room at Smith's public house. I found a bullet which fits the revolver produced. It was lying on the floor. I could find no bullet marks inside the place.

188

"Smith was about forty-five or fifty years of age. He has a wife here. He told me about ten days ago he was often going to commit suicide while travelling through the bush. He was sober when he said this. Smith appeared to be under the influence of drink when I saw him immediately after he shot himself.

"I know of no motive he had for shooting Mr Craig. I have heard he was in Mr Craig's debt. He was in the habit of drinking a good deal. He did not get drunk, but got a good deal excited whilst under the influence of drink."

A packer named James Ferrier gave evidence that he was standing at Solomon's store opposite Smith's public house when he heard a noise inside Smith's place. He heard talking and two shots fired. The next thing he saw was Craig running out of the front door, holding his hand to his breast and shouting out "Murder!", and that he was done for. Smith ran out close behind him and fired two shots at him from a revolver. He then held his hand up quickly towards his breast and shot himself.

"I heard the report and saw him fall and drop or throw the revolver down. He then fell over and I picked the revolver up," said Ferrier. "Smith fell before I got across the street. He said to me: 'Give me a drink of water, old fellow.' Someone got him water. He could not drink it. I saw Craig going into Smith's door about a minute before I heard the shots."

Craig's brother-in-law, William Cochrane, gave evidence that he was behind the grocery counter in Craig's store when he heard two shots fired and heard Craig call out, "Murder! Murder!" He ran outside and saw Craig running across the street from Smith's public house holding his hand to his breast.

"Craig was staggering," said Cochrane. "I caught hold of him and laid him just inside the doorway of his store. He said, 'I am done, Bill.' He died in a few seconds.

"Smith came into the store immediately before the occurrence and asked Mr Craig to go over and he would settle with him. He owed an amount to Mr Craig and I understood Smith to mean he was going to pay him. Mr Craig

189

went over to Smith's public house. They both went out together. I heard the shots a few seconds afterwards.

"Mr Craig and Smith always appeared to be very good
friends."

The Cairns *Advertiser*, in reporting the incident, said
Craig's wife and children had gone south about three weeks
earlier. It described him as one of the most prominent men
in the community. "The corpse was brought into Cairns and
buried at the cemetery, the attendance being very large, and
every house in town was closed. Smith was a man known by
and to all of us. We all are cognisant of recent troubles and
misfortunes which overtook him, although we cannot conceal from ourselves that those troubles have been brought
about by his own passions and irregular conduct."

Old Bill was buried at the end of the main street in Smithfield, close to the main road which he had pioneered.

After that, nothing seemed to go right for Smithfield. The
following 8th March another cyclone roared in from the
Coral Sea and devastated Cooktown, Cairns, and all the far
north coast. Once again the Barron River came roaring
down in a torrent, and for several days Smithfield was under
water. Many were drowned; others had lucky escapes. The
man who was managing Craig's old store was trapped inside
by the rising waters. He managed to hammer a sheet of iron
off the roof and climb out and cling to the top until he was
rescued by a boat. Losses in liquor, merchandise and property were heavy.

Smithfield declined steadily from then on. Many of the
local business men, fearing another flood, moved out to make
a fresh start at a new port which was beginning to flourish
further up the coast—Port Douglas. The man mainly responsible for the founding of Port Douglas was Christie Palmerston, though accounts of how he came to do so vary. Ever
since it had become plain that Old Bill's road from the Hodgkinson could never be any more than a pack track, the miners
of the Hodgkinson had been looking out for a better one,
and another reward had been offered for the man who found
it. Ironically enough, when Palmerston qualified for the reward, he could not claim it because he was wanted by the

police—allegedly for the murder of a Chinaman. A cattle man named John Fraser, who had taken up land in the Mount Molloy area near the headwaters of the Mitchell River, described in his reminiscences how he first heard about it.

"One day when out on the run with a trusted black boy we came on a man in charge of a camp. He was of medium height, of slight build, and very active. He had a black, bushy beard and thick, black curly hair like a Townsville blackfellow. His dress consisted of a red cotton shirt held around the waist by a broad belt glistening with cartridges and holding to his hips a large-sized Colt revolver in an ornamental holster. A Snider rifle hung from his shoulders His moleskin trousers were tucked into knee-boots.

"He had very little to say at first, but after I told him who I was he brightened up and told me he was Christie Palmerston, that he was a miner from the Palmer diggings, and was wanted by the police because he was suspected, with others, of murdering a Chinaman and burning his store. He said he had been out some time and was innocent and that he would not be taken alive.

"He also told me he had blazed a track through the mountains and jungle from the Hodgkinson diggings to the coast, and that his mate was now there to try and get a reward for doing so."

Palmerston's mate on the trip was William Layton. His negotiations were apparently successful, because the two hundred pounds reward subscribed by the business men and mine owners of the Hodgkinson was paid over. Some time later Palmerston came out of hiding and no police action was taken against him.

Warden Mowbray reported the discovery of the new track on 1st June 1877, and the next three months saw a steady flow of Cooktown, Cairns, and Smithfield business men to the new port that was growing up at the seaward end of it. In August a correspondent describing its progress, with stores and pubs going up everywhere, said the town had all the hallmarks of a new gold-rush town. Teams were waiting at the top of the range for the scrub to be cleared over a steep pinch called "the Bump". In the meantime goods were being sent up the range to them by packhorse. But there were tons more goods being put ashore than the horses could handle. In November a parliamentary party looked the place over and named it Port Douglas, after the Premier.

"Thornborough, 1st December: Thirteen teams have arrived from the new port heavily loaded with goods of all kinds, horse feed, beer, and brandy constituting the bulk of it. Byers and Little Brothers, J. V. Mulligan and Co, and Harry Wooster were the principal recipients of the loading. The teams were in splendid condition.

"Ten crushing mills embracing 106 stamps are pounding away full time on the various reefing centres."

Johnny Hogsflesh was on hand as usual to take the first mail from Port Douglas to Thornborough on 12th December.

The dray road followed Palmerston's track up the gorge of the Mowbray River with deviations into small creeks and gullies to make the grade possible. At the Bump it spiralled in double S turns so steep that coach passengers had to get out—the women to walk to the top by a goat track, the men to help push the coach.

Slowly but surely the new port was sucking the life out of both Smithfield and Cairns. Early in 1878 Government officials were transferred from Cairns to Port Douglas. The Cairns branch of the Bank of New South Wales was transferred. Before the end of the year a lighthouse was completed.

In March 1879 yet another cyclone—the worst in years— removed Smithfield from the running for all time. Between 17th and 29th March rain fell in a continuous deluge, the Barron River came down in a roaring torrent of water, and Smithfield vanished beneath it. Most of its inhabitants had fled. The few who had not ran to take shelter in trees and on the high slopes of the gorge. From there they watched the last moments of the town that once had been called "the wickedest town in all Australia". It seemed like Nemesis—as though nature were determined to wipe out all trace of Old Bill Smith and his handiwork.

Bill's old pub, the Beehive, and Craig's old store were both lifted off their stumps about the same time and swept

192

out into the torrent, crashing against trees and swirling about each other in a sort of mad dance of death. Then the pub became snagged in a tree, and the store came wallowing towards it. They met with a splintering crash and disintegrated. Kitty's place, strongly built by Chinese craftsmen, was lifted off its blocks intact and went bobbing away in the torrent to disappear into the waters of Trinity Bay.

When the rain stopped, boats sent up the flooded river from Cairns could see nothing of the town at all. Almost the whole of the town had been swept away. What was left was still under water. But misfortune always benefits someone, it is said. By the end of 1879 the number of Port Douglas's pubs had risen to twenty-one.

16 · THE BATTLE OF LUKINVILLE

In February 1878 the business men of the Palmer goldfield sent a petition to the Minister for Mines protesting against legislation discriminating against the Chinese, and expressing the fear that it would drive the Chinese from the country and spell financial ruin for north Queensland. If the Minister felt some exasperation at the sudden, and complete change of attitude on the diggings, one can sympathize with him. The early months of 1877 had seen a torrent of protest against the Chinese being allowed to flood the goldfields. It had been accompanied by dire warnings of the probable consequences, and supported by almost daily accounts of murder, robbery, and seething discontent. Now, twelve months later, came a petition in support of the Chinese, praise for the part the Chinese had played in developing the colony, and warnings of impending ruin if they were kept out. Rarely has public opinion made such a somersault.

It had all begun back in August 1877, when the Government, stirred by accounts of the Chinese panic, had enacted legislation intended to put a brake on Chinese immigration, and curb their activities on the goldfields. The Chinese Immigration Regulation Act of 1877, assented to on 20th August, placed a poll-tax of ten pounds on every Chinese entering the colony. The Goldfields Act Amendment Act of 1877, assented to on 2nd October, increased the price of a miner's right for Asiatics from ten shillings to three pounds a year, and the price of a business licence for Asiatics from four pounds to ten pounds a year.

194

The Mulligan Highway, following the explorer's old track, crosses the
Palmer River a few miles above the old site of Byerstown

The most substantial building left in Cooktown, the Bank of New
South Wales, which dates back to the roaring days of the gold rush. In
the background is Grassy Hill; at the left, all that the cyclones left of
the Sovereign Hotel

Cooktown, which once covered fifteen square miles, is now mainly vacant spaces. The bush has covered once-busy streets.

Cooktown's once-busy wharves have reverted to mud flats

The first reaction of European diggers—after a brief period of alarm during which they thought the three-pound miner's right fee applied to them too—was one of satisfaction. Business men also saw no reason to complain about their Asiatic competitors having to pay ten pounds against their four. Then the complaints began to come in.

In October Warden Sellheim warned that it would be almost impossible to collect the three-pound fee as, with alluvial yields on the Palmer dropping, not one in fifty of the Chinese on the field would have that much money. If the defaulters were to be imprisoned, he said, the jails of the colony would be filled in a fortnight. Warden Hill reported that even when the ten-shilling fee applied he had to let many Chinese go free because of their utterly destitute condition. The poll-tax, however, was a far more practical measure, and within a few months of its coming into force it became obvious that the Chinese influx was being stopped.

Before long, many who had wanted the Chinese stopped began to have second thoughts about it. Teamsters and packers who had objected to the competition of the Chinese coolie porters remembered that their own most profitable loadings had come from the Chinese merchants, and they began to wonder where next year's loadings were going to come from. European storekeepers at camps where there were ten or a dozen European diggers and several hundred Chinese stopped worrying about their Chinese competitors in trade and began to wonder how they would manage without their Chinese customers. Though the Chinese were not great meat-eaters, a couple of hundred of them still ate a lot more beef than a dozen Europeans. This obvious fact brought some very influential cattle men and butchers onto the Chinese side.

The whole economy of the north had, in fact, become more dependent on the Chinese than most people had realized. Local banks had sought their custom. The Maytown branch of the Queensland National Bank had even accepted a consignment of opium as security for a Chinese merchant.

Chinese property-owners had votes in municipal elections, and in those days payers of rates above a certain amount had three votes. Most of the Chinese business men of Cooktown

195

qualified as "three-deckers" as they were called. By forming a bloc they found themselves able to put a good deal of pressure on councillors and local European business men.

"Now that the Chinese immigration has been stopped," wrote the Cooktown correspondent of the *Queenslander* in September 1877, "a great change may be expected in the state of the district—no more revenues of £10,000 per month."

In October, Cooktown had the novel spectacle of a joint European-Chinese public meeting called to consider the effect on the district of the anti-Chinese legislation.

At Cooktown on 10th November, a Mr Julian Thomas delivered a eulogy on the Chinese and the benefits they conferred on the community. He pointed out that the £9 6s. 8d. a ton import duty on rice which they had paid since 1876 already added 25 per cent to the price of their staple article of food. Accounts of goldfield outrages by Chinese were exaggerated, he said. The meeting was marred by raucous laughter and frequent interruptions from the back of the hall by an old prospector from the Palmer whose opinions of the Chinese, according to the newspaper reporter, "differed from those expressed by the speaker".

Sellheim summed up the effects of the legislation in his report on his sector of the goldfield for the year 1877:

"The population, which at the beginning of the year was 1,500 Europeans and 11,000 Chinamen, was considerably augmented during the first four or five months by the arrival of 7,078 Chinese from China direct, so that at one time there cannot have been less than 18,000 Asiatics on this goldfield.

"Since then, the strict enforcement of the quarantine regulations and the provisions of the new legislation regulating Chinese immigration have considerably diminished the number. During the period—and more particularly so during the past few months—2,162 Chinese have left for China. About 13,000 of those remaining are engaged in alluvial mining and 2,000 in packing, gardening, and trade.

"The European population has considerably decreased during the year and does not exceed 800 at present. Of this number 180 are working quartz."

On the Palmer itself, they now wanted the Chinese to stay.

"Maytown, 23rd February [1878]: A petition to the Minister for Mines is being signed by European storekeepers against the three pounds demanded from the Chinese for miners' rights. It is urged that the ground occupied by the Chinese diggers is now being turned over for the fourth time, and is too poor to admit of the payment. The petition also alleges that inhuman cruelty is practised in the collection of the fees and deprecates its rigid enforcement as calculated to cause a general stampede of Chinese from the field, to the serious loss of storekeepers, besides being highly discreditable to the Colony."

Warden Hill had been transferred, much to his satisfaction, to the more civilized surroundings of the Ravenswood gold-field and had been replaced at Byerstown by Warden Farrelly. Farrelly reported that during February he was obliged to exempt about a hundred Chinamen who were unable to pay the three-pound licence fee and who had nothing to levy on.

Sellheim pointed out in his report for March that though some of the Chinese were working on their own account, many of them were only bondsmen of storekeepers and gambling house proprietors who, in turn, often re-let their bonded countrymen to middlemen who became responsible for providing the miners' rights. The licence fees thus became a matter of considerable importance to the middlemen, and they consequently did everything possible to prevent their collection, by giving their men timely notice of the presence of goldfields officers to enable them to hide, and other expedients. The most successful of these expedients, according to Sellheim, was that of enlisting the sympathies of the European business men who valued their custom.

A result of the petition, said Sellheim, had been the growth among the Chinese diggers of an insolent attitude towards authority, and a number of incidents which, he said, would never have occurred if the Chinese had not realized that they had influential European support. As examples he quoted the entering, working, and removal of gold from No. 1 West Louisa claim by a horde of Chinamen and their beating up of the claim-holders when they remonstrated, and also the assault of the owner of the Heart Content claim while attempting to keep them outside his pegs.

Sellheim toughened his attitude to the Chinese: "Of fifty-three Chinamen found at Jessop's—which is the present refuge of the gambling house keepers since they were induced to leave Maytown—thirty-seven were eventually supplied with miners' rights when it was found that the alternative was imprisonment during the best part of the mining season."

Even the Hodgkinson was having its troubles. In May the Hodgkinson *Miner* reported: "Between 300 and 400 Chinese are fossicking in the neighbourhood of McLeod's Creek. Rumours of a twenty-ounce nugget being found spread, and Chinese flocked in from Byerstown in a stream. The Europeans tried a Roll-up, but only eight answered the call and, considering discretion the better part of valour, left the Chinese unmolested."

It was about this time that the first reports reached the field of the discovery of gold in New Guinea, and many of the old alluvial miners headed out for it. Gold had also been reported on the Coen River, and many had rushed to that. Even good reefing claims were deserted. Large numbers of Chinese joined the rush for Coen, but the campaign against the legislation continued.

Sellheim reported: "Notices have been posted in Chinese—it is supposed by the storekeepers—to the effect that probably the Goldfields Act Amendment Act of 1877 will be repealed, and in consequence those whose licences have expired keep out of the way even more than usual." He was finding it almost impossible to collect fees. Those Chinese who had money lodged it with Chinese storekeepers or gambling-house proprietors, and then claimed they were destitute. He estimated that in July only about 14 per cent of the Chinese in his area had miners' rights. The Act was, in fact, repealed that year, to be replaced by the Goldfields Act Amendment Act of 1878 which banned Chinese from new goldfields for three years after discovery instead of charging them higher fees. Diggers took full advantage of it when a few small strikes were made later, and chased the Chinese off them altogether.

With the Palmer drifting into the doldrums, gold was struck again—by Chinese this time, ironically enough—on a long stretch of the river below Palmerville. Sellheim visited the ground and wired the Minister for Mines: "There are about forty miles of auriferous ground commencing twenty-five miles below Palmerville and extending down the river. The gold is fine and is confined to the bed of the river. Men with cradles are making from two to four pennyweight a day, and some much more occasionally. There are a thousand Chinese on the ground, and the roads are covered with others going there. I expect there will be five thousand there this week. Some Europeans are also going."

Once again the rush was on. Men half way to the Coen heard the news, stopped in their tracks, and turned round. Men in Cooktown who had already paid their passages to New Guinea rolled their swags and once again took the Palmer track. One after another of the stampers at Maytown closed down as reefers abandoned claims and headed down the river.

"Was there ever such a river as the Palmer," wrote the Palmer *Chronicle*. "Five years of hard digging by hundreds of Europeans and thousands of Chinese have failed to exhaust the fabulous wealth of this famed river. The rush extends for 70 miles below Palmerville. The first camp is called the 28-mile, then come the 40-mile, 50-mile and 70-mile camps. The gold is found on the bars of the river. The best is being obtained at the first camp, called by the warden Lukinville, after the Under-Secretary for Mines, Mr George Lukin."

By the middle of August there were about 6,000 Chinese and 150 Europeans on the new diggings. From all over the Palmer the Chinese converged on the lower Palmer in a flood. In the rush for good ground the old tong agreements, which from the beginning had kept the different Chinese groups to their own specified areas, were forgotten, and before long the different factions were fighting over claims. "First they argue," wrote one digger, "then they kick over each other's cradles and billy-cans, then they get to it with their old

199

muzzle-loading guns, and when the supply of powder and lead give out, they throw sticks and stones."

As Chinese continued to fill the field, the fights assumed more serious proportions. Most diggers were in the habit of calling the Chinese cowardly, but this was far from the case. It was all a matter of temperament. In a nerve war, where a mob of painted savages were likely to jump screeching from ambush at any moment, the Chinese were at their worst, and generally took to their heels and ran at the first hint of danger. Many European diggers did the same. In a hot-blooded battle, on the other hand, the Chinese fought like demons.

Anyone who doubted the Chinese as fighters had reason to revise his opinion at the Battle of Lukinville, the bitterest armed clash in the whole history of the Palmer, and one which white diggers had good reason to feel thankful they were out of.

The trouble began when a large group of Cantonese became suspicious that a party of Pekinese working ground near them were quietly cleaning up the Cantonese tail-race and keeping the gold. One dark night they set a watch to check on it. Sure enough, about an hour after the camp had settled down for the night, a party of Pekinese carrying shovels made their appearance and quietly climbed down into the Cantonese tail-race. A couple of carriers with baskets on poles followed, and the gang went to work shovelling the gravel into the carrying baskets which, when full, were lifted gently and carried away to be dumped in a heap at the head of the Pekinese sluice-boxes ready to be run through at leisure.

The Cantonese spies crept away to their camp to discuss the situation. It was decided to wait for the next dark night when they knew the Pekinese would raid the ditch again. This gave them time to plan an attack that would wipe out the gold thieves for all time.

On a night they considered suitable, their tong men rounded up all the hatchet-men they could find in the ranks of the Cantonese in the whole area, and these recruited likely looking fighters from the ranks of their own gangs. The recruits were doped slightly with opium to make them fight better and armed with pick-handles, long-handled shovels, axes, tomahawks, meat choppers, and anything else that could do a suitable amount of damage.

The ambush party took cover in the scrub along the banks of the river and behind the dirt dividing walls that separated the claims. They had chosen their night well. Sure enough, as soon as the camp had settled down for the night the Pekinese raiders arrived with shovels and baskets, dropped into the Cantonese tail-race, and went to work removing the dirt.

The men in hiding waited until they were all hard at it and then, at a signal from one of the tong men, rushed in to the attack. Shrieking and yelling like fiends, the opium-drugged coolies laid about them. A European digger estimated the number of gold thieves at about fifty. They were unprepared for attack, unarmed to resist it, and the skirmish was nothing more than a massacre. All but two of the Pekinese were killed on the spot. The bodies of the rest, many of them horribly mutilated by the shovels of the attackers, were thrown into a heap and left there.

The main body of the Pekinese had meanwhile gathered reinforcements, and early next morning they charged down on the Cantonese camp. The slaughter was considerable on both sides, and after half an hour of fighting both sides were ready to stop.

But the battle was far from over, and during the night fighting broke out again. A short truce was followed by another set-to in daylight. It went on for days. Sellheim and his police, who had been rushed down from Maytown, would stop it one day and it would start all over again the next. Though the European diggers kept out of it, many who gathered around to see the fun came close to being hit by stray bullets. At last about thirty leaders were arrested and jailed as vagrants, and an uneasy truce was arranged.

There was, however, more fighting to come. The Macao men, late arrivals on the Palmer, and suspected pirates, robbers, and standover men, had always been regarded as outsiders among the other Chinese, and they were regularly driven out of Chinese areas where they were heavily out-numbered. A party of them took up ground at a creek near Lukinville and, determined not to be driven out of it, built a strong stockade of logs and posted a regular guard on it. Either by design or accident, the stockade overlooked one of the tracks regularly used by other Chinese prospectors. An exchange of insults led to general abuse, a few shots were exchanged by the holders of the stockade and passing diggers, and soon the Macao men had effectively closed the track. Encouraged by their success, they put a dam across the creek to improve their own water supply, and left Chinese working further down without water.

After many conferences, the tong men from all over the field decided it was time the Macao men were chased out. Every Chinese with any sort of firearm was enlisted, and the attacking forces mustered at dawn for a surprise attack while the Macao men were having their breakfast.

"The first sound of shooting nearly frightened the life out of us whites," one of the European diggers later recalled. "There were only a few of us there and there were thousands of Chinese. We thought they had had a roll-up to drive us off the field. We mustered on high ground and sent off a man on a horse to Maytown to fetch the police.

"More than two thousand Chinese lined up along the western bank of the creek had opened fire on the stockade. The shooting was poor, and after each shot the man who had fired it yelled at the top of his voice and jabbered away to his companions and danced about like a dervish.

"Some of the attackers managed to creep up close to the stockade and hurl in crudely made but very efficient stink pots. Though these were harmless to life, they always scattered everyone within a wide range of where they landed.

"There were several counter-attacks from the stockade during the day, but the marksmanship was bad on both sides. One man was killed. All that night the firing and yelling continued. We could not sleep because of it.

"On the second day those on the inside of the stockade burst out to meet a party of the enemy who were advancing across the creek. Another party managed to get behind them, and there was a lively skirmish in which one man was killed and four wounded."

During the fighting a Northern Irelander called Belfast Jack found a way to make some money out of it. Waiting for a lull in the battle, he hurried down the creek and worked his way among the excited Chinese, warning both sides that the wounded would have to be treated, and explaining that, fortunately for them, he himself had some skill in first aid. The leaders of both sides agreed to let Belfast Jack attend to the wounded at five pounds a head.

On one occasion a Chinese from the stockade found himself surrounded by members of the attacking party and there seemed little chance of his getting out of it alive. Belfast Jack grabbed a Snider in one hand and an axe in the other and fought his way into the centre of the fray to the side of the hard-pressed Chinaman.

"Hold on, you yellow heathens," he yelled, as he grabbed the lone Chinaman who was already bleeding from several knife wounds. "You aren't going to kill him if I can help it; a wounded Chow is worth a fiver to me but a dead one is worth nothing."

Late on the third night Warden Sellheim arrived with a party of police from Maytown and took charge of the field. He divided his forces and ordered them to circle round the Chinese and bring them into the largest clear spot on the field. When the Chinese saw what was happening many of them raced towards their claims and tried to hide. But the police soon found them and dragged them out.

Later in the day about three thousand Chinese were herded together on a stretch of ground below the white diggers' camp, and the Riot Act was read to them. Then the native troopers were ordered to disarm them. Within minutes they had grabbed the firearms from the Chinese, removed the bolts, and smashed the barrels against the rocks. All other weapons—knives, picks, and axes—were also collected. The Chinese, after being warned against further fighting, were allowed to return to their claims. There many of them found that while they had been fighting at the stockade white diggers had gone through their camps and stolen every speck of gold to be found. Belfast Jack collected fifty-five pounds from the Chinese for his medical services.

After that, although there were still occasional skirmishes among the Chinese, they were on a much smaller scale, and the new field settled down. "Europeans have their own township and have drawn a line across the river below which no Chinese will be allowed to pass," one digger wrote.

By the middle of September there were about ten thousand Chinese and five hundred Europeans on the field, which by now extended almost down to the junction of the Palmer with the Mitchell River. Each of the main centres—Lukinville, Fox's Camp, and Stuart's Camp, strung out along the river at five- or six-mile intervals—was based around a rocky, granite bar across the river. These bars spread the water to a width of three hundred yards or more, and caught a good deal of fine gold. Lukinville had become a fair-sized town with a large teamsters' camp, hotel, stores, several shanties, and Chinese opium dens and gambling houses. As in most Chinese centres, gardens provided melons, bananas, and an abundance of fruit and vegetables.

Though a good deal of gold was got from it, the field was past its peak by the end of the year. The Europeans began to drift back to the reefs, and then the Chinese began to scatter and dwindle away. The poll-tax had stopped the influx of Chinese, and the amendments to the Goldfields Act made it harder for them to make a living on a Queensland goldfield, but it was the exhaustion of the alluvial gold deposits that finally drove the Chinese from the Palmer. They scattered at first to newly discovered smaller fields to the north and south. Many made a living in the newly opened tin fields. Many found other occupations, like market gardening. But every day more of them left for home.

The Chinese invasion was over.

17 · THE PALMER SLEEPS

"COOKTOWN, 25th April [1879]: A large and important public meeting was yesterday held here at which the Mayor presided. The object was to express disapproval of the continued financial neglect of the Cooktown district by the Government."

"Cooktown, 2nd May: A meeting was held here on Thursday for the purpose of taking steps towards petitioning the Government for a grant of £5,000 to be spent in prospecting the Cook district for gold and other minerals, under the management of a central committee to be elected by the ratepayers of Cooktown."

These were not the kind of news items one saw in Cooktown newspapers in the boom days. The fact was that by the close of the 1870s the Palmer's payable alluvial gold deposits had been worked out. A few European fossickers and a tiny remnant of the Chinese horde scratched its threadbare gullies for a bare subsistence.

Several strikes were made in the far north and in previously neglected creeks and gullies, but the gold that came from them was only a trickle compared with the Palmer flood. More men turned to the once-ignored tin deposits, and a few to bêche-de-mer fishing.

At Maytown and on the Hodgkinson the reefs were still bearing, and for those who had good claims there were still years of prosperity ahead. But the Hodgkinson gold went to Port Douglas, and the reefs of Maytown were nothing to the alluvial deluge that had built Cooktown. Of about one million ounces of gold that had been recovered from the Palmer field until that time, more than 90 per cent was alluvial. The Chinese had smuggled out as much alluvial again that was never recorded.

Gradually the old diggers were drifting away. New Guinea took some of them. Others pushed up the peninsula to Coen, the Wenlock River, and other fields that were no more than pale ghosts of the mighty Palmer.

Mulligan, whose restless probing had opened up the whole of the field, soon tired of reefing on the Hodgkinson, and headed out again for new country. He discovered the first Queensland silver-lead deposits at Silver Valley, west of Herberton, in 1880. These and Herberton tin took more men from the Palmer.

Mulligan married at Brisbane on 5th March 1903, and bought the Mount Molloy Hotel. He died on 24th August 1907, of injuries received while trying to stop a brawl. An inscription on a headstone at the local cemetery reads: *Sacred to the memory of James Venture Mulligan, prospector and explorer, died at Mt. Molloy aged 69 years. R.I.P. Erected by a few old friends.*

Christie Palmerston, the enigma, continued to prowl the trackless scrub until the last. He induced John Fraser's brother, Harry, to go with him to try to find a new goldfield, and they became the first white men to visit the headwaters of several rivers south of Cooktown. He found gold, and for a while new alluvial fields flourished on the headwaters of the Russell and Johnstone rivers among the tangled rain forest between the Atherton Tableland and the coast. But these, also, were small fields.

Palmerston's fossicking opened several tracks from the hinterland to the sea, and in the end killed Port Douglas, the town he had been mainly responsible for founding. Herberton tin and a developing pastoral industry called for a rail link with the coast, and Cairns and Port Douglas battled to become the seaport. Palmerston found a track; Cairns got the railway. Port Douglas languished, and when the reefs of the Hodgkinson began to cut out, died.

By then Palmerston also was dead. In 1886, at Townsville, he had married and bought a hotel with the idea of settling down. Soon after, he told a friend he was too generous to make a good publican, and left for Malaya where he died of fever in 1893 while prospecting for tin.

By 1883—ten years after the beginning—the Palmer was finished. When Mulligan's friend, W. O. Hodgkinson, was transferred there as warden in 1883, he wrote that most of the enterprising miners had left the place and that those who remained were notable mainly for their thirsts, which supported one hotel—not counting shanties—to every fourteen men. All over the field, once thriving camps were deserted and reverting to the bush, often marked by no more than hundreds of empty bottles, mammoth heaps of beef bones, and scores of jam, butter, and sardine tins.

Cooktown still pushed the Government to spend some money in opening up the north. Since the roaring days of 1875 and 1876, its leaders had been campaigning for a railway line to link it with the interior. The plan for the railway was brilliant in its conception, and, if pushed through in the days of prosperity, would have changed the history of the north. It was to serve the whole Palmer diggings, and then go on to Chillagoe and open up all the pastoral and mineral land from Cooktown to the Gulf. Then it was to turn north, link up with Coen and the Wenlock River, and continue on to a new outlet port for peninsula timbers, cattle, and minerals at Somerset, or somewhere else high up on the Gulf of Carpentaria.

But there was too much debate and too little action. The plan was stifled by political and parochial jealousies, shortsighted economies, and tropical lethargy. By the time the first sod was turned it was April 1884; by the time the first section of thirty-one miles was opened it was November 1885. Laura (sixty-seven miles from Cooktown) was reached in October 1888. There were eighty-nine wooden bridges and countless culverts to get the line across the country's maze of river and creek beds.

At Laura the river was liable to floods sixty or more feet high between steep banks. So £21,000 was spent on a five-span steel bridge to cross it. When the bridge was finished a single locomotive was driven across to test it—and that was all that ever did cross it. For years the magnificent Laura railway bridge was to be famous as the great white elephant of the north.

The reefs of Maytown had been declining through the 1880s and were almost finished. The first purpose of the line had disappeared. Where was it to go now? For years the argument dragged on. Should it turn north to Coen, or south to the new copper fields of Mungana. The result of all the arguments was—*mañana*.

In March 1940 a record flood wrecked the white elephant bridge, sending its three centre spans crashing into the river. Another flood in 1957 did the clean-up job nobody had bothered to do, and swept away the rest of it.

The Palmer's last chapter, by then, had already closed. In the 1930s, dredging produced some alluvial, but not enough to make it worth persisting with. In 1949 Maytown's last inhabitant, the caretaker at the Louisa mine, left when the machinery was dismantled and removed to Ravenswood. The last of the buildings, long empty, were pulled down by graziers and carted away for the sake of their iron.

Today only heaps of bottles, a few bricks, and scraps of rusting machinery remain on the banks of the Palmer to mark the site of what was once a thirteen-hotel town of ten thousand people. Mr J. Berry, a mining inspector, wrote to Mr J. H. Binnie: "Echotown is quite deserted. At German Bar, where the mill was, are a couple of old pipes screwed together and a stonework system at the rear end of where the boiler was and where you had the chimney."

In its peak year—1875—the Palmer produced a recorded 250,400 ounces of gold. From the time of its discovery until the end of 1954 it produced a recorded 1,334,000 ounces, valued at more than £5,666,000. The Chinese, in the peak years, must have taken away at least as much again that was never recorded.

The Cooktown-Laura railway, for a while, had a daily train service, but it dropped back gradually to a weekly round trip by rail motor. Then this was stopped, and a few years ago the rails were taken up and used for telephone posts and other things. Anyone who wants to go to Palmerville or the Maytown area today needs a four-wheel-drive vehicle and dry weather—or a packhorse, like Kennedy had. The going is just as rough today as it was then.

Cooktown, in spite of a trickle of gold, some tin, fishing, bêche-de-mer, and a little farming, declined with the gold boom that made it. By the 1890s a visitor was writing: "In the deserted streets, lean goats try to exist on empty bottles and jam tins, and retire for their siesta to the verandas of public buildings."

The place was so far gone in its decline that when it was devastated by a cyclone in 1907 no one bothered to repair what had been blown down. What was left was roughly patched; over the years, what was useful was carried away, until there were more vacant blocks than buildings in the town which, with its outlying bullockies' camps and shanties, once sprawled over more than fifteen square miles. Grass and weeds, and then trees, pressed in from the fringes to cover the scars, and in the cool of the mornings kangaroos came back to graze in Charlotte Street.

The substantial Bank of New South Wales building remains as a monument to past glories. Half the old Soverign Hotel remains; a second big cyclone in 1949 took the rest of it. Two others of the original ninety-four hotels are still open for business. On the walls of one of them—the West Coast—dry rot is beginning to destroy a painted mural showing the lively life of the gold rush days. Across the street no trace of Chinatown remains except the great joss-house bell, a gong, some carved screens, and other relics now housed in the town's small museum.

Cooktown today is a shabby shell in which about five hundred contented people potter about, fish, and sip an occasional beer with a few fossickers who will not forget the good days and still pan gravel in some of the back creeks of the Conglomerate and further north.

There is still a little gold left in the Palmer and, if a man has the pension to keep him going, there is still the chance of finding that forgotten pocket of alluvial. Today it is worth about fourteen pounds an ounce, against less than four pounds at the peak of the rush. The possibility keeps alive the old art of twirling gravel in a tin dish, and keeps a few sun-browned old-timers working the old ground.

Cooktown's future, if it has one, is right at its door. The rich soil along the banks of the Endeavour will grow anything from oranges to bananas. Some of the Barrier Reef's best fishing is just off its shores. Cooktown could be the garden of Australia, a tropical haven of rest from the never-ending rat-race, a tourist resort without equal.

Out in the Palmer country there are signs that the recent decades of slumber may be nearing their end. New life is stirring in the tablelands as international cattle interests take up land for development. Perhaps modern technology may leave a mark where thirty-five thousand gold-hungry men left none.

NEWSPAPERS AND BOOKS CONSULTED

The *Australasian Sketcher*, the Cooktown *Herald*, the *Queenslander*, and other newspapers and journals of the period.

Binnie, J. H., *My Life on a Tropic Goldfield* (Melbourne, 1944)

Browne, Reginald Spencer, *A Journalist's Memories* (Brisbane, 1927)

Corfield, W. H., *Reminiscences of Queensland 1862-1899* (Brisbane, 1921)

Dick, James, *The Mineral Resources of the Cook District* (Port Douglas, 1910)

Hill, W. R. O., *Forty-five Years' Experiences in North Queensland* (Brisbane, 1907)

Jack, R. Logan, *Northmost Australia* (London, 1921)

Meston, Archibald, *Geographic History of Queensland* (Brisbane, 1895)

Mulligan, James Venture, diaries and reminiscences, published in the *Queenslander* at the time of the Palmer gold rush and shortly after it.

Palmer, Edward, *Early Days in North Queensland* (Sydney, 1903)

Pike, Glenville, *The Men Who Blazed the Track* (Cairns, 1956)

Abelsen, Peter, 9-11, 73, 125, 127
Aborigines, cannibalism, 4-5, 26, 52-3, 64, 69, 70-1, 93-4, 108, 123, 127, 131; whites attacked by, 8-9, 16-7, 24, 41, 49, 62-4, 72-3, 94, 107, 122-3, 149, 164; attacked by whites, 16-7, 25, 32, 38; killing of whites, 21, 24, 52, 66-8, 70-1; weapons, 25, 36, 107-8; killed by whites, 31, 131-2, 150, 158; attack at Battle Camp, 32-6; attacks on Chinese, 64, 69, 94 (see also cannibalism); horses and bullocks killed by, 64, 71-2, 108, 131, 159; punitive measures against, 107-10, 150; piccaninnies abandoned, 107-8; and wild whites, 150-1; killed by Chinese, 156
Abrahams, Jens, 102-3
Ada, reefing claim, 118
Adria, ship, 87, 89
Alexandra, reefing claim, 155
Alliance, reefing claim, 118
Anglo-Saxon, reefing claim, 74

Band of Freedom, reefing claim, 168
Barron River, 125, 182-3, 187, 190, 192
Battle Camp, 32-6
Beardmore, F. W. J., 86
Beehive Hotel, 185, 192
Belfast Jack, 203-4
Big Oaky Creek, 30-1
Binnie, J. H., and family, 157-60, 165-6
Blackbird, ship, 114, 130-1
Blackfellow's Creek, 131
Blair, John, 70
Bloomfield River, 27
Boomerang, ship, 45-6
Bouel, Charles. See French Charley
Bowen, 27

Bowen, ship, 171
Brandt, Albert, 9
Brown, Peter. See Abelsen
Bullock teams, 42-3, 46
Burdekin River, 6
Bushfires, 20
Butcher's Creek, 47
Byers, John, 124, 165, 185
Byerstown, 124, 126-7, 132, 168

Cairns, 184, 206
Caledonian, reefing claim, 118
Caledonian No. 1, reefing claim, 119
Callaghan, Patrick, 75
Cameron, Murdo, 22-3
Cannibalism. See Aborigines
Canton, 86
Cape River, 6
Cape York Peninsula, 2
Cardnow, Jack, 162
Cardwell, 14-15, 26-7
Carpentaria, Gulf of, 3
Carriage, cost of, 45
Carriers, 42, 120
Carstenz, J., 3
Cattle prices, 21
Charlotte Street, Cooktown, 53, 138-41
Charters Towers, 6, 16
Chinese, on track, 30, 33-4, 91-3, 139-40; eaten by blacks, 64, 72, 93-4, 127, 131; opposition to, 77, 80, 87-90, 172-4; rush to Palmer, 78; legislation against, 78, 194; spread over Palmer goldfield, 79, 81, 90, 95, 119-20, 127, 155-6, 166, 169, 172-80; working methods, 79; lynching of, 80; lynching threat to, 175; mass immigration of, 86-7, 170-1; tongs, 90; killed by whites, 92; in Cooktown, 93, 140-1, 144-7, 177; die of disease, 95; at

Chinese—*continued*
Chinky Creek, 95-6; attacked by whites, 105-6; killing of blacks, 156; on Hodgkinson goldfield, 168, 175-6, 198; crime among, 170, 173-80, 197-8; rioting by, 171; in quarantine, 171-2; march on Cooktown feared, 174; drastic punishment of, 178-9; support for, 196-7; leave the Palmer goldfield, 196-7, 204; at Lukinville, 199-203
Chinese Immigration Regulation Act, 194
Chinky Creek, 95-6
Clohesy, Sub-Inspector, 62-3
Cobb and Co, 139
Coen River, 198, 206
Conglomerate Tableland, 13, 38-9, 96
Connor, Lieutenant, 27
Cook, Captain James, 3
Cooktown, Hann near site of, 8; founded, 28; in December 1873, 44-5; in February 1874, 53-7; fever at, 100; dysentery epidemic, 126; in boom days of 1875, 138-47; Chinese in, 86, 144-7, 177; in decline, 205-9
Coquette, ship, 26
Corfield, W. H., 42-7, 65-6, 68, 108-10, 121-2
Courier, Cooktown, 55
Coward, mining warden, 124, 126, 128, 179-80
Cradle Creek, 11, 13, 157
Craig, Robert Jackson, 185, 187-90
Cranley, J. J., 31, 36, 40
Crossland, Edwin, 46, 186
Crushing machinery, 114, 116, 157, 166, 168, 192
Cyclones, 187, 190

Daintree, Mount, 7, 39
Daintree, Richard, 6
Daintree River, 27
Dalrymple, George Elphinstone, 26-8
Dead Dog Creek, 85, 97, 115, 124
Death on the track, 16, 52, 55-8
Deighton River, 37
Devil's Kitchen, 94
Devil's Staircase, 60
Dick, James, 56, 138
Doherty, Big Bill, 120
Doughboy Creek, 173
Douglas, Sub-Inspector Alexander, 59, 85, 162-3, 182-3
Douglas's new track, 85

Douglas's track, 59-61
Dowdell, James, 9, 125
Doyle, John, 162
Drought, 41
Duff, Jack, 75
Dutch explorers, 3
Duyfken, ship, 3
Dyas, Sub-Inspector, 30, 41
Dysentery, 25, 50, 126

Echotown, 157-8, 165, 208
Edwards, Jack, 21, 47, 75, 91, 102, 116, 118, 157, 166
Edwardstown, 47, 73, 83-4, 91, 111-13, 114. *See also* Maytown
Emu Creek, 126-7
Endeavour River, 3, 27-8
Etheridge River, 6-8, 16
Explorer, reefing claim, 168

Fahey, Bartley, 145-6
Fairview Plains, 37
Fanning, William, 161
Farrelly, mining warden, 197
Fever, 76, 100
Fish Creek, 16
Fitzroy, ship, 184
Fitzroy Island, 171-2
Flannery, James, 68
Florence Irving, ship, 56
Flying Fish, ship, 26
Fossilbrook Station, 7
Fox's Camp, 204
Fraser, Harry, 206
Fraser, John, 191, 206
French Charley, 141-2
Galley of Lorne, ship, 171-2
Georgetown, 9, 12-13, 15
German Bar, 23, 166, 208
Gilbert River, 6, 16
Gold, escort attacked, 62; sent to China, 140; prices, 45, 147, 209; total Palmer River production, 208. *See also* Gold discoveries
Gold discoveries: at Gympie, 6; Cape River, 6; Gilbert River, 6; Percy River, 6; Etheridge River, 6; Ravenshoe, 6; Charters Towers, 6 On Palmer River: at Warner's Gully, 7; Cradle Creek, 11; Left-hand Branch, 12; Sandy Creek, 12; Fish Creek, 16; Oaky Creek, 19; McLeod's Creek, 19; Greasy Bill's Creek, 19; Stony Creek, 19; McGann's Creek, 19; White Horse Creek, 19; Sweeny's Creek, 19; Revolver Point, 23; German Bar, 23; Jessop's Gully, 24; Butcher's

Gold discoveries—*continued*
    Creek, 47; Pine Creek, 74; on
    headwaters of Palmer (Dead Dog
    Creek, Byerstown area), 82; Ed-
    wardstown (reefs), 83; Emu Creek,
    126; Lukinville, 199
    At Normanby River, 85; Chinky
    Creek, 96
    On Hodgkinson River, "traces" of
    gold, 82; "tolerable show", 127;
    reported, 128; at McLeod's Creek,
    134
    At Coen, 198; Wenlock River, 206
    In New Guinea, 198
Golden Age, newspaper, 157
Golden horseshoes, 186-7
Goldfields Act Amendment Act, 194,
    198
Granite Range, 125
Grassy Hill, 3, 29, 56, 145-6
Greasy Bill. *See* Little, William
Greasy Bill's Creek, 19
Grove Creek, 162
Gympie, 6

Hamilton, Dr Jack, 76-7, 154, 165
Hamilton, Thomas, 55
Hann, Frank, 6
Hann, William, 6-9, 62, 77
Hartley, W. J., 149-50
Harvey, William, 125
Hawkins, George, 120
Heart's Content, reefing claim, 83,
    198
Hell's Gate, 59-60, 62-3, 68-70, 94,
    99
Herald, Cooktown, 55
Herberton, 206
Hill, W. R. O., 128, 133, 143, 150,
    172-8, 197
Hit or Miss, reefing claim, 119
Hodgkinson, W. O., 82, 207
Hodgkinson River, 82, 127, 128-33,
    154-5, 161, 165, 167-8, 192, 205
Hogsflesh, Johnny, 118, 192
Hong Kong, 86

Ida, reefing claim, 115
Ingham, William Bairstow, 183-4

Jansz, W., 3
Jardine, Alex, 5
Jardine, Frank, 5
Jerry, William Hann's black boy,
    7-8, 29-31
Jessop, prospector, 23
Jessop's Creek, 24, 172, 198

Jessop's Gully, 24
Johnstone, Sub-Inspector Robert, 26,
    162, 183
Johnstone River, 26
Jumping George, 121
Junction Creek, 21

"Kangaroo Courts", 104, 133-4
Kennedy, Edmund, 4-5, 7
Kennedy, Hugh, 127
Kennedy River, 38-9
Kersley, George, 120
Killarney, ship, 171
Kingsborough, 165
Knight, J. W., 146
Kortum, Dr, 76

Laura railway, 207-8
Laura River, 37, 60, 207
Layton, William, 191
Left-hand Branch (Palmer River),
    11, 13, 20, 22, 40, 47
Leichhardt, ship, 27-9, 46, 183
Leichhardt, Ludwig, 2, 4, 7
Leslie, Tom, 74
Little, William (Greasy Bill), 124,
    162-3, 165
Little Laura River, 37
Lone Star, reefing claim, 165-6
Lord Ashley, ship, 15, 46
Louisa, reefing claim, 208
Louisa, ship, 183, 186
Lukinville, 199, 200-3
Lynching, 20, 80, 135-6, 175
Lynd River, 7, 9

McAuley, family, 155
McDonald, Captain, 171-2
McGann's Creek, 19
McLeod, William, 23, 127, 134
McLeod River, 82
McLeod's Creek, on Hodgkinson,
    134-5, 198; on Palmer, 19, 23
Macmillan, A. C., 27-31, 36-9, 41
Macmillan's track, 59, 64
Macquarie brothers (Hugh and
    Dan), 69-70
Mann, Alexander, 71
Mareeba, 125
Mary Grant, ship, 114
Mary River, 6
Maryborough, 44
Maryvale Station, 6
Maytown, 114-20, 155, 205, 208
Merkin tribe, 4. *See also* Aborigines
Mitchell, Sir Thomas, 2
Mitchell River, 2, 4, 7, 9, 43, 46,
    131-2

Molloy, Mount, 191
Moran, Jack, 125
Moresby River, 27
Mosman, Hugh, 96
Mosman, prospector, 95-6
Mosman River, 96
Mount Daintree, 7, 39
Mount Mulgrave, 9
Mount Mulligan, 82
Mount Surprise Station, 7, 9, 14, 21
Mowbray, William, 167, 182, 188, 191
Mowbray River, 192
Mulgrave, Mount, 9
Mulgrave River, 27
Mulligan, James Venture, at Etheridge River, 9; finds payable gold on Palmer River, 10; reports, 13; warns against rush, 14; leads first rush, 15; on Left-hand Branch, 20; threats to lynch, 20, 135-6; attacked by blacks, 73; finds gold at Pine Creek, 74; criticizes Chinese, 80; exploring, 81; reports on Edwardstown reefs, 83-4; receives Government grant, 97; on Hodgkinson, 125-6; reports gold, 128; registers claims, 129; leads rush, 130; opens store, 160; reefing interests, 165, 167-8; death, 206
Mulligan, Mount, 82
Mulligan Highway, 82
Murder, on Hodgkinson River, 153, 154-5, 165; at Smithfield, 187
Murdering Lagoons, 68, 158

Nash, James, 6
Native police, 25, 49, 67, 70, 107-10
Neil, Mrs, 42
Neil, Ned, 42
New Guinea, 198, 206
Normanby, ship, 171
Normanby River, 31-2, 85
Normanby Woman, 151

Oaky Creek, 19, 75, 77, 85
O'Connor, Sub-Inspector, 108-10, 150
Old Bill. See Smith, William

Palmer, Arthur Hunter, 6-7
Palmer Kate, 44, 53, 147
Palmer Kitty, 53, 185-6
Palmer River, tributary of Mitchell, 2; Hann discovers gold on, 7; Mulligan finds payable gold on, 10; rush, 15 (see also Gold discoveries, on Palmer River); first township, 19; women on, 42, 48, 66, 101, 111-12, 116, 157-60; in flood, 51, 118; diggings abandoned to Chinese, 133; Chinese leave, 204; gold finished, 206, 208; total gold production, 208. See also Left-hand Branch (Palmer River)
Palmerston, Christie, 104; attacks Chinese, 105-6, 147; helps diggers, 106; in Cooktown, 147; hideout of, 148; singing voice, 149; finds track to Port Douglas, 190-1; finds track to Cairns, 206; death, 207
Palmerston's track, 190-1, 192, 206
Palmerville, 40, 43, 47
Paluma, ship, 172
Pearl, ship, 27
Pera, ship, 3
Percy River, 6
Pine Creek, 74, 81
Poole, Harry, 142-3
Porpoise, ship, 183
Port Douglas, 125, 190, 192-3, 206
Port Essington, 4

Queen of the North, reefing claim, 83-4, 115, 119
Queen of the North No. 3, reefing claim, 118

Rations, shortage, 20, 40; cost on Palmer, 41-2; cost in Cooktown, 45
Ravenswood, 6
Reefing claims, in Edwardstown (later Maytown) area, 83-4, 113, 115-16, 118-19; at Echotown, 160; on Hodgkinson, 128-9, 161, 165, 167-8; at Byerstown, 168
Revolver Point, 23, 157
Robberies, notable, 102-3
Robinson, David, 9
Rockingham Bay, 4, 26
Runge brothers, 23

St George, Howard, on Etheridge, 13; on Cooktown–Palmer River rush, 27, 30, 38-9; on Palmer, 41-2, 47-8, 73; appointed to Cooktown, 73; warns on Chinese, 78; defends Mulligan, 136; on Hodgkinson, 160, 162; at Smithfield founding, 184
St George River, 38, 74
Sandy Creek, 12, 19, 74, 80, 85
Saunders, Captain, 27
Sea Wah, 144-5
Sefton, Robert, 127
Sellheim, P. F., 27, 73, 114, 172, 201, 203

Shanties, 45, 49, 100-2
Sharkey, Commissioner J.P., 183
Silver Valley, 206
Singapore, ship, 87, 89
Sluicing methods, 79
Smith, William (Old Bill), 143, 161-3, 182-6, 187-90
Smith's Creek, 183
Smith's Landing, 162, 183
Smith's track, 184-5
Smithfield, 184-7, 190, 192-3
Snider Gully, 77
Snider rifle, 35
Somerset, 5
Sovereign Hotel, 142
Starvation, 52
Steam Packet Hotel, 143
Stony Creek, 19, 99
Strau, Johan, 66
Stuart Town, 165
Stuart's Camp, 204
Sweeny's Creek, 19
Sykes, Captain, 149-50

Tate, Dr Thomas, 7-8
Tate River, 7, 9
Taylor, Norman, 7
Thompson's Range, 13
Thornborough, 161, 163-5, 168, 184
Tongs, Chinese, 90
Toughtville, 81

Townsend, Sub-Inspector, 142-3, 162
Townsville, 16, 27
Trinity Bay, 162, 164, 182-4

Union Camp, 165

Victoria, ship, 86

Walsh, W. H., 7
Walsh River, 7
Warner, Frederick, 7, 97, 125, 162, 184
Warner's Gully, 7
Waterford, 165
Watson, Alexander, 9
Webb, William J., 29-32, 34-5, 37-8, 42
Welch, George Batton, 30-1
Welcome Waterholes, 37, 65
Wellesley, 165
Wenlock River, 3, 206
West Louisa, reefing claim, 197
Wet, the, 49-54, 83
White Horse Creek, 19
"Wild" whites, 150-1
Williams, W., 127
Wilson, William, 42-5, 47
Woodville, 165

Yates, William, 46

919.43
H

DU 280 .P3 H6 1967

Holthouse, Hector

River of gold;the story of
the Palmer River gold rush

69- 010297

lmer River gold rush.

.ust.

(Aus 67–1536)

SEO Library Center
State Library of Ohio
40780 Marietta Road, Caldwell, OH 43724

l mining—Queensland—

68–85086

Library of Congress   [2]